成田インスペクテッド

JAPAN GRAPHIC DESIGN COMPILER

NARITA INSPECTED

EDITED COMPILED AND DESIGNED BY BÜRO DESTRUCT BERN

TRANSLATIONS BY JUNKO TOZAKI

PUBLISHED BY DIE GESTALTEN VERLAG BERLIN

NARITA INSPECTED
THE JAPAN GRAPHIC DESIGN COMPILER
EDITED, COMPILED AND DESIGNED BY LOPETZ01
IN BURO DESTRUCT BERNE CAPITAL.
WWW.BURODESTRUCT.NET
WWW.BURODESTRUCT.NET/BD/NARITA-UPLOADED/

TYPED WITH BD BDR MONO AND HELVETICA NEUE.
TRANSLATIONS BY JUNKO TOZAKI.
JAPANESE TYPESET BY M.HANZAWA (PGX)
PHOTOS AND KIRIBARI SYU BY LOPETZ:BD
(1999-2001)
ADDITIONAL PHOTOS BY HEIWID:BD

PUBLISHED BY DIE GESTALTEN VERLAG, BERLIN
WWW.DIE-GESTALTEN.DE
PRINTED BY MEDIALIS OFFSET, BERLIN

DIE DEUTSCHE BIBLIOTHEK - CIP-
EINHEITSAUFNAHME
NARITA INSPECTED / LORENZ GIANFREDA, ILL.
LOPETZ. HRSG. ROBERT KLANTEN. -
BERLIN: DIE-GESTALTEN-VERL., 2001
ISBN 3-931126-61-7

© DIE GESTALTEN VERLAG GMBH, BERLIN.
ALL RIGHTS RESERVED. NO PART OF THIS
PUBLICATION MAY BE REPRODUCED OR
TRANSMITTED IN ANY FORM OR BY ANY MEANS,
ELECTRONIC OR MECHANICAL, INCLUDING
PHOTOCOPY OR ANY STORAGE AND RETRIEVAL
SYSTEM, WITHOUT PERMISSION IN WRITING
FROM THE PUBLISHER.

PAGE #

CONTENTS

002	CONTENTS
004	NARITA EXPRESS BY TORU HACHIGA
005	NARITA CENSORED BY KIYONORI MUROGA
006	7/16 HOURS INTO THE FUTURE BY LOPETZ
007	LOGOFOLIO
008	FURI FURI COMPANY
012	FONTGRAPHIC.COM
016	KIRIBARI #1
017	KIRIBARI #2
018	SATOLABO
022	PHOTOGRAPHICA #1/2
024	617
028	MANIACKERS DESIGN
032	KIRIBARI #3
033	KIRIBARI #4
034	KORATERS.
038	JOSURE
042	PHOTOGRAPHICA #3/4
044	DEVILROBOTS
048	KIRIBARI #5
049	KIRIBARI #6
050	ZETUEI FONTS
054	PHOTOGRAPHICA #5/6
056	PIROMI.COM
060	TYCOON GRAPHICS
064	KIRIBARI #7
065	KIRIBARI #8
066	NOBODY DESIGN PRODUCTS
070	KENTARO «ANI» FUJIMOTO (NENDO)
074	PHOTOGRAPHICA #7/8
076	TSUYOSHI KUSANO (NENDO/LEVEL1)
080	KIRIBARI #9

NARITA
成田インスペクテッド
NARITA INSPECTED

PAGE #		PAGE #		PAGE #	
81	NARITA SELECTED	161	KIRIBARI #14	193	KIRIBARI #18
129	KIRIBARI #10	162	POWER GRAPHIXX	194	TGB DESIGN
130	SUNDAY VISION	166	IIS (ITSUO ILLUSTRATION SERVICE)	198	PHOTOGRAPHICA #17/18
134	PHOTOGRAPHICA #9/10	170	PHOTOGRAPHICA #13/14	200	ASTRO GRAPHICA
136	CYCLONE GRAPHIX	172	FJD (FUJITA JIRO DESIGN)	204	KAITEKI
140	GHS WEB GRAPHICA	176	KIRIBARI #15	208	KIRIBARI #19
144	KIRIBARI #11	177	KIRIBARI #16	209	KIRIBARI #20
145	KIRIBARI #12	178	GROOVISIONS	210	LIVING TD.
146	TSUYOSHI HIROOKA (LEVEL1)	182	HIDEKI INABA DESIGN	214	EXTRA DESIGN
150	PHOTOGRAPHICA #11/12	186	PHOTOGRAPHICA #15/16	218	PHOTOGRAPHICA #19/20
152	ENLIGHTENMENT	188	BOLD INK.	220	IMAITOONZ
156	PAT DETECTIVE	192	KIRIBARI #17	224	YUTANPO SHIRANE
160	KIRIBARI #13			228	NARITA RESPECTED

TORU HACHIGA

Became freelance after having worked at the graphic books publishing company «P.I.E. Books Co., Ltd.»,.. Has worked on planning and magazine articles mainly for design magazines «Design Plex», «Axis» etc. Launched a bilingual graphical magazine «+81» in 1997, and served as chief editor up until issue no.11 in the summer of 2001. Right now he is working on a new project producing motion graphics and DVDs. He is scheduled to launch a new magazine in 2002.

蜂賀亨

グラフィック書籍出版社(ピエブックス)を経て、その後フリーに。デザイン雑誌、デザインプレックス、アクシスなどを中心に企画・ライターなどを手がける。97年バイリンガルグラフィカルマガジン「+81」を創刊。2001年夏11号まで編集長を勤める。現在は新しいプロジェクトとして映像・DVDを製作中。2002年には新しい雑誌を創刊予定。

BIOGRAPHY ↑
NARITA EXPRESS ↓

For several years, or even several decades, I have rarely regarded Japanese design as «this is exactly what Japanese design is», and rarely had a chance to think of such art work easily. In 2001, the exhibition of Japanese art and design happened to be held in England, United States, and Korea. But for those of us actually living in Japan it was just a story from overseas, and attention was focused on its topicality rather than the definition of Japanese design.

However, it's nothing special. There has been almost no opportunity to discuss whether Japanese design is superior or if this is what Japanese design can do. Whether it's in Japan, the United States or England, design keeps changing in people's lives and ways of living, and many designers keep creating outstanding and interesting works and occasionally silly. Design is needed in civilized countries, all over the earth, and people are designing there. The essence of design itself should raise questions more often. Borders and language are no longer considered to be the big issue now.

But, of course, there is design which can only exist as Japanese. Communication design which uses Japanese is impossible to create in other countries, and the design is different because of the differences in historical and cultural background. There is also an originality which only the Japanese can create. I see some foreign designers design a Japanese character using Katakana or Hiragana for the art work, but to be honest I have rarely found an example which is legible, or as well-designed as a Japanese character. If you think it's okay as long as it's visually interesting then that's fine. But the ones who can design more beautiful, legible and interesting Japanese characters are the Japanese people and those designers who understand Japan very well.

Unquestionably there's a language, or cultural, problem. However, as mentioned earlier, the question is why is Japanese design getting attention from around the world. You can say it's because Japanese design is simply interesting. In other words, it's not because it's from Japan or Japanese design, it is by chance that Japanese design is now interesting worldwide.

We sometimes judge design by whether we have experienced it visually or not. When you compare a Japanese artwork, which you have already seen many times, to a foreign artwork, which you have never seen before, the newness is obviously different. Admittedly, whatever you have seen for the first time seems more interesting than the other.

People who have visited Japan for the first time will probably take the Narita Express train from Narita Airport to Tokyo, from Shibuya to Shinjuku station, and get to see the view which gives you a feeling of riding on a vehicle at Disneyland or some kind of amusement park. Buildings, billboards, cars, neon signs and a variety of graphics etc. The street will be full of graphics that you have never seen before.

Even package design for the lunch you ate on the train has a value. The Narita Express will surely run like a rollercoaster all over town in Tokyo. But not all of them who revel in the scenery outside the window are people from other countries. Even a Japanese man like myself realizes anew that Tokyo is interesting on the way from Narita Airport to Shinjuku after coming back from a business trip abroad. I get that feeling at such moments, while looking at the scenery through the window.

«Japan and Tokyo are interesting».

It's not too much to say that it's simply interesting, since the normal Japanese who live here think so.

Like the view of the chaotic town that you see from a train, you will find something that you feel with your own vision and senses from the abundance of design in various fields of Tokyo, Japan. Although it may sound funny for a Japanese person like me to say so, what is introduced in this book is merely only some of the Japanese designers and a portion of their art work. In a chaotic place like Japan, design continues to change and it's fast like an express train.

If you ever have the chance then I want you to come to Japan and take a ride on the Narita Express. This may help you to understand visually what I am trying to say here. And I hope you will enjoy experiencing much more of Japanese design here.

日本のデザインについて、ここ数年いやここ数十年「これこそ日本のデザインだ」というようなことを意識したことはほとんどないし、すぐにそういった作品を思い出すこともない。たまたま2001年にはイギリス、アメリカ、韓国などで日本デザインやアートをテーマにした展覧会等が開催されたが、現実的に日本で生活している私達にとって、それは結局のところ海の向こうでの話であり、日本のデザインについてといった定義よりは話題性のほうに注目が集中してしまったようだ。

しかし、それは当たり前の話であって、日本のデザインが優れているかどうかとか、あるいは日本のデザインだからこそといったような論議が成立すること自体がほとんどなくなってきたからである。日本だろうが、アメリカだろうが、イギリスだろうが、常に人々の生活や暮らしのなかでデザインは変化し続け、そして多くのデザイナー達がたくさんの優れた、面白い、そして時には愚劣なデザイン作品を作り続けているのである。文明のあるところ、地球上の至るところでデザインが求められているし、そしてデザインされている。デザインそのものの本質を問われることが多くなってきており、現在ではもはや国境や言葉などはあまり大きな問題とは言えないのである。

とはいえ、日本だからこそのデザインというものはもちろん存在する。日本語を使ったコミュニケーションデザインは他国ではあり得ないし、歴史や文化といったバックグラウンドが違えばデザインだって当然違ってくる。日本だからこそのオリジナリティもある。時々海外のデザイナーがカタカナやひらがなを使って日本語をデザインをしている作品があるが、正直言ってしっかりと可読性があるものや、あるいは日本語として美しくデザインされたような例を見たことはほとんどない。ヴィジュアル的に面白ければそれでいいといってしまえばそれだけだが、やはり日本語を美しく、読みやすく、あるいはもっと面白くデザインすることができるのは、日本人あるいは日本のことを詳しく知っているデザイナーなのではないだろうか。

そういった言語や文化の問題等は確かにあることはある。しかし、先述したように、なぜ日本のデザインが世界から注目されているのだろうか。それは日本のデザインが単純に面白いからではないだろうか。それは言い直せば、日本だから、日本のデザインだからではなくて、たまたま日本のデザインが世界的に今、面白いということでもある。

時々、私たちは視覚体験があるかどうかでデザインを判断してしまうということがある。日本のデザイナーの作品で何回も見ているものと、たまたま海外のデザインではじめて見たものとの場合では新鮮さが当然違ってくる。正直言って初めて見たもののほうが面白いと感じてしまうのである。

日本を初めて訪れた人達はきっと、成田エキスプレスに乗って、成田空港から東京、渋谷それから新宿駅まで、まるでディズニーランドや遊園地の乗り物にでも乗っているような風景を見ることになるだろう。ビルディング、看板、クルマ、ネオンサイン、そして様々なグラフィックなど、街中は初めて見るデザインで一杯だろう。電車の中で食べるお弁当のパッケージデザインだって捨てたもんじゃない。成田エクスプレスはジェットコースターのように東京の街中を駆け抜けるに違いない。でもそんな窓の外の風景に見とれているのはなにも海外の人たちばかりとは限らないのである。仕事で海外に出かけて、そして成田から新宿への帰り道、日本人である私もやはり東京は面白いなと改めて実感したりするのである。そんなときふと電車の窓から外の景色を見ながら思うのである。

「日本が、そして東京が面白い」と。

普段生活している日本人がそう思うくらいだから、きっとシンプルに面白いといっても間違いではないだろう。

KIYONORI MUROGA (IDEA MAGAZINE)

室賀清徳

Born in 1975. Has engaged in editorial work for graphic design magazine «IDEA» since 1999.

1975年生。1999年よりグラフィックデザイン誌「アイデア」の編集に携わる。

BIOGRAPHY ↑
NARITA CENSORED ↓

Many of the designers appearing on this book were born in the 1970's and they are in their twenties now. I, myself, was also born in 1975, belonging to the first generation who had a computer at the very beginning of its involvement in design. It is not exactly wrong to consider us as a vanguard even if we are not the war criminal who has joined the flood of «the ego trip and superficial graphic design», as a prudent man would say.

In the early days of 1990's, those of us who had a creative preference for Tokyo got excited about the Macintosh, which finally became affordable. One of my friends was moaning, «Although a teacher might laments that we cannot even use a drafting pen well, those who would say such a thing can only use a drafting pen». First of all, the impact of radical designers like Neville Brody from London, Emigre from the United States, and David Carson was brought to Japan. At the same period in Japan, designers like Gento Matsumoto of Saru Burunei, who developed an original approach in digital design, Hajime Tachibana, who was a charismatic man also as a musician, and Tycoon Graphics, who also appear in this book, were highly valued as star designers of a new era. The Exhibition shop of the digital art work «Flokke» (the coinage of floppy and market) was opened for anyone who wants to submit, and it sparked the boom of making original fonts in Japan. The number of indies magazines or free papers by DTP also increased rapidly. The underground music scene like House or Techno has also made a steady breakthrough, and piles of flyers were all over at the same period. This situation was somewhat common to other countries like the US and Europe.

The fever of the early 90's was engaged in the expansion of club culture, and in the entire movement involving the possibility of a computer including interactive work and internet rather than what happened only to so-called design proper. What somebody like me, who has grown up in such circumstances, realizes is that the reality of graphic design had appeared in harmony with personal reality in a D.I.Y. way of thinking, like designing T-shirts that you want to wear yourself. The discipline of «traditional» graphic design was only one of many. Even if it's called an «ego-trip», it seemed to have no problem as long as the market or the community was formed with a mutual understanding.

A decade has passed since then. Even the young men who used to enjoy making party flyers for friends began to establish themselves as a professional designers. «The new phase of design was greeted by the arrival of the Macintosh». «By development of information and communication technology, graphic design is getting globalized increasingly». With my self-examination, there are such phrases that appear routinely in books or magazines related to graphic design, yet they are not repeated as if insatiable. It is natural to point out that the design-related statement itself is immature. Incidentally, these points have been repeated for a long time. It just creates an illusion of running on the conveyor belt. One of the founders of Emigre, Rudy Vanderlands, has said in an interview for one of these magazines, «I am sick of the future».
There is surely also the «boring» situation here in Tokyo. But there are still lots of people coming here with the excitement of new participation. If it's too boring for you, then you don't have to look. As they have a right to create freely, you have a right to turn your eyes away. But there sre also peculiar circumstances which don't let you get bored, like the American guy, Rudy. It is something we, as Japanese, have to face right in front of a book like «Narita Inspected», which asks the question «what Japan is?».

Where do we stand in the network of visual communication transgressing national borders? It seemed real to us in the 90's that both graphic design and music both realized communication across countries, through the movement of subculture in those days. In this optimistic view, you could say that cultural problems, chronicically inherent in Japanese culture, were passed over in advance. But the fact is that the occurrence which originates in being Japan was also observed in the development of comtemporary Japanese graphic design.

For example, the work of the Designers Republic must have been accepted sensationally here more than in Western countries. They have succeeded in incorporating Japanese Katakana (one of the japanese phonetic languages) into the design in a way that Japanese could never conceive. The figurative interpretation of the Japanese character by tDR has demonstrated the feasibility of new design treatments of Japanese characters which were considered ill-shaped and too restless for design, and inverted the paradoxical value that Katakana is cool. We were also very much excited about Japanese anime, manga and video games which happened to have been evaluated globally. There was even a sudden upsurge of cultural nationalism. This was because young Japanese people were almost severed from the history and tradition of their own country by the national modernization at the end of the 19th century and the national reform after World War II. They are not able to find an identity there, so some of them saw anime and games to be the real culture that they could be proud of. None of the Japanese traditional art and entertainment which are currently introduced in overseas Japan travel guidebooks can not be found in our life here. It's undeniable that the style, having a «Japanese» appearance which can be seen in young designers' work, is in fact also the result of some kind of inversion. But that's the reality we feel. That's what made us find the small strength in the games, manga, anime having spread globally, and the possibility of communication through these. For us, Japan as a tradition is an object to be «rediscovered». If you find something traditionally Japanese in the new graphic design from Japan in some way, it may be a result of the actual structure, fraught with modern Japan, not the aesthetic feeling of stereotyped Japanese tradition severed from reality.

The word «design» in Japanese has been used and pronounced in the same way as English, as it is a foreign word. Since «design» has its origin in Western countries, it seems that the hegemony of the concept is not likely to exist in Japan. Until the middle of the 20th century, the history of modern graphic design in Japan was simply the history of experiment and practice, applying the idea of «design» in specific terms (i.e the word «design» has been conceived as a plan in art, especially in context of the history of modern design, like that from the Arts and Crafts movement to Bauhaus, Swiss Typography and so on. Expressions like «designer drugs» often perplex Japanese.) So Japanese are often confined in using Japan as a background. Although this long standing feud seems to have been dissolved in technology and globalism, the opportunity to become conscious of «the political thing» will increase since cultures have begun to live together side by side. On the other hand if you now look down widely upon the whole graphic design community in Japan, there are practically no frameworks for discussion or bases for evaluation for designers to share. The central organization and the goal which has led Japanese graphic design have turned into an exclusive political forum and become a mere shell. When business is good, the design-related policy of a state or a cultural sector becomes extravagant, but then it is the first thing to be discarded when business is declining. Cultural? Companies go crazy trying to sell design as a consumer product. Design-related journalism is expanding based on a completely different logic from «How to create a virtual beauty» and «Typography Now» to «Successful tips! Image strategy of IT era».

The reality of graphics has been increasingly fractionated like this, along with Japanese society and the ways of individual being, and the recovery of oneness in graphic design is an anachronistic fantasy. The «diversity» which is often used as a positive meaning is another expression of this «estrangement». The Japanese designers in their twenties are going their own ways under these circumstances. Most people are living happily in their own world. Although it is too late to turn back, I also think that in this age of young kids desiging websites, Japanese «Design» might have become «design» as a general verb/noun from «Design» in a capital with the limited meaning for the first time, I think. Of course, easy future predictions or analysis are to be carefully avoided. Reality is always one step ahead of what we get to know.
As it is often said that Japanese people like to talk about Japanese, my hang-ups like these are very Japanese. age quod agis. Hey, let's get back to work.

本書に納められているデザイナーの多くが1970年代に生まれて、現在20代。僕自身も1975年生まれ。デザインとの関わりのそもそもの最初にコンピュータがあった最初の世代に属する。心ある人が言うところの、「自己満足的で表層的なグラフィックデザイン」の氾濫に加わってきた戦犯ではないにせよ、先兵であることに間違いはない。

1990年代の初め頃、ようやく手が届くようになったマッキントッシュに、東京のクリエイティブな嗜好を持つ僕たちは興奮していた。僕のある友人は「教師は僕たちをカラス口も満足に扱えないくせにと嘆くが、そういう彼らはカラス口しか使えないんだよ」と言って、息巻いていた。ロンドンのネビル・ブロディ、アメリカのエミグレ、デビット・カーソンといった先鋭的デザイナーの衝撃は直ちに日本にもたらされた。同時期の日本では、デジタル・デザインに独創的なアプローチを展開したサルブルネイの松本弦人や、ミュージシャンとしてもカリスマ的な存在だった立花ハジメ、本書にも収録されているタイクーン・グラフィックスなどが新たな時代のスター・デザイナーとしてもてはやされていた。誰でも出品できるデジタル作品の展示販売会「フロッケ」が開かれ、日本の自主制作フォントブームの口火を切った。DTPによるインディーズマガジンやフリーペーパーも急激に増えた。同時期にハウスやテクノといったアンダーグラウンドの音楽シーンも着実な進展を見せ、フライヤーの山が築かれることになったのは、ヨーロッパやアメリカでも事情は一緒だろう。

90年初頭の熱狂はいわゆるデザイン・プロパーだけの出来事というよりは、クラブカルチャーの展開、インタラクティブ作品やインターネットなども含めて、コンピュータの可能性に絡んだ動向全般に連動するものだった。こういう状況に育った、例えば僕のような人間の実感としては、グラフィックの持つリアリティは自分の着たいTシャツを自分でデザインするようなD.I.Y.的な発想とともに、個人的なリアリティとの協調のなかで立ち現れていた。「伝統的な」グラフィックデザインのディシプリンは多の中の一つにすぎなかった。「自己満足的」と言われようと、それを理解しあえる共同体や市場が成立している分には何も問題が無いように思えた。

あれから10年経った。仲間内のパーティー・フライヤーを作って喜んでいた若者たちも、今では職業的なデザイナーとして身を立て始めている。「マッキントッシュの到来によってデザインの新たなフェイズを迎えた」「情報通信技術の発展で、グラフィックデザインはますますグローバル化していく」自戒を込めて言うのだが、グラフィックデザインに関係する本や雑誌の誌面には決まってこういったフレーズが決まって表れ、未だ飽きることを知らぬかのように繰り返されている。デザインにまつわる言説自体が未成熟だからというのはもっともな指摘だが、ついでに言えば、この指摘も同じくらい長い間繰り返されている。僕たちはずっとベルトコンベアで走っているような錯覚さえ覚える。エミグレの創設者の一人、ルディ・バンダーランズはある雑誌のインタビューでこう語っている。「未来にはうんざりしている」、と。

ここ東京でも確かに「うんざりする」状況は形成されている。それでもそれぞれの興奮を持って、新たに参加してくる人は絶えない。そんなにうんざりするなら、見なければいい。彼らが自由な創作をする権利があるのと同様、あなたには目を背ける権利がある。だが、日本にはアメリカ人のルディと全く同じようにうんざりするわけにいかない、特殊な事情も存在する。それは例えばこの『Narita Inspected』のような本を前にした瞬間に直面せざるを得ない、日本とは何か？ という問いである。

国を越えたヴィジュアルコミュニケーションのネットワークのなかで、僕たちはどこに立っているのだろうか？　グラフィックデザインでも音楽でも90年代のサブカルチャーの展開には、国を越えてコミュニケートしている実感があった。この楽観的な見方のなかでは、日本という場所が潜在的に抱えてきた部分はあらかじめ不問にされていたと言っていい。だが実際には、90年代のグラフィックデザインの展開のなかでも、ここが日本であることに起因する出来事が確かに起こっている。

例えばザ・デザイナーズ・リパブリックの作品は欧米以上に衝撃的に受け取られたはずである。彼らは日本のカタカナをその僕たちの思いもよらない使い方でデザインに組み込んでみせた。tDRによる日本の文字の造形解釈は、これまでカッコよくなくデザイン的にも落ち着きが悪いと思っていた日本語に新しいデザイン処理の可能性を感じさせ、カタカナがカッコイイという逆説的な価値観の転倒をもたらした。折しも日本のアニメ、漫画、ビデオゲームが世界的に評価されていたことにも、僕たちは少なからず沸き立った。にわかに文化的なナショナリズムの高揚の動きすらあった。というのは、19世紀末の近代国家化と第二次大戦後の国家改編を経て自国の歴史や伝統からほとんど断絶され、そこにアイデンティティを見いだせない日本の若者にとって、アニメやゲームこそが自分たちの誇れる文化だと感じられたからだ。海外の日本旅行のガイドブックに紹介されている日本の伝統芸術や芸能など、僕たちの生活のどこにもない。若いデザイナーの作品にみられる一見和風なスタイルも、実はある種の転倒の結果だということは否めない。だが、これが僕たちが感じるリアリティである。だからこそ、僕たちは自分たちのゲームや漫画、アニメが世界的に広がったことにささやかな拠り所を感じ、これらを通じたコミュニケーションに可能性を見いだした。伝統としての日本は僕たちにとって「再発見」される対象なのである。いま日本発の新しいグラフィックデザインに日本が何らかのかたちで見いだされるとすれば、それは現実から断絶された紋切り型の日本伝統の美意識ではなく、近代日本の孕む構造そのものと言っていい。

デザインという語は、日本語では音読みでそのまま使用されている。デザインが欧米に起源を持つものである以上、その概念のヘゲモニーは日本には無いみたいだ。20世紀の真ん中を過ぎるあたりまで、日本のモダングラフィックデザインの歴史は「デザイン」という思想を日本を舞台に具体的応用する、実験と実践の歴史だった。この長い確執はテクノロジーとグローバリズムのなかで解消されたように見えるが、文化と文化がすぐ隣り合って同居するようになったからこそ、「政治的なもの」が意識される機会は増えていく。振り返って、日本国内のグラフィックデザイン界全体を広く俯瞰してみると、デザイナーたちが共有できる議論のフレームワークや評価基盤は無いに等しい。それまで日本のグラフィックデザインを牽引してきた中心的な機関や賞は閉鎖的な政治の場と化して、形骸化している。国家や文化機関のデザイン政策は景気がいい時は度を越して派手になるが、不景気時には真っ先に切り捨てられる。企業は消費財としてのデザインを売りまくる。デザインを巡るジャーナリズムも「3D美少女の作り方」から「タイポグラフィ・ナウ」、「売れる！ IT時代のイメージ戦略」まで、それぞれまったく別の論理に基づいて展開している。

こんな具合に日本の社会と個人の在り方とともにグラフィックの持つリアリティはますます断片化していて、グラフィックデザインにおける全体性の回復は時代錯誤な夢である。よくポジティブな意味で使われる多様化とはこの断絶の別の表現だ。日本人の20代のデザイナーたちは、このような状況のなかでそれぞれの道を歩んでいる。大抵の人はそれぞれの世界でハッピーにやっている。もう後戻りはできないが、僕はこうも思っている。小学生がウェブサイトをデザインする現代になって初めて、日本のデザインは大文字のデザイン(Design)から一般動詞・名詞としてのデザイン(design)になり得たんじゃないか、と。安易な未来予想や分析は禁物だ、現実は常に僕らの知りうる一歩先にある。

日本人は日本人論が好きだといわれるが、このような僕の悩みも極めて日本人的だ。age quod agis。さあ、仕事に戻ろう。

LOPETZ (BÜRO DESTRUCT)

With the aim to encourage and promote young artists, HGB Fideljus created the «Destruct Agentur» in 1992. Teaming up with graphic designer Lopetz in 1994, the «art agency» changed into the graphic design «Büro Destruct», as it's known today. The current crew consists of five members. In 1999 the book «Büro Destruct», published by «Die Gestalten Verlag», Berlin/Germany, offered a sort of retrospective on the their work from 1994 to 1999. The ever so popular «Electronic Plastic» book followed this up in 2000. Even though Büro Destruct often seems weird and precise enough to be Japanese, they're still located in Berne, the small and unsuspecting capital of Switzerland.

ロペス（ビュロ デストラクト）

1992年、若手アーティストを奨励、促進する目的で、HGB Fideljusがアート・エージェンシーDestruct Agenturを設立。94年にグラフィックデザイナーのロペスと協力、今日のグラフィックデザインburo destructとなる。現在5名のメンバーによって構成。ドイツ、ベルリンのゲスタルテン社から99年に出版された「buro destruct」では、彼らの94年から99年までの作品を振り返ることが出来る。これに続き2000年、今やベストセラーとなった「Electronic Plastic」も出版される。よく日本人ではないのかと思われるほど風変わりで几帳面なBuro Destructだが、今もなお、小さなスイスの首都、ベルンを拠点に活動。

BIOGRAPHY ↑
7 AND 16 HOURS INTO THE FUTURE ↓

The Japanese live in the future. Compared to Europe they're ahead by seven hours, to America the difference clocks in at an impressive sixteen hours. The advantage seems slight but remains decisive – the moniker «land of the rising sun» is by no means a coincidence.

This kind of reasoning is a little silly, of course. Not to be dismissed, on the other hand, is the fact that a new strain of graphic designers has emerged from this cradle of electronic and technological progress, nurtured directly at the source of brand new electronic entertainment and infotainment. And this is very much reflected by their work.

In a country where it is common to see grown-up adults obsessing over their Gameboy Advanced during train journeys or considering characters we would have banished to the nursery really cute, visual language has always had a long and important tradition.

By using three different «alphabets», Kanji, Hiragana and Katakana as well as a Japanised English called Romaji, the Japanese are trained from birth to quickly distinguish the subtle visual differences in letters that, to us Westerners, seem incredibly complex and unfathomable. They have been brought up with a sense for detail. And this obsession is ubiquitous in Japanese graphic design, simultaneously clashing with the aesthetic translation of abstraction and reduction. This is a trait normally associated with Swiss graphic styles, where similar virtues rule: patience and diligence in search of perfection. For example, the Japanese cherish their business cards, to be handed over politely with both hands – figuratively this is how they submitted their graphic files for this book.

With this book I attempt to convey a poignant insight, not a comprehensive overview. In Tokyo alone there are at least three times as many graphic designers as in all of Switzerland.

Besides presenting examples from 33 different studios my main concern was to provide a sneaky glimpse of the Japanese work environment and visual surroundings.

Due to lack of space and exorbitant rents a lot of young graphic designers work from home, with laptop and net access within their private collector's heaven. A visit to a Japanese studio will often trigger a speedy tidying session by the owners. On this occasion, I would like to extend a very warm thank you to all the participants. They have allowed us an exciting peek at Japanese life and graphic design.

日本人は未来に生きている。欧州と比べると7時間も先を進み、米国と比べるとまさに16時間にも及ぶ時差である。取るに足らない利点であるかもしれないが、「日いづる国」という決定的な愛称も、決して偶然の一致ではないと思われる。

言うまでもなく、この手の推理は少し馬鹿げているだろう。とは言うものの忘れてはならないのは、真新しいデジタル・エンターテイメントと情報エンターテイメントの情報源で育まれ、エレクトロニックやテクノロジー進化の発祥地であるこの国から、グラフィックデザイナーの新しい素質が現れているという事実だ。そしてこれらは彼らの作品に、強く反映されているのである。

電車に乗っている間、ゲームボーイに夢中になっている大人たち、幼児向けだと私たちが思うようなキャラクターをとても可愛いと思う大人たちを見かけることが普通であるこの国では、常にビジュアル・ランゲージが長く大切な伝統とされてきた。

ローマ字と呼ばれる和風英語だけでなく、漢字、ひらがな、カタカナとそれぞれ3つの文字を使いながら、私達、欧米人には信じられないほど複雑で不可思議な文字の中で、微妙なビジュアルの違いを素早く見分けるよう、日本人は生まれた時から鍛えられている。彼らはディテールに相応しい感覚で育てられてきたのだ。そしてこの執着は、抽象と還元の審美的な解釈とぶつかり合いながら、日本のグラフィックデザインに偏在するのである。完成されたものを求める中での根気と努力、といった同じような美徳が良しとされるスイスのグラフィックスタイルを想わせてもおかしくない特色である。例えば、日本人が名刺を大切なものとし、礼儀正しく両手で差し出すように、彼らの作品も同じように本書に提出されたのだろう。

私はこの本書で、包括的な概観ではなく要を得た洞察を伝えようと試みている。少なくともスイスの3倍以上のグラフィックデザイナーが居ると言われている、この東京で。

33名、各スタジオの作品紹介の他に、日本人の作業環境やビジュアル環境を垣間見れるものにすることが、今回の主な関心であった。

不十分なスペースと法外な家賃のため、多くの若いグラフィック・デザイナーはラップトップとネット・アクセスを用いて、彼らのコレクターズアイテムに埋もれながら自宅で作業を行っている。彼ら日本人のスタジオへの訪問は、素早く整理整頓をさせてしまうきっかけともなるのだ。この機会を利用して、全ての参加者に心から感謝の気持ちを表したいと思う。彼らのお陰で、日本人の生活、そしてグラフィックデザインの一端を垣間見ることが出来たのだから。

FURI FURI COMPANY

Formed by Ryosuke Tei and Miho Sadogawa in January, 1998. Established Furi Furi Company in July that same year. With the original style of Furi Furi Comapany, they have provided the planning, development, and design which capitalizes on all kinds of media such as a character, website, motion graphics, books, goods, events etc. Have aggressively expanded the field here and abroad with the international members and the wide variety of design works. Right now, in order to make concrete the color of Furi Furi Company, they are working in four different divisions including Furi Furi, DV4, Yamada Taro, Erotic Dragon. Currently they have 10 members.

1998年1月程亮弼、佐戸川美穂の2名で結成。同年7月、有限会社フリフリカンパニーを設立。フリフリカンパニー独自のスタイルによって、キャラクター、ウェブサイト、映像、書籍、商品、イベントなどあらゆるメディアを最大限にいかした企画、開発、デザインを供給している。国際色豊かなメンバー、バラエティーに富んだデザインワークで、フリフリカンパニーは国内外問わず積極的にフィールドを拡大している。現在、フリフリカンパニーの持つカラーを明確化するために「フリフリ」「DV4」「ヤマダタロウ」「EROTIC DRAGON」の4ディビジョンを内部に構成し活動を行っている。現在メンバー10名。

BIOGRAPHY ↑
10 QUESTIONS/ANSWERS ↓

HOW DOES JAPAN SMELL TODAY?
The smell of wet asphalt. A smell filled with ion.

HOW DOES YOUR DAY START AND HOW DOES YOUR DAY END?
I am woken by a cawing crow and the noise of a garbage truck. I spend my daytime working on design, having meetings, and having silly conversations. At night, I have dinner with my girlfriend, and we have sweet dreams together, then my day ends. How about that? Isn't it romantic?

IS THERE SOMETHING THAT YOU REALLY LOVE AND THAT YOU REALLY HATE ABOUT JAPAN?
I don't really have anything that I love or hate about Japan in general, but I do love Tokyo. A lovable Tokyo, stylish Tokyo, cool Tokyo, sad Tokyo, cruel Tokyo, I love them all. What I hate is there are too many crows. Somebody please help us!

WHAT DO YOU THINK ARE THE DIFFERENCES BETWEEN AMERICAN, EUROPEAN AND JAPANESE PEOPLE?
American people maintain a life sheltering behind the law. European people maintain a life depending on knowledge. Japanese people maintain a life only in a group.

WHAT DO YOU THINK IS THE DIFFERENCE BETWEEN JAPANESE, AMERICAN AND EUROPEAN DESIGN?
American people design with different passion from European people. European people design with different passion from American people. Japanese people design with the passion.

WHAT WOULD YOU DO, IF GRAPHIC DESIGN DID NOT EXIST?
I would be a rich man.

CAN YOU TELL US YOUR 3 MOST IMPORTANT THINGS/OBJECTS/ACTIVITIES?
People whom I love. People that love me. People that love each other.

WHAT IS BEAUTIFUL AND WHAT IS UGLY?
Children are beautiful, and adults are ugly. Our minds have been distorted.

TO WHICH QUESTION YOU WOULD NEVER GIVE AN ANSWER?
Bunch of question about money. «How much is your salary? How much is your office rent? How much is your annual income»? What are you going to do with it?

IS THERE ANYTHING YOU WOULD LIKE TO TELL THE READERS OF THIS BOOK?
Don't just sit there and work on design all day. You should spend more time with the one you love, and go on a trip! Working on design all day is totally unhealthy. In general, pleasure can be toxic for your body.

(interview by Ryosuke Tei)

Q1: 今日の日本はどんな匂いがしますか？
A1: 雨に濡れたアスファルトのニオイ。イオンが満ちたニオイ。

Q2: あなたの1日はどの様に始まり、どの様に終わりますか？
A2: カラスの鳴き声と清掃車のノイズで1日がスタート。日中はデザインと打合せとバカ話で過ごし、夜はガールフレンドと一緒に食事をして一緒に良い夢を見て1日が終わる。どう？ロマンティックでしょ？

Q3: 日本の好きな部分、嫌いな部分を挙げて下さい。
A3: 日本という括りでは特に好きも嫌いもないけど、東京は大好き。カワイイ東京もオシャレな東京もカッコイイ東京も悲しい東京も残酷な東京も全部まとめて大好き。大嫌いなところはカラスが多すぎるところだね。誰かなんとかしてくれよ！

Q4: アメリカ人、ヨーロッパ人、日本人の違いは何だと思いますか？
A4: アメリカ人は法を盾に生活を営みます。ヨーロッパ人は知識に依存して生活を営みます。日本人は集団の中だけで生活を営みます。

Q5: 日本のデザイン、アメリカのデザイン、ヨーロッパのデザインの違いは何だと思いますか？
A5: アメリカ人はヨーロッパ人と違った情熱でデザインをする。ヨーロッパ人はアメリカ人と違った情熱でデザインをする。日本人は情熱を持ってデザインをする。

Q6: グラフィックデザインが存在していなかったら、あなたは何をしていますか？
A6: 金持ちになってます。

Q7: あなた大事なことを3つ教えて下さい。
A7: 愛する人達。愛してくれる人達。愛し合える人達。

Q8: 何が美しくて、何が醜いと思いますか？
A8: 子供達は美しく、大人達は醜い。僕たちの心は歪んでしまっている。

Q9: あなたが絶対に答えない質問は何でしょう？
A9: お金に対する一連の質問。「給料はいくら？ 事務所の家賃はいくら？ 年収はいくら？」聞いてどうするの？

Q10: 読者に何か伝えたいことがあれば書いて下さい。
A10: デザインばかりしてないで、愛する人ともっと仲良くしよう。そして旅に出よう！ デザインは健康に良くないよ。概して楽しい事は身体に毒だしね。

(インタビュー: 程亮弼)

NAME OF DESIGN COMPANY: FURI FURI COMPANY
NAMES/YEAR OF BIRTH: RYOSUKE TEI (68)/MIHO SADOGAWA (70)/OSAMU IWASAKI (74)/KAZU HIRAI (74)/TARO YAMADA (68)/HANDSOME (73)/KLAUS LYNGGAARD HOUGESEN (78)/HAWKEN LOGAN BRIGHT-ROBERTS (78)/KATSURA ARAI (77)/KUMAGAI SHIGEHIKO (76)
COMPANY SINCE: 1998
ADDRESS: 2-1-10-202 SENDAGAYA, SHIBUYA-KU, TOKYO 151-0051, JAPAN
WEBSITE: HTTP://WWW.FURIFURI.COM/
EMAIL ADDRESS: TEI@FURIFURI.COM
FAX: +81 (0)3-5414-5448

デザイン会社名：フリフリカンパニー
メンバー名（生年）：程亮弼(68年)/佐戸川美穂(70年)/岩崎理(74年)/平井カズ(74年)/山田タロウ(68年)/ハンサム(73年)/Klaus Lynggaard Hougesen(78年)/Hawken Logan Bright-Roberts(78年)/あらいかつら(77年)/熊谷滋彦(76年)
会社設立日：1998年
住所：〒151-0051 東京都渋谷区千駄ヶ谷2-1-10-202
ウェブサイト：http://www.furifuri.com/
Eメールアドレス：tei@furifuri.com
ファックス番号：+81 (0)3-5414-5448

PROFILE ↑
BUSINESS CARD →
SELFPORTRAIT ↓

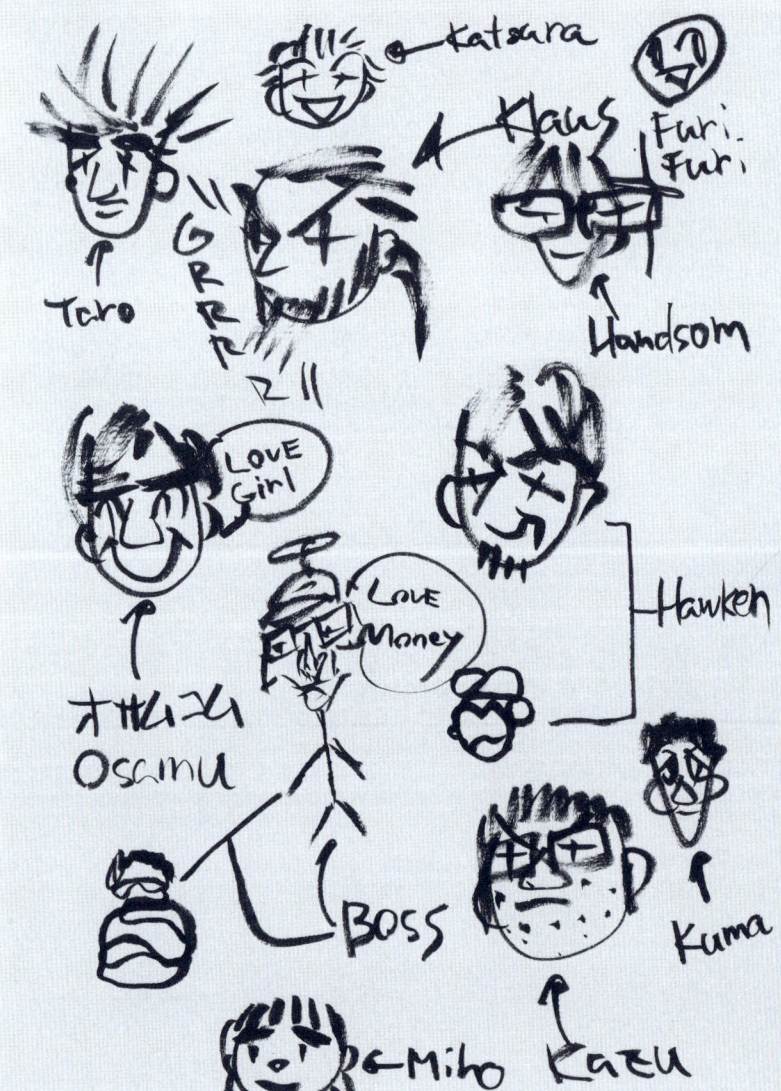

FURI FURI COMPANY フリフリカンパニー

WORKSPACES ↓   LOGOTYPE ↑

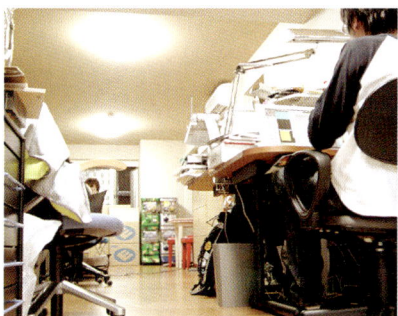

TITLE OF WORK: CLOTHIES FOR A SICK WORLD
POSTCARDS
DESIGN COMPANY: FURI FURI COMPANY
YEAR: 2001
CLIENT: RETREAD THREADS

TITLE OF WORK: ARCADE GAME CHARACTERS
DESIGN COMPANY: FURI FURI COMPANY
YEAR: 2000
CLIENT: SEGA ENTERPRISE, LTD.

TITLE OF WORK: ARCADE GAME CHARACTER STUDY
DESIGN COMPANY: FURI FURI COMPANY
YEAR: 2000
CLIENT: SEGA ENTERPRISE, LTD.

© SEGA enterprises, Ltd., 2000 / © 2000 FuriFuri Co.

FONTGRAPHIC.COM

After graduating from Musashino Art University and working on graphic design such as advertising, book covers, and typography etc., started getting engaged in corporate web design and educational activities for digital design in a vocational school. Having the motto to create design, he considers that the web is the contact surface between people and PC screen, precisely what functions normally as the interface, and develops the web visualization fitted to client's taste with user friendly navigation and a readable character in mind. Has used the websites such as zx26.com and fontgraphic.com as a self-promotion for font or web design, kept the original detailed style of web design with the original font as its core.

武蔵美卒業後、広告、装丁、タイポ等グラフィック全般の仕事を経て現在、企業WEBデザイン制作や専門学校でのデジタルデザイン教育活動に携わる。デザイン制作のモットーとして、WEBは人間とPC画面の接触面、すなわちインターフェイスとして正常に機能するものであると考え、わかりやすいナビゲーションと読みやすい文字を心掛けながら、クライアントの雰囲気に合わせたWEBビジュアライズを構築する。FONTやWEB制作のセルフプロモーションとしてzx26.comやfontgraphic.comを運営し、オリジナルFONTを核とした独自の緻密なWEBデザインスタイルを持つ。

BIOGRAPHY / 10 QUESTIONS/ANSWERS

HOW DOES JAPAN SMELL TODAY?
The change from analog to digital.

HOW DOES YOUR DAY START AND HOW DOES YOUR DAY END?
Peacefully.

IS THERE SOMETHING THAT YOU REALLY LOVE AND THAT YOU REALLY HATE ABOUT JAPAN?
How everything is new. How everything is miscellaneous (Sometimes good).

WHAT DO YOU THINK ARE THE DIFFERENCES BETWEEN AMERICAN, EUROPEAN AND JAPANESE PEOPLE?
Color.

WHAT DO YOU THINK IS THE DIFFERENCE BETWEEN JAPANESE, AMERICAN AND EUROPEAN DESIGN?
Japan: a circle. America: a star. Europe: a square.

WHAT WOULD YOU DO, IF GRAPHIC DESIGN DID NOT EXIST?
Cockpit design.

CAN YOU TELL US YOUR 3 MOST IMPORTANT THINGS/OBJECTS/ACTIVITIES?
Time. Computer. Human Activity.

WHAT IS BEAUTIFUL AND WHAT IS UGLY?
Light and shadow (Sometimes vice versa).

TO WHICH QUESTION YOU WOULD NEVER GIVE AN ANSWER?
None.

IS THERE ANYTHING YOU WOULD LIKE TO TELL THE READERS OF THIS BOOK?
Thank you.

(interview by Hideaki Ohtani)

Q1: 今日の日本はどんな匂いがしますか？
A1: アナログからデジタルへの変革期。

Q2: あなたの1日はどの様に始まり、どの様に終わりますか？
A2: 平和。

Q3: 日本の好きな部分、嫌いな部分を挙げて下さい。
A3: 新しいところ、雑多なところ(それが良い場合もある)。

Q4: アメリカ人、ヨーロッパ人、日本人の違いは何だと思いますか？
A4: 色。

Q5: 日本のデザイン、アメリカのデザイン、ヨーロッパのデザインの違いは何だと思いますか？
A5: 日本—丸。アメリカ—星。ヨーロッパ—四角。

Q6: グラフィックデザインが存在していなかったら、あなたは何をしていますか？
A6: コックピットの設計。

Q7: あなた大事なことを3つ教えて下さい。
A7: 時間。コンピューター。人間活動。

Q8: 何が美しくて、何が醜いと思いますか？
A8: 光、影(逆の場合もある)。

Q9: あなたが絶対に答えない質問は何でしょう？
A9: ない。

Q10: 読者に何か伝えたいことがあれば書いて下さい。
A10: よろしく。

(インタビュー: オオタニヒデアキ)

NAME OF DESIGN COMPANY: FONTGRAPHIC.COM
NAME/YEAR OF BIRTH: HIDEAKI OHTANI (64)
COMPANY SINCE: 1999
ADDRESS: 1-33-10-304 OHOKAYAMA, MEGURO-KU, TOKYO 152-0033, JAPAN
WEBSITE: HTTP://WWW.FONTGRAPHIC.COM
EMAIL ADDRESS: INFO@FONTGRAPHIC.COM
FAX: +81 (0)3-3725-7476

デザイン会社名：フォントグラフィック・ドット・コム
メンバー名(生年)：オオタニヒデアキ(64年)
会社設立日：1999年
住所：〒152-0033 東京都目黒区大岡山1-33-10-304
ウェブサイト：http://www.fontgraphic.com
Eメールアドレス：info@fontgraphic.com
ファックス番号：+81 (0)3-3725-7476

PROFILE / BUSINESS CARD / SELFPORTRAIT

FONTGRAPHIC.COM　　　　　　　　フォントグラフィック・ドット・コム

fontgraphic.com
フォントグラフィックコム

WORKSPACES ↓　　　　　　　　　　　　　　　　　LOGOTYPE ↑

成田インスペクテッド

TITLE OF WORK: WEB SITE
DESIGNER: HIDEAKI OHTANI
DESIGN COMPANY: FONTGRAPHIC.COM
YEAR: 2000

TITLE OF WORK: WEB SITE
DESIGNER: HIDEAKI OHTANI
DESIGN COMPANY: 2X26.COM
YEAR: 2000

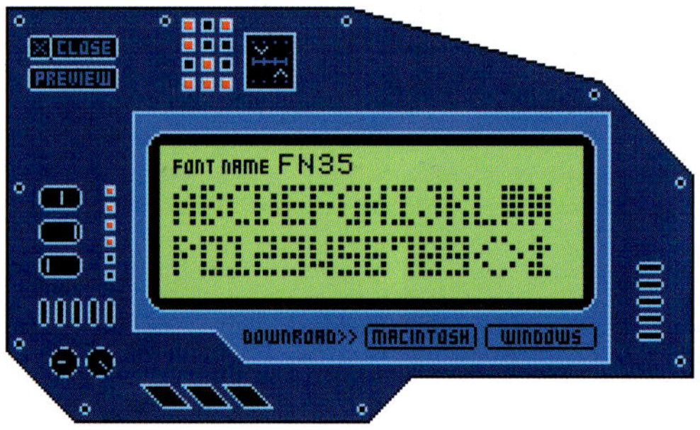

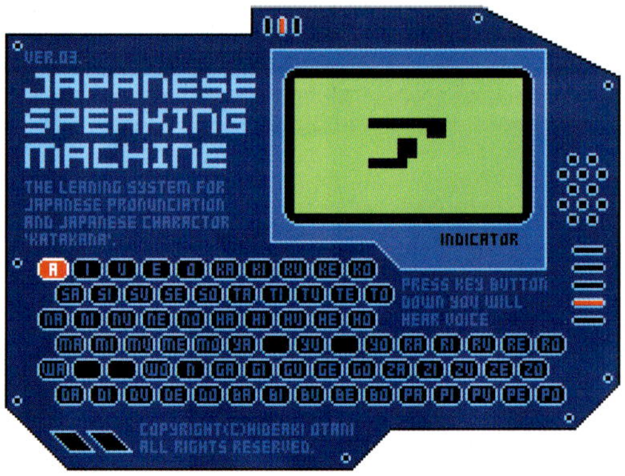

TITLE OF WORK: WEB SITE
DESIGNER: HIDEAKI OHTANI
DESIGN COMPANY: FONTGRAPHIC.COM
YEAR: 1999
CLIENT: K10K.NET

TITLE OF WORK: WEB SITE
DESIGNER: HIDEAKI OHTANI
DESIGN COMPANY: FONTGRAPHIC.COM
YEAR: 2000

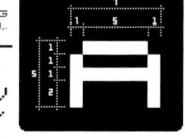

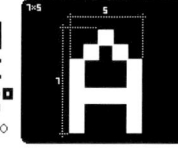

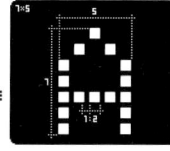

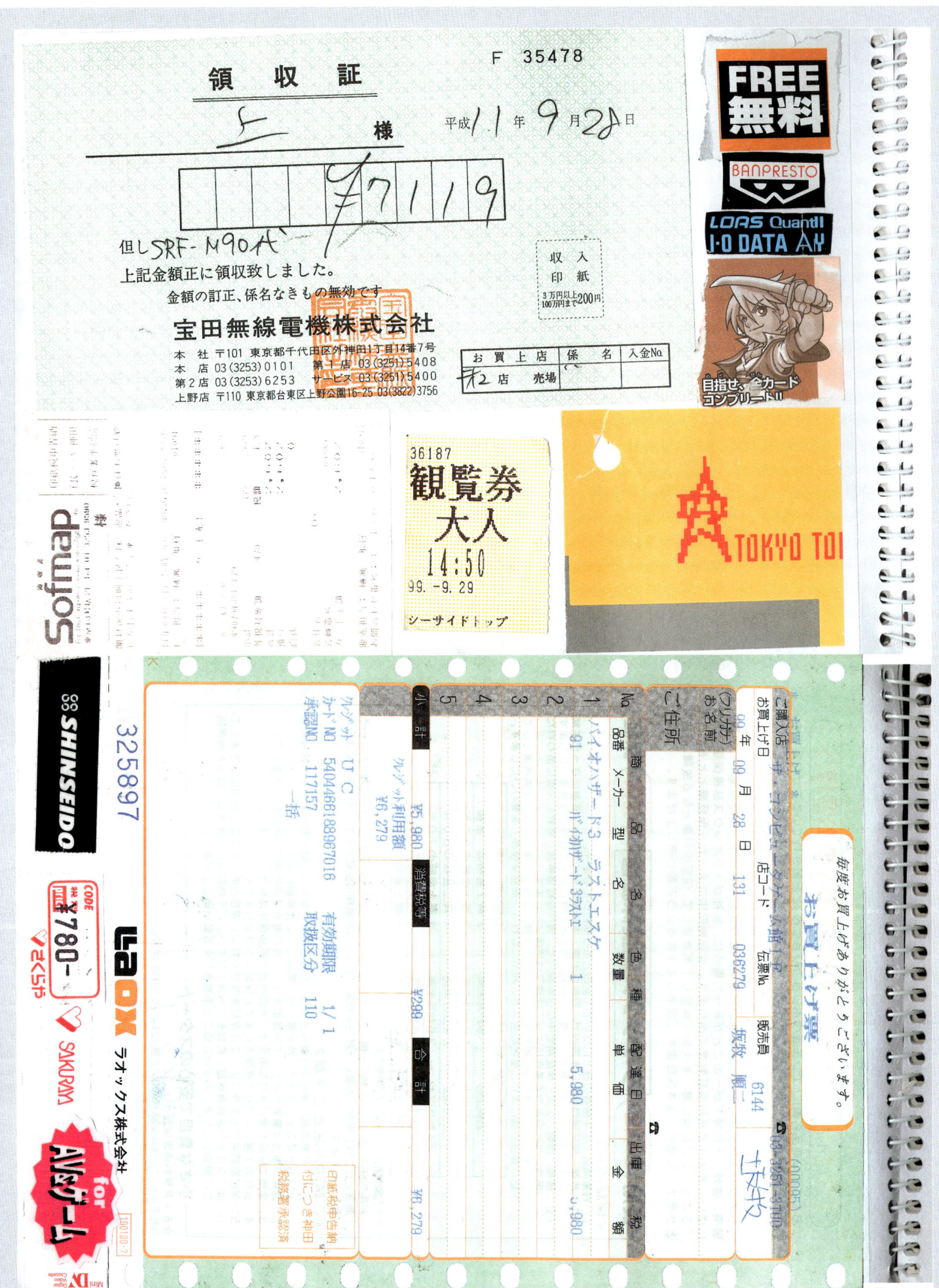

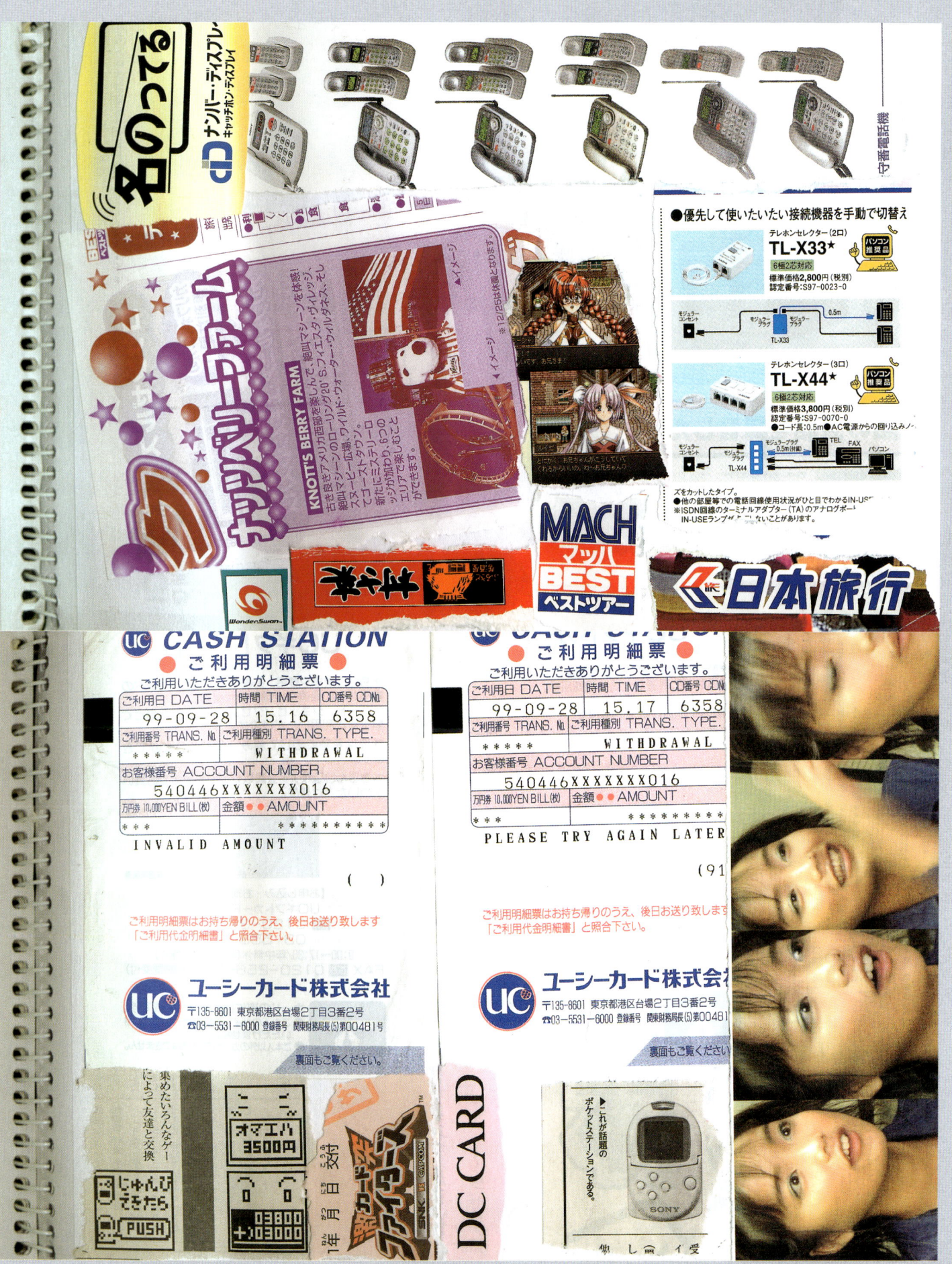

SATOLABO

In 1996, started working on 2D/3D character design, illlustration etc. as a freelancer. The range of activity was extended from 1999 mainly by web design. Contributed the illustration for the art space of the club event «CLUB-SPOTTING» in Italy, 2000. Recent work includes a web design for J-WAVE spring campaign «Living in Tokyo», AVEX character design, ENIX network game etc. Also a visual production for Hip-Hop unit «Street Peddlers» from Miami.

株式会社シンコー・ミュージックより刊行している月刊音楽雑誌「音楽と人」のアートディレクション&デザイン、Sony Communication Network Corporation提供のフリーグリーティングカードサイト「CARTOLINA」のWEBデザイン。IBMから発売している「ホームページ・ビルダーベストデザインテンプレート」制作に参加。プレイステーション等の各種ゲームソフトや多種多様の媒体にオリジナルフォント提供、i-modeの携帯コンテンツやボディケア商品等の各種ロゴデザイン。クラブイベントでのフライヤーデザイン、VJ、T-SHIRTデザインなど愉快で楽しいデザインをモットーに活動は多岐に渡る。

BIOGRAPHY / 10 QUESTIONS/ANSWERS

HOW DOES JAPAN SMELL TODAY?
It smells of Helvetica.

HOW DOES YOUR DAY START AND HOW DOES YOUR DAY END?
10:00am: I jump out of bed with a sense of urgency and start my work. 03:00am: I deliver the data, and end my work. After I remind myself to wake up at 07:00am tomorrow, I go to bed.

IS THERE SOMETHING THAT YOU REALLY LOVE AND THAT YOU REALLY HATE ABOUT JAPAN?
Love: convenient in all respects.
Hate: to criticize others often.

WHAT DO YOU THINK ARE THE DIFFERENCES BETWEEN AMERICAN, EUROPEAN AND JAPANESE PEOPLE?
When Americans see art work, they can immediately say either «I Love It!!» or «So Bad!!». Europeans always want to ask about the background and technique of a piece of work. Japanese people wait and see, then react nervously.

WHAT DO YOU THINK IS THE DIFFERENCE BETWEEN JAPANESE, AMERICAN AND EUROPEAN DESIGN?
I don't really notice the difference because they've interpenetrated each other. However, when it comes to production budget, Japan may have a low level budget.

WHAT WOULD YOU DO, IF GRAPHIC DESIGN DID NOT EXIST?
«Wall painting», even if I am not good at it.

CAN YOU TELL US YOUR 3 MOST IMPORTANT THINGS/OBJECTS/ACTIVITIES?
Relaxation. Memory. Keeping clean and neat.

WHAT IS BEAUTIFUL AND WHAT IS UGLY?
Beautiful: fingers. Ugly: hard luck story.

TO WHICH QUESTION YOU WOULD NEVER GIVE AN ANSWER?
«Are you busy lately?» – I don't know what the standard is...

IS THERE ANYTHING YOU WOULD LIKE TO TELL THE READERS OF THIS BOOK?
I would like to send my appreciation to the staff and readers of this book.

(Interview with Satoshi Matsuzawa)

Q1: 今日の日本はどんな匂いがしますか?
A1: Helveticaの匂い。

Q2: あなたの1日はどの様に始まり、どの様に終わりますか?
A2: 10:00am—切迫感で飛びおきて仕事開始。3:00am—データを送って、仕事終了。明日こそ7:00amに起きようと誓い、寝る。

Q3: 日本の好きな部分、嫌いな部分を挙げて下さい。
A3: 好き—全ての面で便利。
嫌い—他人の事で評論めく。

Q4: アメリカ人、ヨーロッパ人、日本人の違いは何だと思いますか?
A4: 例えばデザインを見た時の反応が瞬時にビックリマークつきで「I Love It!」又は「So Bad!」と言えるのがアメリカ人。作品の背景や手法をつっこみたがるのがヨーロッパ人。時間をおいて様子をみてから反応するのが日本人かな。

Q5: 日本のデザイン、アメリカのデザイン、ヨーロッパのデザインの違いは何だと思いますか?
A5: 浸透し合っているので、特に違いは意識してません。ただ制作予算については日本は低レベル。

Q6: グラフィックデザインが存在していなかったら、あなたは何をしていますか?
A6: 下手でも壁画。

Q7: あなた大事なことを3つ教えて下さい。
A7: リラックス。記憶。整理整頓。

Q8: 何が美しくて、何が醜いと思いますか?
A8: 美しい—人の指。醜い—苦労話。

Q9: あなたが絶対に答えない質問は何でしょう?
A9: 「最近忙しい?」— 基準がわからない…。

Q10: 読者に何か伝えたいことがあれば書いて下さい。
A10: この本のスタッフと読者に感謝します。

(インタビュー: マツザワサトシ)

PROFILE / BUSINESS CARD / SELFPORTRAIT

NAME OF DESIGN COMPANY: SATOLABO
NAME/YEAR OF BIRTH: SATOSHI MATSUZAWA (67)
COMPANY SINCE: 1996
ADDRESS: JAPAN
WEBSITE: WWW.SUNFIELD.NE.JP/~SARU/
EMAIL ADDRESS: SARU@SUNFIELD.NE.JP

デザイン会社名:サトラボ
メンバー名(生年):マツザワサトシ(67年)
会社設立日:1996年
住所:日本
ウェブサイト:http://www.sunfield.ne.jp/~saru/
Eメールアドレス:saru@sunfield.ne.jp
ファックス番号:—

SATOLABO サトラボ

WORKSPACES

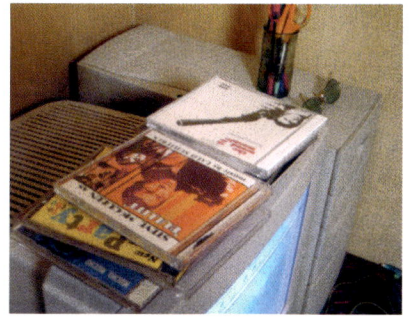

TITLE OF WORK: CHASE CHASE
DESIGNER: SATOSHI MATSUZAWA
DESIGN COMPANY: SATOLABO
YEAR: 2000
CLIENT: ENIX

TITLE OF WORK: NO TITLE
DESIGNER: SATOSHI MATSUZAWA
DESIGN COMPANY: SATOLABO
YEAR: 2001
CLIENT: KIWI

TITLE OF WORK: MEE-MEE (FUJIKO-TIC)
DESIGNER: SATOSHI MATSUZAWA
DESIGN COMPANY: SATOLABO
YEAR: 1998
CLIENT: MEE-MEE

617

617 name was set up around 1997 to put together work made for a friend and present it on the website. Have worked on graphic design including posters, font creation and exhibition displays, mainly in the area of indie brands and shops etc. The latest work includes the art direction of the free magazine «tiger», published in Germany in the winter of 2000, Breath Font & Ripple Font design etc. Planned this year are the collaboration on a digital medium with Jun Tsuzuki, the group exhibition with French artist Alundale in New York and a release of a new font.

それまで友人の為に制作してきたデザイン作品群をまとめてサイト上で公開する為、1997年頃、617名義を発足。主にインディーズブランドやショップなどを中心に、ポスターを初めとするグラフィックデザイン、フォント作りやエキシビジョンのディスプレイ等を行う。最近の作品は、2000年の冬にドイツで発刊したフリーペーパー「tiger」のアートディレクション、Breath Font & Ripple Fontの書体デザイン等。今年はツヅキジュンとのデジタル媒体上でのコラボレーション活動、フランスのAlundaleとN.Y.にて共同展、そして新作の書体を予定。

NAME OF DESIGN COMPANY: 617
NAME/YEAR OF BIRTH: TAKESHI HAMADA (70)
COMPANY SINCE: 1997
ADDRESS: 9-1-7-#617 AKASAKA, MINATO-KU, TOKYO 107-0052, JAPAN
WEBSITE: HTTP://64.124.215.177/617/
EMAIL ADDRESS: 617@GMX.NET
FAX: +81 (0)3-3475-0214

デザイン会社名：617
メンバー名(生年)：浜田武志(70年)
会社設立日：1997年
住所：〒107-0052 東京都港区赤坂9-1-7 秀和レジデンシャル617
ウェブサイト：http://64.124.215.177/617/
http://www.tigermagazine.org/jump/
Eメールアドレス：617@gmx.net
ファックス番号：+81 (0)3-3475-0214

BIOGRAPHY
10 QUESTIONS/ANSWERS

HOW DOES JAPAN SMELL TODAY?
I would say Tokyo smells like absolute despair and hope. I think it's very exciting.

HOW DOES YOUR DAY START AND HOW DOES YOUR DAY END?
I usually have a sort of direction line which heads for design crawling in my consciousness. Otherwise I have lots of things going on every day.

IS THERE SOMETHING THAT YOU REALLY LOVE AND THAT YOU REALLY HATE ABOUT JAPAN?
There is nothing that I hate about Japan right now. I love Japan because I have no trouble talking to people in Japanese.

WHAT DO YOU THINK ARE THE DIFFERENCES BETWEEN AMERICAN, EUROPEAN AND JAPANESE PEOPLE?
I think they are basically the same. The biggest difference is language. I guess the structure of language and custom have overall influence on individual character.

WHAT DO YOU THINK IS THE DIFFERENCE BETWEEN JAPANESE, AMERICAN AND EUROPEAN DESIGN?
I wouldn't make any comments on that because it's hard to tell without understanding each history and cultural background. In terms of attitude however, not the superficial trend of color or form of design, there are no borders to the feeling of thinking what's good is good. And I think everyone bears a longing for something faraway.

WHAT WOULD YOU DO, IF GRAPHIC DESIGN DID NOT EXIST?
I am scared because I might be doing something wrong.

CAN YOU TELL US YOUR 3 MOST IMPORTANT THINGS/OBJECTS/ACTIVITIES?
To create something. To meet with other people's work. To talk with girls.

WHAT IS BEAUTIFUL AND WHAT IS UGLY?
I think that something created happily is beautiful. But something created while pretending to create happily is the ugliest.

TO WHICH QUESTION YOU WOULD NEVER GIVE AN ANSWER?
Personal questions, except for work.

IS THERE ANYTHING YOU WOULD LIKE TO TELL THE READERS OF THIS BOOK?
Please visit my website.

(Interview with Takeshi Hamada)

Q1: 今日の日本はどんな匂いがしますか？
A1: 東京に関して言えば徹底的な絶望と希望の匂いがします。とてもエキサイティングだと思います。

Q2: あなたの1日はどの様に始まり、どの様に終わりますか？
A2: デザインに向かう方向線のようなものがいつも意識に走っています。それ以外は毎日違う出来事が起こっています。

Q3: 日本の好きな部分、嫌いな部分を挙げて下さい。
A3: 今、大嫌いな点はありません。大好きな点は、日本語が通じるというところ。

Q4: アメリカ人、ヨーロッパ人、日本人の違いは何だと思いますか？
A4: 根っこの部分ではほとんど同じだと思います。一番大きい事は言葉の違いだと思います。言葉の構造や習慣が個人個人の性格に全体的な影響を与えていると思います。

Q5: 日本のデザイン、アメリカのデザイン、ヨーロッパのデザインの違いは何だと思いますか？
A5: それぞれの歴史、文化的背景を理解せずに言うのは難しいのでノーコメントです。ただ、表面的なデザインの色彩や形態の傾向では無く、意識の部分だけに絞ると、良いものを良いと感じる気持ちに国境は全く無いような気がします。そして遠いものに対する憧れというのはみんな持っていると思います。

Q6: グラフィックデザインが存在していなかったら、あなたは何をしていますか？
A6: 何か間違った事をしていそうで怖いです。

Q7: あなた大事なことを3つ教えて下さい。
A7: 作ること。人の作品に触れる事。女の子と喋る事。

Q8: 何が美しくて、何が醜いと思いますか？
A8: 楽しく作られている物は美しいと思います。楽しく作っているフリをして作られている物は一番醜く思います。

Q9: あなたが絶対に答えない質問は何でしょう？
A9: 作品以外の個人的な事。

Q10: 読者に何か伝えたいことがあれば書いて下さい。
A10: 良かったらサイトに遊びに来て下さい。

（インタビュー：浜田武志）

HAMADA TAKESHI
617-Akasaka Residential, 9-1-7 Akasaka, Minato-ku, Tokyo, 〒107-0052 / Japan
Telephone and Facsimile. 凸一呵, 弓夕叱冎
617@gmx.net — http://64.124.215.177/617/

617

6 1 7

WORKSPACES ↓   LOGOTYPE ↑

This is my working space.

I am very sorry.

I cannot show you any photos of my room

because I am moving each time

when I work recently.

617

TITLE OF WORK: A POSTER FOR A ROOM OF MY FRIEND
DESIGNER: TAKESHI HAMADA
DESIGN COMPANY: 617
YEAR: 2000

TITLE OF WORK: JETZT
DESIGNER: TAKESHI HAMADA
DESIGN COMPANY: 617
YEAR: 2001
CLIENT: JETZT MAGAZIN (SÜDDEUTSCHE ZEITUNG)

TITLE OF WORK: SASQUATCH POSTER
DESIGNER: TAKESHI HAMADA
DESIGN COMPANY: 617
YEAR: 1998
CLIENT: SASQUATCH

MANIACKERS DESIGN

The art direction and layout design of monthly music magazine «Ongaku to Hito», published by Shiko Music Pub. Co. Ltd. A web design for a free greeting card site «CARTOLINA», sponsored by Sony Communication Network Corp. Participation in the production of «homepage builders best design template» released by IBM. Contributed original fonts to various Playstation game softwares and a variety of media, and various logo designs to i-mode mobile contents and body care goods. Wide range of activity includes a design for club event flyer, VJ and T-shirt etc. with the motto, «joyous and happy design».

株式会社シンコー・ミュージックより刊行している月刊音楽雑誌「音楽と人」のアートディレクション&デザイン、Sony Communication Network Corporation提供のフリーグリーティングカードサイト「CARTOLINA」のWEBデザイン、IBMから発売している「ホームページ・ビルダーベストデザインテンプレート」制作に参加。プレイステーション等の各種ゲームソフトや多種多様な媒体にオリジナルフォント提供、i-modeの携帯コンテンツやボディケア商品等の各種ロゴデザイン。クラブイベントでのフライヤーデザイン、VJ、T-SHIRTデザインなど愉快で楽しいデザインをモットーに活動は多岐に渡る。

BIOGRAPHY / 10 QUESTIONS/ANSWERS

HOW DOES JAPAN SMELL TODAY?
I can smell the refreshing scent of fresh green.

HOW DOES YOUR DAY START AND HOW DOES YOUR DAY END?
I turn on my Macintosh, and I turn off my Macintosh at the end of day. This is my daily life

IS THERE SOMETHING THAT YOU REALLY LOVE AND THAT YOU REALLY HATE ABOUT JAPAN?
What I love about Japan is delicious food, what I hate about Japan is it's an insular country.

WHAT DO YOU THINK ARE THE DIFFERENCES BETWEEN AMERICAN, EUROPEAN AND JAPANESE PEOPLE?
I think the appearances are slightly different from each other. That's it. Other than that, we are all the same.

WHAT DO YOU THINK IS THE DIFFERENCE BETWEEN JAPANESE, AMERICAN AND EUROPEAN DESIGN?
I think that design style changes delicately with the history or background of each country, or the environment and scenery that we live in now. As a matter of fact, I think there is no difference.

WHAT WOULD YOU DO, IF GRAPHIC DESIGN DID NOT EXIST?
I would be doing product design.

CAN YOU TELL US YOUR 3 MOST IMPORTANT THINGS/OBJECTS/ACTIVITIES?
To enjoy everyday life. Macintosh (you can create design, listen to music, or browse the Internet, or do anything you want!). To communicate with many people through design.

WHAT IS BEAUTIFUL AND WHAT IS UGLY?
I think the heart is beautiful and the heart is ugly.

TO WHICH QUESTION YOU WOULD NEVER GIVE AN ANSWER?
Well... it's a hard question because there are lots of things I could not give an answer to... Therefore this is the question I wouldn't answer.

IS THERE ANYTHING YOU WOULD LIKE TO TELL THE READERS OF THIS BOOK?
I hope this book will please, interest, surprise, influence, and impress as many people as possible. And I would like people to get to know the existence of Maniackers Design from Japan.

(interview with Masayuki Sato)

NAME OF DESIGN COMPANY: MANIACKERS DESIGN
MEMBERS: MASAYUKI SATO (74)/MAYUMI KAKEGAWA (75)/JUNYA YAMADA (75)/MASASHI KATO (73)
COMPANY SINCE: 1997
ADDRESS: #102 SERENADE, 27-10 FUTABA, TAKASAKI, GUNMA 370-0843, JAPAN
WEBSITE: HTTP://MKS.JP.ORG
EMAIL ADDRESS: SATO@MKS.JP.ORG
FAX: +81 (0)27-310-6380

Q1: 今日の日本はどんな匂いがしますか？
A1: 清々しい新緑の香りがします。

Q2: あなたの1日はどの様に始まり、どの様に終わりますか？
A2: マッキントッシュを立ち上げて、マッキントッシュをシステム終了して終わる。これが基本的な日常です。

Q3: 日本の好きな部分、嫌いな部分を挙げて下さい。
A3: 日本の好きな部分は料理がとても美味しいところ。日本の嫌いな部分は島国なところ。

Q4: アメリカ人、ヨーロッパ人、日本人の違いは何だと思いますか？
A4: ちょっと見た目が違うと思う。ただそれだけ。中身は同じだ!!

Q5: 日本のデザイン、アメリカのデザイン、ヨーロッパのデザインの違いは何だと思いますか？
A5: それぞれの国が築き上げてきた歴史やその背景、または現在生きているそれぞれの環境、風景によってデザインのスタイルは微妙に違って来ると思う。でも結局のところは違いなんて無いと思う。

Q6: グラフィックデザインが存在していなかったら、あなたは何をしていますか？
A6: プロダクトデザインをしている。

Q7: あなた大事なことを3つ教えて下さい。
A7: 毎日を楽しくいられること。マッキントッシュ。(デザインもできるし、音楽も聴けるし、インターネットもなんでも出来る!) デザインを通じてたくさんの人達とコミュニケーションをしていくこと。

Q8: 何が美しくて、何が醜いと思いますか？
A8: 心が美しくて、心が醜いと思う。

Q9: あなたが絶対に答えない質問は何でしょう？
A9: うーん。色々答えられない事があって難しい質問ですね…。よってこの質問が答えない質問です。

Q10: 読者に何か伝えたいことがあれば書いて下さい。
A10: この本によって出来る限り大勢の人達が楽しんだり、面白がったり、驚いたり、影響を受けたり、記憶に残してくれれば嬉しい。そして日本のマニアッカーズデザインの存在を知って欲しい。

(インタビュー：佐藤正幸)

マニアッカーズデザイン

デザイン会社名：マニアッカーズデザイン
メンバー名(生年)：佐藤正幸(74年)/掛川真由美(75年)山田純也(75年)/加藤雅士(73年)
会社設立日：1997年
住所：〒370-0843 群馬県高崎市双葉町27-10 セレナーデ102
ウェブサイト：http://mks.jp.org
Eメールアドレス：sato@mks.jp.org
ファックス番号：+81 (0)27-310-6380

PROFILE / BUSINESS CARD / SELFPORTRAIT

MANIACKERS DESIGN

マニアッカーズデザイン

WORKSPACES ↓ LOGOTYPE ↑

TITLE OF WORK: CUTE VEGETABLES AND FRUIT
DESIGNER: MASASHI KATO
DESIGN COMPANY: MANIACKERS DESIGN
YEAR: 2001
SELFPROMOTION

TITLE OF WORK: MANIACKERS DESIGN GRAPHIC 2001 POSTER
DESIGNER: MASAYUKI SATO & MAYUMI KAKEGAWA & JUNYA YAMADA & MASASHI KATO
DESIGN COMPANY: MANIACKERS DESIGN
YEAR: 2001
SELFPROMOTION

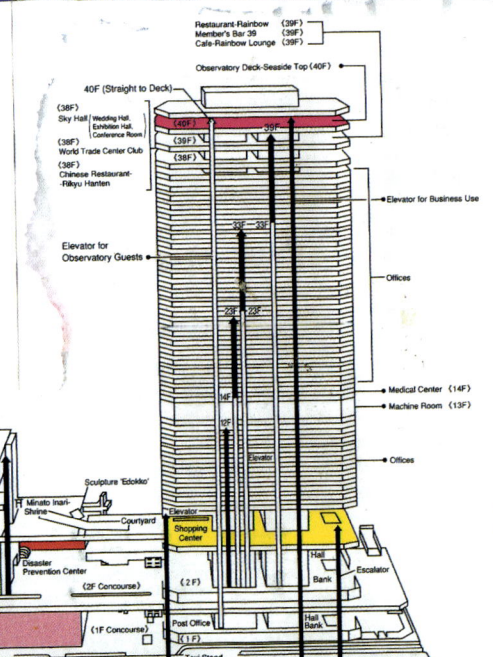

KORATERS.

Under the influence of her mother, who was a good artist, she started to enjoy drawing from early childhood. At the age of 4 she decided to become an artist in the future, and graduated from the Department of Art and Design in Joshibi University of Art and Design. Went freelance as graphic designer after working on package design for candy etc. Made a comeback to the field of illustration in January, 2001 through activities such as graphic design, character design, illlustration, logo design etc. Works mainly on character design and illustration now.

絵の上手だった母の影響で、幼少の頃から絵を描く楽しさを知る。4才にして将来は絵描きになると決心する。女子美術短期大学造形科卒業後、グラフィックデザイナーとしてお菓子のパッケージデザインなどを手掛け、フリーとなる。グラフィックデザイン、キャラクターデザイン、イラスト、ロゴデザインなど、幅広くこなしていたが、2001年1月、イラストレーションの道へ回帰、現在に至る。主にキャラクターデザイン、イラストレーションを手掛ける。

コラッターズ

NAME OF DESIGN COMPANY: KORATERS.
NAME/YEAR OF BIRTH: SHOKO NAKAZAWA ('72)
COMPANY SINCE: 2001
ADDRESS: JAPAN
WEBSITE: HTTP://WWW.KORATERS.COM/
EMAIL ADDRESS: SHOKO@KORATERS.COM

デザイン会社名：コラッターズ
メンバー名(生年)：ナカザワショーコ(72年)
会社設立日：2001年
住所：日本
ウェブサイト：http://www.koraters.com/
Eメールアドレス：shoko@koraters.com
ファックス番号：—

BIOGRAPHY ↑
10 QUESTIONS/ANSWERS ↓

HOW DOES JAPAN SMELL TODAY?
Like rain.

HOW DOES YOUR DAY START AND HOW DOES YOUR DAY END?
My day starts and ends up with taking care of my kitten...

IS THERE SOMETHING THAT YOU REALLY LOVE AND THAT YOU REALLY HATE ABOUT JAPAN?
Love: cherry blossom. Hate: too small.

WHAT DO YOU THINK ARE THE DIFFERENCES BETWEEN AMERICAN, EUROPEAN AND JAPANESE PEOPLE?
Soul.

WHAT DO YOU THINK IS THE DIFFERENCE BETWEEN JAPANESE, AMERICAN AND EUROPEAN DESIGN?
Spirit.

WHAT WOULD YOU DO, IF GRAPHIC DESIGN DID NOT EXIST?
Voice actress.

CAN YOU TELL US YOUR 3 MOST IMPORTANT THINGS/OBJECTS/ACTIVITIES?
My lovely kitten. My memories. To continue drawing.

WHAT IS BEAUTIFUL AND WHAT IS UGLY?
Beautiful: nature. Ugly: destroying nature.

TO WHICH QUESTION YOU WOULD NEVER GIVE AN ANSWER?
I will answer anything honestly!

IS THERE ANYTHING YOU WOULD LIKE TO TELL THE READERS OF THIS BOOK?
I just want to draw pictures leisurely without any restrictions, day after day.

(interview with Shoko Nagasawa)

Q1: 今日の日本はどんな匂いがしますか？
A1: 雨。

Q2: あなたの1日はどの様に始まり、どの様に終わりますか？
A2: 子猫の世話に始まり、子猫の世話に終わる…。

Q3: 日本の好きな部分、嫌いな部分を挙げて下さい。
A3: だいすき―桜。
    だいきらい―狭すぎ。

Q4: アメリカ人、ヨーロッパ人、日本人の違いは何だと思いますか？
A4: 魂。

Q5: 日本のデザイン、アメリカのデザイン、ヨーロッパのデザインの違いは何だと思いますか？
A5: 精神。

Q6: グラフィックデザインが存在していなかったら、あなたは何をしていますか？
A6: 声優。

Q7: あなた大事なことを3つ教えて下さい。
A7: 愛猫、思い出、絵を描き続けること。

Q8: 何が美しくて、何が醜いと思いますか？
A8: 美しい―自然のもの。
    醜い―自然を破壊すること。

Q9: あなたが絶対に答えない質問は何でしょう？
A9: 何でも素直に答えます！

Q10: 読者に何か伝えたいことがあれば書いて下さい。
A10: 何にも束縛されず、毎日のんびりただ絵を描いていたい。

（インタビュー：ナガサワショーコ）

PROFILE ↑
BUSINESS CARD →
SELFPORTRAIT ↓

KORATERS.

コラッターズ

KORATERS.

WORKSPACES ↓   LOGOTYPE ↑

TITLE OF WORK: THERE ARE
DESIGNER: SHOKO NAKAZAWA
DESIGN COMPANY: KORATERS.
YEAR: 2001

TITLE OF WORK: KORAT VILLAGE
DESIGNER: SHOKO NAKAZAWA
DESIGN COMPANY: KORATERS.
YEAR: 2001

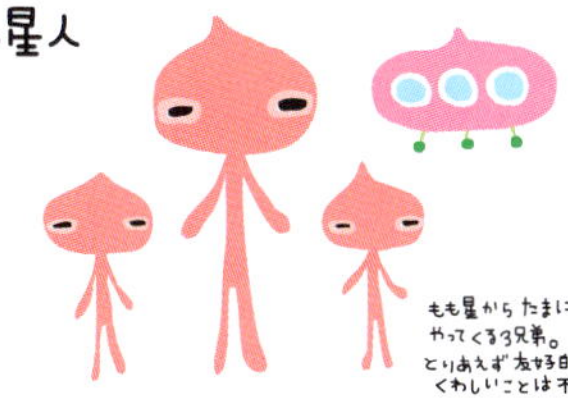

→/→→/→→→
TITLE OF WORK: A BAD FELLOW/MOMO/MOGORO
DESIGNER: SHOKO NAKAZAWA
DESIGN COMPANY: KORATERS.
YEAR: 2001

→/→→/→→→
TITLE OF WORK: HEBI KUN/MUSI KUN/KORATTA
DESIGNER: SHOKO NAKAZAWA
DESIGN COMPANY: KORATERS.
YEAR: 2001

→/→→/→→→
TITLE OF WORK: KORAKKO/NAMATARO/TAMATEN
DESIGNER: SHOKO NAKAZAWA
DESIGN COMPANY: KORATERS.
YEAR: 2001

JOSURE

The members of Josure made a decisive encounter in their high school days. Launched Youth Company label to devote themselves to music activities at the time. Learned several things through this Youth Company and music. Started recognizing the importance of creation, and having an interest in graphic design. Shifted from music to design, and continue to the present day.

ジョシュアの決定的な出会いは高校時代。当時、レーベル青春社を発足し音楽活動に没頭。この青春社を通し、そして音楽を通して幾つか学ぶ事になる。この頃から制作する事の重要性を認識、グラフィックデザインに興味を抱き、音楽からデザインへとシフトして現在に至る。

NAME OF DESIGN COMPANY: JOSURE
NAME/YEAR OF BIRTH: HIRSK.EXE (79)/VENDON (79)/MULTI (79)
COMPANY SINCE: 2000
ADDRESS: 4-13-37-201 MURE, MITAKA-CITY, TOKYO 181-0002, JAPAN
WEBSITE: HTTP://WWW.JOSURE.COM/
EMAIL ADDRESS: JOSURE@JOSURE.COM

デザイン会社名：ジョシュア
メンバー名（生年）：ヒロシクンドットエグゼ(79年)/ヴェンドン(79年)/マルチ(79年)
会社設立日：2000年
住所：〒181-0002 東京都三鷹市牟礼4-13-37-201
ウェブサイト：http://www.josure.com/
Eメールアドレス：josure@josure.com
ファックス番号：―

BIOGRAPHY ↑
10 QUESTIONS/ANSWERS ↓

HOW DOES JAPAN SMELL TODAY?
Although a single misstep could result in a dangerous situation, it seems to give off a smell of mind-blowing reality. Also success and failure may depend on how well you do. Through the development of an information network, everyone seems to be in the situation where they can get a chance easily. On the other hand, there may be a honeyed trap lurking. (VENDON)
Comfortable or uncomfortable, it's a smell of chemical material. (multi)

HOW DOES YOUR DAY START AND HOW DOES YOUR DAY END?
My day starts and ends with checking my e-mail. Although I basically have an unhealthy life-style, I've noticed that I haven't been ill for more than a year. Josure is unhealthy, but a healthy style. It's a dying young style.com. (HiRSK.exe)
I start my day with checking today's fortune on the morning news, and end with brushing my teeth. (VENDON)
My day starts and ends before I notice it. (multi)

IS THERE SOMETHING THAT YOU REALLY LOVE AND THAT YOU REALLY HATE ABOUT JAPAN?
We've never thought about it before.

WHAT DO YOU THINK ARE THE DIFFERENCES BETWEEN AMERICAN, EUROPEAN AND JAPANESE PEOPLE?
Although we're basically all the same and we're all different, if we have to name one difference it is in the education.

WHAT DO YOU THINK IS THE DIFFERENCE BETWEEN JAPANESE, AMERICAN AND EUROPEAN DESIGN?
In respect of design, its own particular culture or history may be automatically creating the differences to other countries. In respect of sense, we don't think there is much difference.

WHAT WOULD YOU DO, IF GRAPHIC DESIGN DID NOT EXIST?
I would probably be involved in music. (HiRSK.exe)
I'd like to be a mathematics teacher or a teen idol. (VENDON) I think I would be drawing a picture no matter what. (multi)

CAN YOU TELL US YOUR 3 MOST IMPORTANT THINGS/OBJECTS/ACTIVITIES?
Sense. Relationship. Positive attitude. (HiRSK.exe)
Simplicity. Extremity. Intrepidity. (VENDON)
Family. Friends. Fuji Rock Festival. (multi)

WHAT IS BEAUTIFUL AND WHAT IS UGLY?
People. (HiRSK.exe)
Michael Jackson. (VENDON)
Woman. Architecture. Feeling. (multi)

TO WHICH QUESTION YOU WOULD NEVER GIVE AN ANSWER?
About inferiority complex. (HiRSK.exe)
Complicated (mental) calculation of 3 or more figures which is given unexpectedly. (VENDON)
About annual income. (multi)

IS THERE ANYTHING YOU WOULD LIKE TO TELL THE READERS OF THIS BOOK?
We will do the thing we had never thought about before. You will be definitely seeing it in our work. And it just gives us an excited feeling.

(interview with HiRSK.exe/VENDON/multi)

Q1: 今日の日本はどんな匂いがしますか？
A1: 一歩間違えれば大変危険ではありますが、大変刺激的なリアルを発しているように感じます。自分次第で成功や失敗が左右されるでしょう。情報網の発達により、一人一人が容易に機会を手に入れる事ができる状況にあると思えます。その反面では甘酸っぱい罠が潜んでいるのではないでしょうか。(ヴェンドン)
心地良くも悪くも化学物質的な匂い。(マルチ)

Q2: あなたの1日はどの様に始まり、どの様に終わりますか？
A2: メールチェックで始まり、メールチェックで終わります。基本的に不健康な生活リズムを繰り返していますが、ここ一年以上病気にかかっていないことに気付きました。ジョシュア、不健康だけど健康スタイル。それは早死にスタイルドットコム。(ヒロシクンドットエグゼ)
朝のニュースで今日の運勢をチェックして始まり、歯を磨いて終わります。(ヴェンドン)
いつの間にか始まって、あっという間に終わります。(マルチ)

Q3: 日本の好きな部分、嫌いな部分を挙げて下さい。
A3: 考えた事もなかったです。

Q4: アメリカ人、ヨーロッパ人、日本人の違いは何だと思いますか？
A4: 基本的にみんな同じであり基本的にみんな違うと思いますが、強いて言うならば教育の違いを感じます。(全員)

Q5: 日本のデザイン、アメリカのデザイン、ヨーロッパのデザインの違いは何だと思いますか？
A5: デザイン面ではその国特有の文化や歴史が、無意識に他の国との違いを醸し出しているかもしれません。感覚面ではそれほど違いは無いように思えます。

Q6: グラフィックデザインが存在していなかったら、あなたは何をしていますか？
A6: 音楽に携わっていると思います。(ヒロシクンドットエグゼ)
数学の先生かアイドルだと良いですけど。(ヴェンドン)
仕事に限らず絵を描いていると思います。(マルチ)

Q7: あなた大事なことを3つ教えて下さい。
A7: 感覚。繋がり。積極性。(ヒロシクンドットエグゼ)
簡単。極端。大胆。(ヴェンドン)
家族。友達。Fuji Rock。(マルチ)

Q8: 何が美しくて、何が醜いと思いますか？
A8: 人。(ヒロシクンドットエグゼ)
マイケル・ジャクソン。(ヴェンドン)
女性。建築。感情。(マルチ)

Q9: あなたが絶対に答えない質問は何でしょう？
A9: 本気でコンプレックスに思う事。(ヒロシクンドットエグゼ)
突然出された3桁以上の計算（暗算型）の問題。(ヴェンドン)
年収。(マルチ)

Q10: 読者に何か伝えたいことがあれば書いて下さい。
A10: 私達自身考えもなかったような事をこれからやっていきます。それは間違いなく私達の作品からお知らせする事になるでしょう。そしてそれはどうしようもなく私達を興奮させるのです。

(インタビュー: ヒロシクンドットエグゼ/ヴェンドン/マルチ)

PROFILE ↑
BUSINESS CARD →
SELFPORTRAIT ↓

DESTRUCT AND CONSTRUCT
We want to react to various cultural activities and to send a signal by the medium called the design. Conversely, it is moved by the design.

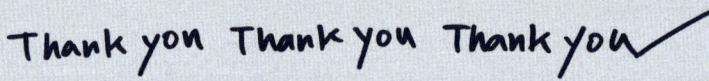

JOSURE	ジョシュア

WORKSPACES ↓	LOGOTYPE ↑

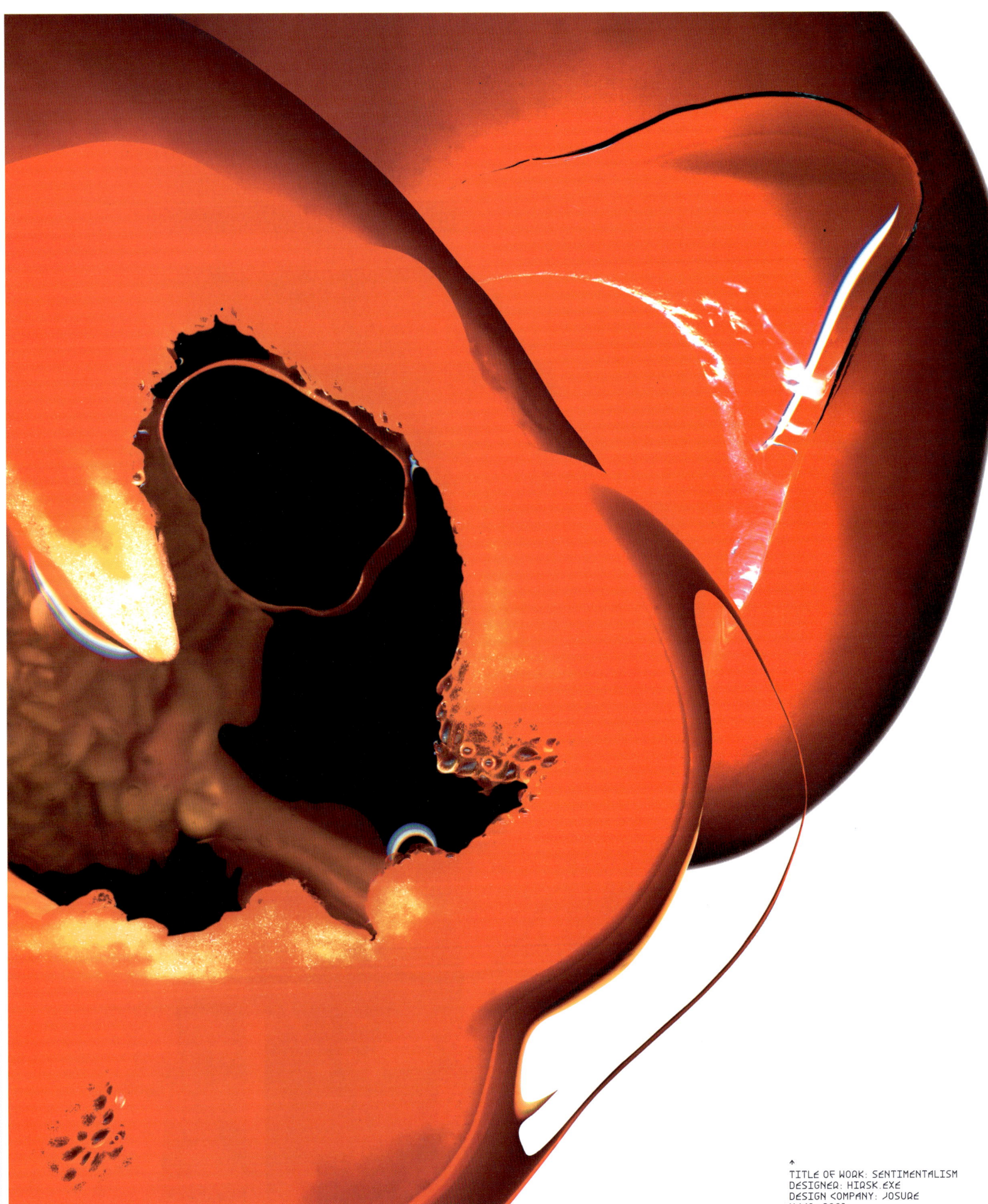

↑
TITLE OF WORK: SENTIMENTALISM
DESIGNER: HIRSK.EXE
DESIGN COMPANY: JOSURE
YEAR: 2001

歪曲インスペクテッド

P#41

«NARITA INSPECTED»

TITLE OF WORK: BOY MEETS GIRL
DESIGNER: HIRSK.EXE
DESIGN COMPANY: JOSURE
YEAR: 2001

BD/DGV/01

DEVILROBOTS

Devilrobots works on graphic design, character design, illustration, clothing, goods, motion graphics, web design etc, and consists of 6 members - Shinichiro Kitai, Kenji Saito, Seikou Kato, Yoshizo Yoshimura, Takeshi Ikegami, and Toshiyuki Ushikubo. While doing well at their own pace, activities have expanded recently into new areas. The World Exhibition Tour, the project of the mascot character «Tofu Family» figure, and the original clothing brand called «evirob» are scheduled to launch very soon. Although the naughty plan for the future is veiled, it's ready to be exposed to the light of day.

キタイシンイチロウ、サイトウケンジ、カトウセイコウ、ヨシムラヨシゾー、イケガミタケシ、ウシクボトシユキの6人が揃ったデビロボは、グラフィック、キャラクター、イラスト、ウェア、グッズ、映像、WEBページなどの制作を手掛けています。結構マイペースだけど、最近はアクティブさを増し、新しい分野にちゃっかり顔を出しています。World Exhibition Tourのスタート、看板キャラ「トーフ親子」のフィギュア化、オリジナルウェアブランド「evirob」の立ち上げとボーダレスに展開中。この先、何をやらかすかは秘密だけど、少しずつ白日のもとにさらされていくのでお楽しみに。

BIOGRAPHY
10 QUESTIONS/ANSWERS

HOW DOES JAPAN SMELL TODAY?
It is the smell of an old dude and cheap candy. The smell probably comes from having only dudes in the office, and I carry my favorite cheap candy. But I like the smell. It's cloudy outside.

HOW DOES YOUR DAY START AND HOW DOES YOUR DAY END?
I unconsciously wake up, and go to the office. I start work after checking my e-mail. I browse the internet during lunch (either bread or rice ball), and I try to finish up my work around 9pm to go to a sports gym nearby. After an hour of exercise, I go back home, have dinner, watch TV, read manga, and play with my cat. Then I draw some illustrations, or play with clay, and go to sleep. That's how my day is lately.

IS THERE SOMETHING THAT YOU REALLY LOVE AND THAT YOU REALLY HATE ABOUT JAPAN?
Love: having plenty of different things. Hate: having plenty of different things.

WHAT DO YOU THINK ARE THE DIFFERENCES BETWEEN AMERICAN, EUROPEAN AND JAPANESE PEOPLE?
Language. Currency. Color of skin.

WHAT DO YOU THINK IS THE DIFFERENCE BETWEEN JAPANESE, AMERICAN AND EUROPEAN DESIGN?
There is not much difference, I think. Cool stuff is cool and corny stuff is corny. I think it's common to have design as work containing the client's idea as well as the design created freely for the portfolio.

WHAT WOULD YOU DO, IF GRAPHIC DESIGN DID NOT EXIST?
I would be probably be searching for something similar to design or making something. For example, making bread in various shapes at a bakery.

CAN YOU TELL US YOUR 3 MOST IMPORTANT THINGS/OBJECTS/ACTIVITIES?
To stick with Devilrobots' policy of «doing things by halves». My Macintosh (necessary equipment for work). Activity as Devilrobot.

WHAT IS BEAUTIFUL AND WHAT IS UGLY?
Beautiful: all living things except human beings.
Ugly: human beings.

TO WHICH QUESTION YOU WOULD NEVER GIVE AN ANSWER?
«Are there any designs (or designers) you like, or designs (or designers) you don't like?» etc.

IS THERE ANYTHING YOU WOULD LIKE TO TELL THE READERS OF THIS BOOK?
I hope you will find it cute, or corny, or interesting, or whatever to see our work.

(interview with Shinichiro Kitai)

NAME OF DESIGN COMPANY: DEVILROBOTS
NAME/YEAR OF BIRTH: SHINICHIRO KITAI (71)/ KENJI SAITO (69)/SEIKOU KATO (70)/ YOSHIZO YOSHIMURA (68)/TAKESHI IKEGAMI (78)/ TOSHIYUKI USHIKUBO (71)
COMPANY SINCE: 1999
ADDRESS: 4-28 MURAKAMI-BLDG. 2F, SUIDO-CHO, SHINJUKU-KU, TOKYO 162-0811, JAPAN
WEBSITE: HTTP://WWW.DEVILROBOTS.COM
EMAIL ADDRESS: DEVIL@DEVILROBOTS.COM
FAX: +81 (0)3-3267-7338

デザイン会社名：デビルロボッツ
メンバー名(生年)：キタイシンイチロウ(71年)／サイトウケンジ(69年)／カトウセイコウ(70年)／ヨシムラヨシゾー(68年)／イケガミタケシ(78年)／ウシクボトシユキ(71年)
会社設立日：1999年
住所：〒162-0811 東京都新宿区水道町4-28 村上ビル2F
ウェブサイト：http://www.devilrobots.com/
Eメールアドレス：devil@devilrobots.com
ファックス番号：+81 (0)3-3267-7338

PROFILE
BUSINESS CARD →
SELFPORTRAIT

Q1: 今日の日本はどんな匂いがしますか？
A1: おっさんと駄菓子の匂いです。男のみの男臭い事務所と、大好物の駄菓子のせいでしょう。でも好きな匂いです。外は曇ってます。

Q2: あなたの1日はどの様に始まり、どの様に終わりますか？
A2: なんとなく起きて事務所に行き、メールのチェックをしてから仕事が始まります。昼ご飯(パン、おにぎり)の間にホームページを見て、21時くらいになると仕事を片づけて近所のスポーツジムに行きます。1時間くらい運動をしたら家に帰り、ゴハンを食べて、TVを見て、マンガを読んで、ネコと遊びます。そして手描きのイラストを描いたり、粘土で遊んだりして寝ます。最近はこの繰り返し。

Q3: 日本の好きな部分、嫌いな部分を挙げて下さい。
A3: 好き―いろんなモノが溢れているところ。
嫌い―いろんなモノが溢れているところ。

Q4: アメリカ人、ヨーロッパ人、日本人の違いは何だと思いますか？
A4: 言葉。通貨。肌の色。

Q5: 日本のデザイン、アメリカのデザイン、ヨーロッパのデザインの違いは何だと思いますか？
A5: 特に違いはないと思います。カッコイイものはカッコイイと思うし、ダサイものはダサイと思います。それなりにクライアントの考えも入った仕事としてのデザインもあれば、自由なアイデアで作られた作品としてのデザインもあったりという部分は世界共通だと思います。

Q6: グラフィックデザインが存在していなかったら、あなたは何をしていますか？
A6: きっとデザインに近い事やモノを作る事を探していると思います。パン屋でいろんなカタチのパンを作ってるとか。

Q7: あなた大事なことを3つ教えて下さい。
A7: デビルロボッツのポリシー「中途半端な感じ」を貫くこと。自分のMAC(仕事道具)。デビルロボッツとしての活動。

Q8: 何が美しくて、何が醜いと思いますか？
A8: 美しい―人間以外の生きているもの。醜い―人間。

Q9: あなたが絶対に答えたくない質問は何でしょう？
A9: 「好きなデザイン(デザイナー)、嫌いなデザイン(デザイナー)は？」とか。

Q10: 読者に何か伝えたいことがあれば書いて下さい。
A10: ボクタチの作品を見て、カワイイとかダサイとかオモシロイとかいろいろ何か感じてもらえたらウレシイです。

(インタビュー：キタイシンイチロウ)

art director
shinichiro-kitai
キタイシンイチロウ

4-28 Murakami-Bldg.2F,Suido-cho,Shinjuku-ku,
Tokyo,Japan zip162-0811

Telephone:03-3267-7336
Facsimile:03-3267-7338
Portable:090-1957-3725

e-mail : kitai@devilrobots.com
URL:http://www.devilrobots.com

有限会社　デビルロボッツ
〒162-0811　東京都新宿区水道町4-28　村上ビル2F

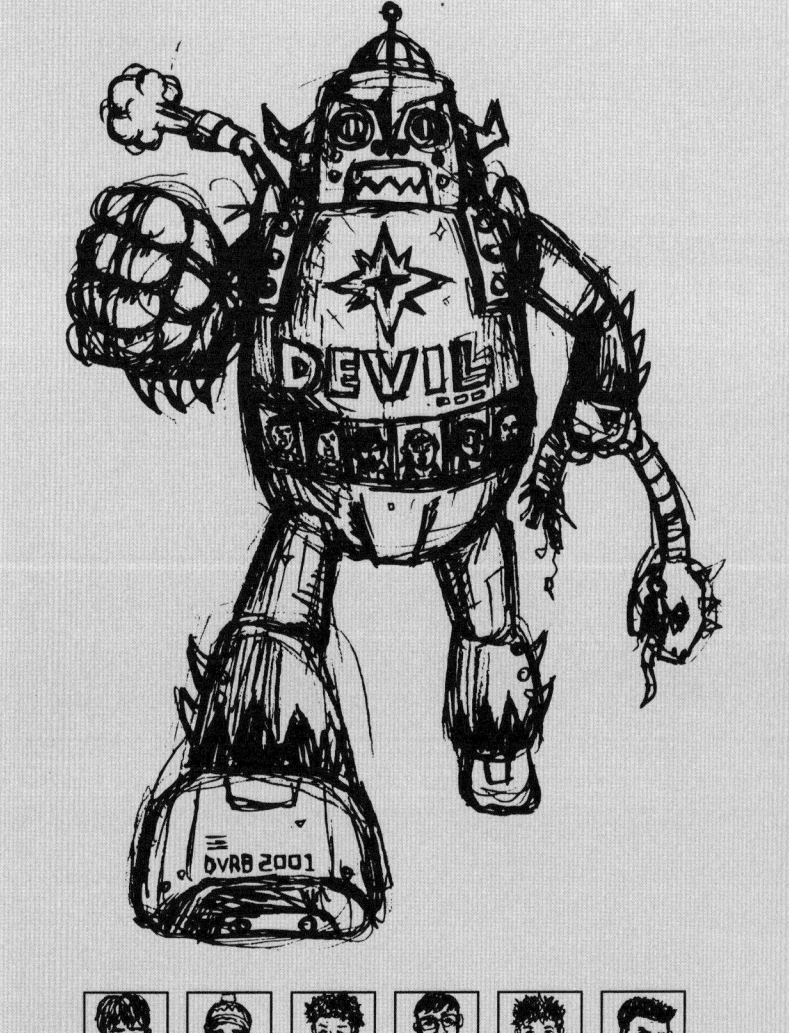

Shinichiro Kitai | Kenji Saito | Seikou Kato | Yoshizo Yoshimura | Takeshi Ikegami | Toshiyuki Ushikubo

DEVILROBOTS

デビルロボッツ

WORKSPACES ↓   LOGOTYPE ↑

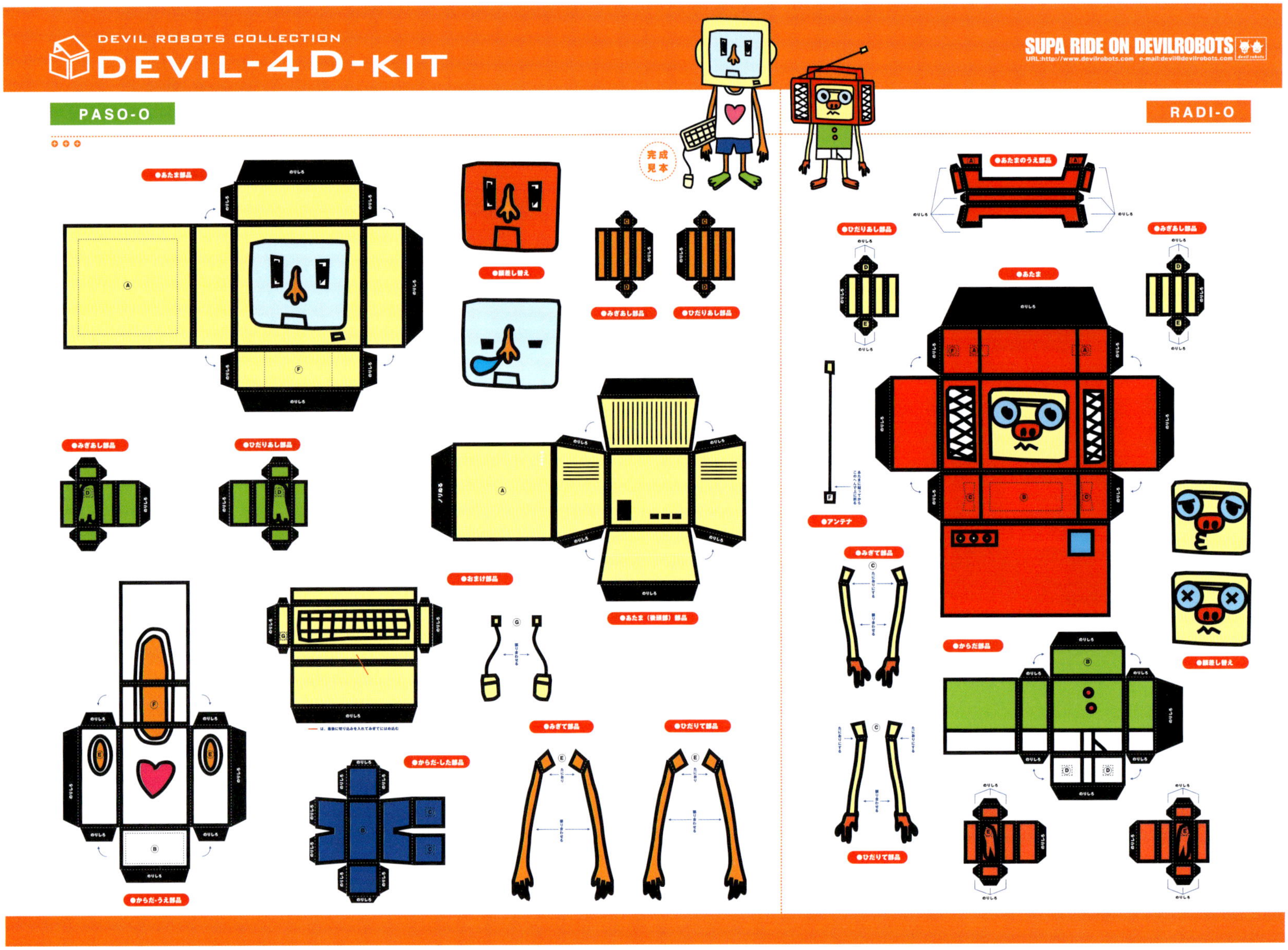

TITLE OF WORK: F4DKIT
DESIGN COMPANY: DEVILROBOTS
YEAR: 2000

TITLE OF WORK: LABOR
DESIGN COMPANY: DEVILROBOTS
YEAR: 2000
CLIENT: BNN

TITLE OF WORK: ZAKKA BOOK COVER
DESIGN COMPANY: DEVILROBOTS
YEAR: 2001

TITLE OF WORK: TO-FU FAMILY
DESIGN COMPANY: DEVILROBOTS
YEAR: 2000
SELFPROMOTION

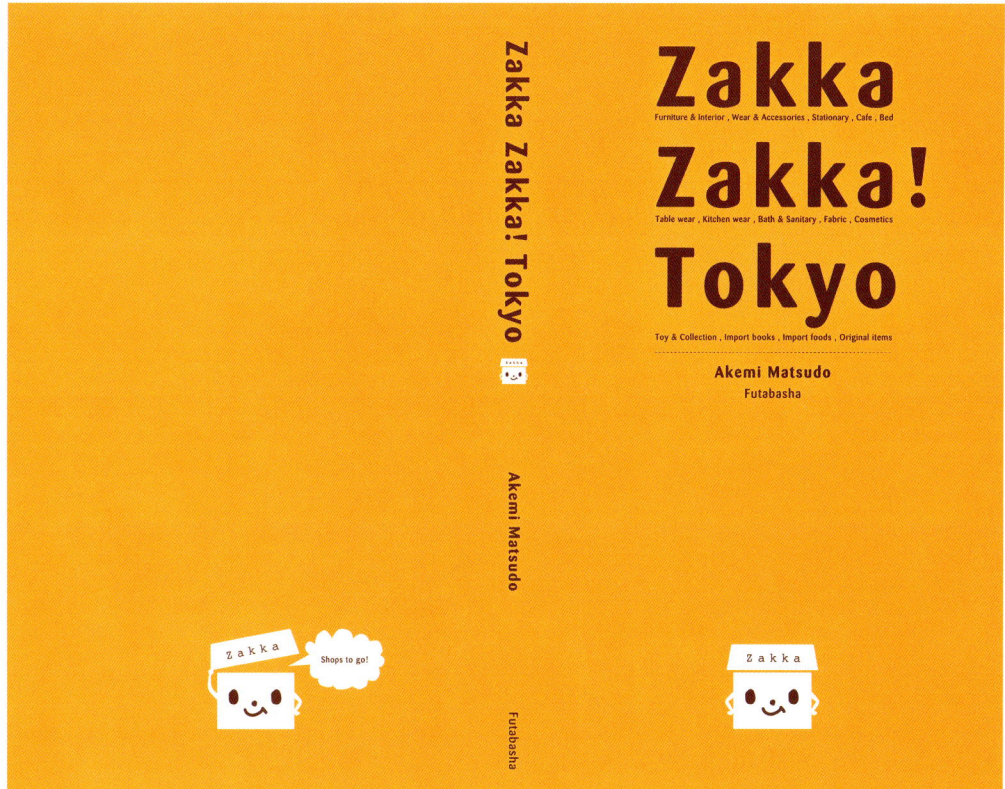

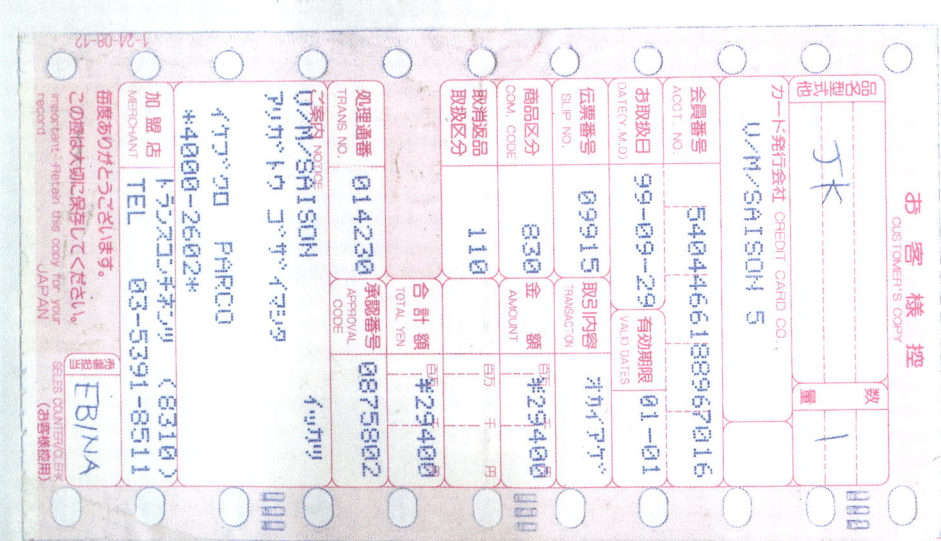

ZETUEI FONTS

08/1996--Established ZETUEI FONTS
08/1999--Published a booklet «Thai Language Lessons»
01/2000--Published a booklet «Declaration of Zetuei the Conquest of the Moji World»
10/2000--Started a free paper «Quarterly Teikoku-Gaho Free Graphic Magazine»
08/2001--Published a booklet «a Library of Teito Re-construction Plan»

1996年08月―ZETUEI FONTS設立
1999年08月―小冊子「泰國語講座」発行
2000年01月―冊子「絶影文字世界征服宣言」発行
2000年10月―無料誌「季刊 鼎國画報」発行開始
2001年08月―冊子「鼎都再開発計画叢書」発行

絶影

BIOGRAPHY ↑
10 QUESTIONS/ANSWERS ↓

HOW DOES JAPAN SMELLS TODAY?
Tasteless and odorless today. Different one from yesterday and the day before yesterday.

HOW DOES YOUR DAY STARTS AND HOW DOES YOUR DAY ENDS?
I naturally wake up at the same time everyday, eat some food, look at a character, read a character, get a good sunlight, ride on a bicycle, check today's change, write a character, explain a character, check a character, type a character, proofread a character, place a character, print out a character, pass a character, send a character, ride on a bicycle, check today's change, eat some food, and get some sleep.

IS THERE SOMETHING WHAT YOU REALLY LOVE AND WHAT YOU REALLY HATE ABOUT JAPAN?
I love experience of change by extraordinary speed for all things. I hate the system which makes all standards obscure and puts all problems off.

WHAT DO YOU THINK ARE THE DIFFERENCES BETWEEN AMERICAN, EUROPEAN AND JAPANESE PEOPLE?
American: gathering. European: integration. Japanese: group. The difference in a form of converging.

WHAT DO YOU THINK IS THE DIFFERENCE BETWEEN JAPANESE, AMERICAN AND EUROPEAN DESIGN?
Japanese design is functionally contained within the limits of it. American design is splendidly embellished even outside of the limits. European design does not show the existence of the limits. The difference in a way of looking at the limits.

WHAT WOULD YOU DO, IF GRAPHIC DESIGN DID NOT EXIST?
I would be a calligrapher.

CAN YOU TELL US YOUR 3 MOST IMPORTANT THINGS?/OBJECTS/ACTIVITIES?
Bicycle commute. Hope to be inoccupation (which means not to have specific occupation). Conquest of moji(typeface) world.

WHAT IS BEAUTIFUL AND WHAT IS UGLY?
White is beautiful and black is ugly. It is the most beautiful when white and black are compounded.

TO WHICH QUESTION YOU WOULD NEVER GIVE AN ANSWER?
The question about background and future plan.

IS THERE SOMETHING YOU WOULD LIKE TO TELL THE READERS OF THIS BOOK?
What is a good font? A good font is excellent in readability, and universal and functional. However, it may be the result of omitting individual information from many typeface information included in the handwritten typeface. What I think is that the information of his idea, thought, philosophy, thesis, and life is all included just in the omitted part. At the best moment of character input by a computer, now handwritten typeface cannot be replaced with font as it is. In the age of digital input, you should get your own typeface alternative to handwriting without depending on the existing digital font.

(interview with Yoshiyuki Kano)

Q1: 今日の日本はどんな匂いがしますか?
A1: 今日は無味無臭。昨日とも一昨日とも違う無味無臭。

Q2: あなたの1日はどの様に始まり、どの様に終わりますか?
A2: 毎日決まった時間に自動的に目を覚まして、食って、字を眺めて、字を読んで、太陽浴びて、自転車で走って、今日の変化を確認し、字を書いて、字を説明して、字を確認して、字を打って、字を校正して、字を判別して、字を印刷して、字を渡して、字を送って、自転車で走って、今日の変化を確認し、食って、寝る。

Q3: 日本の好きな部分、嫌いな部分を挙げて下さい。
A3: あらゆるものの尋常でない早さでの変化の体験を愛し、あらゆる基準が曖昧で、あらゆる問題を先送りする体制を憎む。

Q4: アメリカ人、ヨーロッパ人、日本人の違いは何だと思いますか?
A4: アメリカ人は集合。ヨーロッパ人は集積。日本人は集団。集まる形の違い。

Q5: 日本のデザイン、アメリカのデザイン、ヨーロッパのデザインの違いは何だと思いますか?
A5: 日本のデザインは、その範囲内に機能的に収納される。アメリカのデザインは、その範囲外まで華麗に装飾される。ヨーロッパのデザインは、その範囲の有無を感じさせない。その範囲の捉え方の違い。

Q6: グラフィックデザインが存在していなかったら、あなたは何をしていますか?
A6: 書道家。

Q7: あなた大事なことを3つ教えて下さい。
A7: 自転車通勤。無職希望(特定の仕事を持たないの意)。文字世界征服。

Q8: 何が美しくて、何が醜いと思いますか?
A8: 白が美しく、黒が醜い。白と黒が合わさる時、最も美しい。

Q9: あなたが絶対に答えない質問は何でしょう?
A9: 過去の経歴、未来の予定。

Q10: 読者に何か伝えたいことがあれば書いて下さい。
A10: 良い書体とはなんであるか、可読性に優れ、普遍的で、機能的な書体である。しかしそれは手書きの文字に含まれた多くの文字情報以外の個人的情報を切り捨てた結果であろう。その切り捨てられた部分にこそ、その人の考え、思想、主義、主張、人生の全ての情報が含まれていると考える。コンピュータでの文字入力が全盛の今、手書きの文字をそのまま書体に置換することはできない。デジタル入力時代には手書きに代わる自分自身の文字、既存のデジタルフォントに頼らない自分自身の唯一の文字を手に入れ、自分自身を表現すべきである。

(インタビュー: 加納佳之)

NAME OF DESIGN COMPANY: ZETUEI FONTS
NAME/YEAR OF BIRTH: YOSHIYUKI KANO (76)
COMPANY SINCE: 1996
ADDRESS: 2-3-8-#201, MINAMISUNA, KOTO-KU, TOKYO 136-0076, JAPAN
WEBSITE: HTTP://WWW.ZETUEI.COM
EMAIL ADDRESS: INFO@ZETUEI.COM
FAX: +81 (0)3-3615-2501

デザイン会社名: 絶影
メンバー名(生年): 加納佳之(76年)
会社設立日: 1996年
住所: 〒136-0076 東京都江東区南砂2-3-8-201
ウェブサイト: http://www.zetuei.com
Eメールアドレス: info@zetuei.com
ファックス番号: +81 (0)3-3615-2501

PROFILE ↑
BUSINESS CARD →
SELFPORTRAIT ↓

ZETUEI FONTS 絶影

WORKSPACES ↓ LOGOTYPE ↑

FONTNAMES:
NIJIKAKARU-ALP/KAT [ALPHABET/KATAKANA] 2001
ZETUEI FAMILY [ALPHABET/KATAKANA/HIRAGANA] 1999
TYPOCAPSULE-ALP [ALPHABET] 1999
DESIGNER: KANO
DESIGN COMPANY: ZETUEI FONTS

FONTNAMES:
DEBUGRATORS [ALPHABET] 1999
MECH-GOTHIC [ALPHABET] 1999
RYZEEM [ALPHABET] 1999
ZETUEIALP01-ROUND [ALPHABET/KATAKANA/HIRAGANA] 2001
MECANICULES [HIRAGANA] 2001
DAMARA A [BON-JI] 1999
DESIGNER: KANO
DESIGN COMPANY: ZETUEI FONTS

| FONT NAME | Nijikakaru-ALP | FONT TYPE | ALPHABET |

| FONT NAME | Nijikakaru-KAT | FONT TYPE | KATAKANA |

| FONT NAME | ZetueiALP00 | FONT TYPE | ALPHABET |

| FONT NAME | Zetuei-HIR | FONT TYPE | HIRAGANA |

| FONT NAME | Zetuei-KAT | FONT TYPE | KATAKANA |

| FONT NAME | Typocapsule-ALP | FONT TYPE | ALPHABET |

| FONT NAME | DebugRators | FONT TYPE | ALPHABET |

| FONT NAME | MECH-Gothic | FONT TYPE | ALPHABET |

| FONT NAME | RYZEEM | FONT TYPE | ALPHABET |

| FONT NAME | ZetueiALP01-Round | FONT TYPE | ALPHABET+(KATAKANA/HIRAKANA) |

| FONT NAME | MEcanicules | FONT TYPE | HIRAGANA |

| FONT NAME | Damara-A | FONT TYPE | BON-JI |

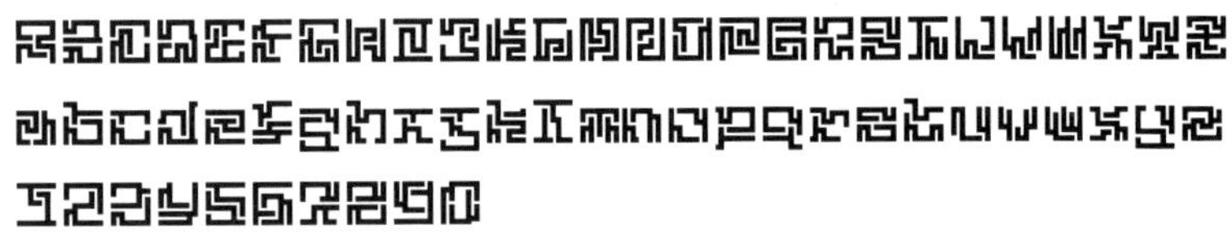

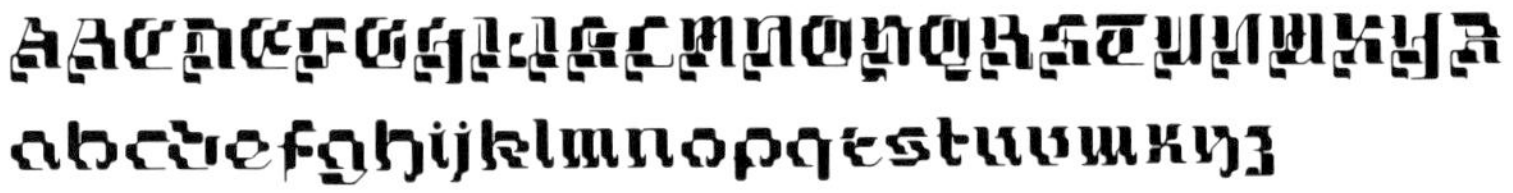

«NARITA INSPECTED»

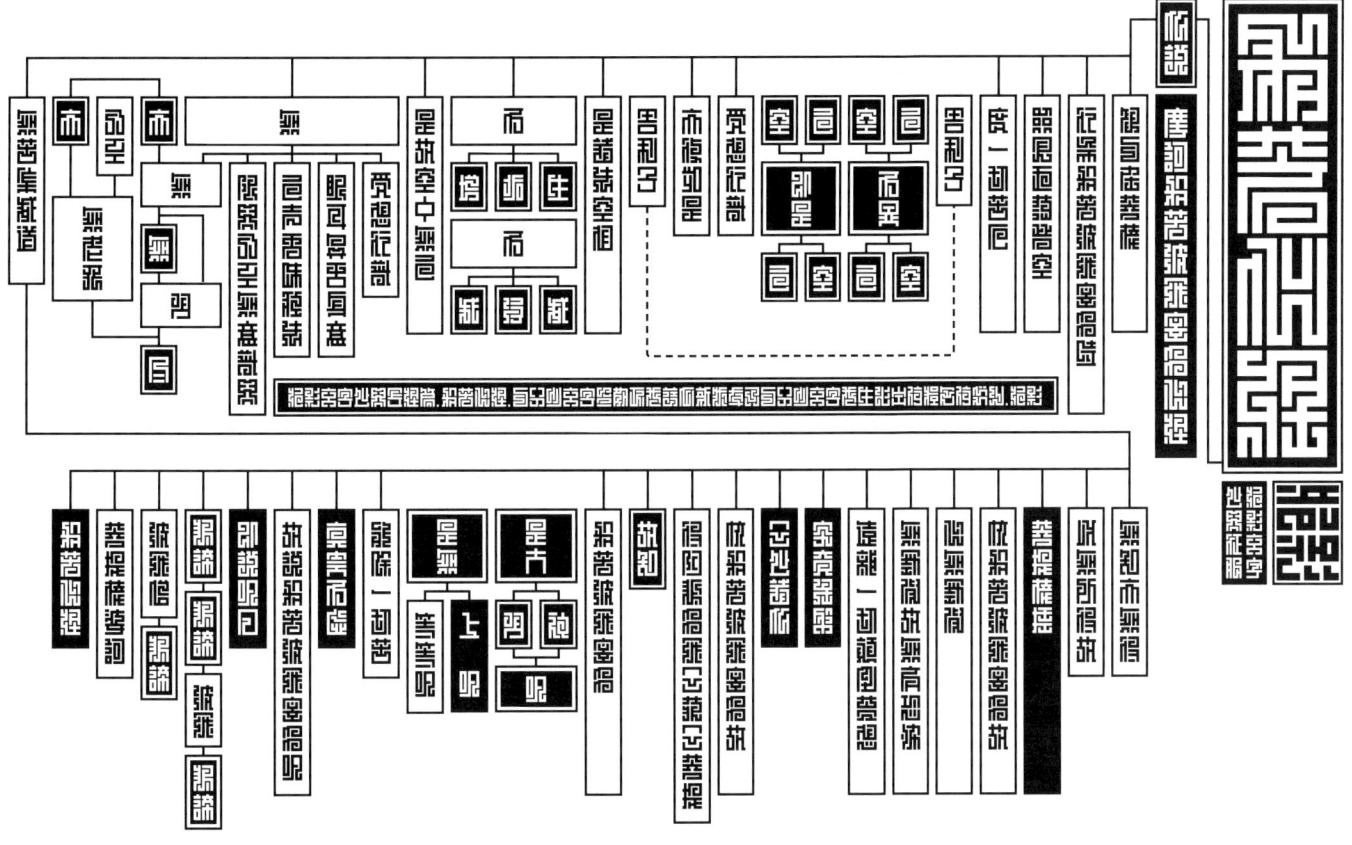

TITLE OF WORK: PARTS OF DESIGN/ZETUEI HANNYA SHINKYO
DESIGNER: KANO
DESIGN COMPANY: ZETUEI FONTS
YEAR: 2001

TITLE OF WORK: EXPAND KANJI'S DOMAIN FLYER
DESIGNER: KANO
DESIGN COMPANY: ZETUEI FONTS
YEAR: 1998

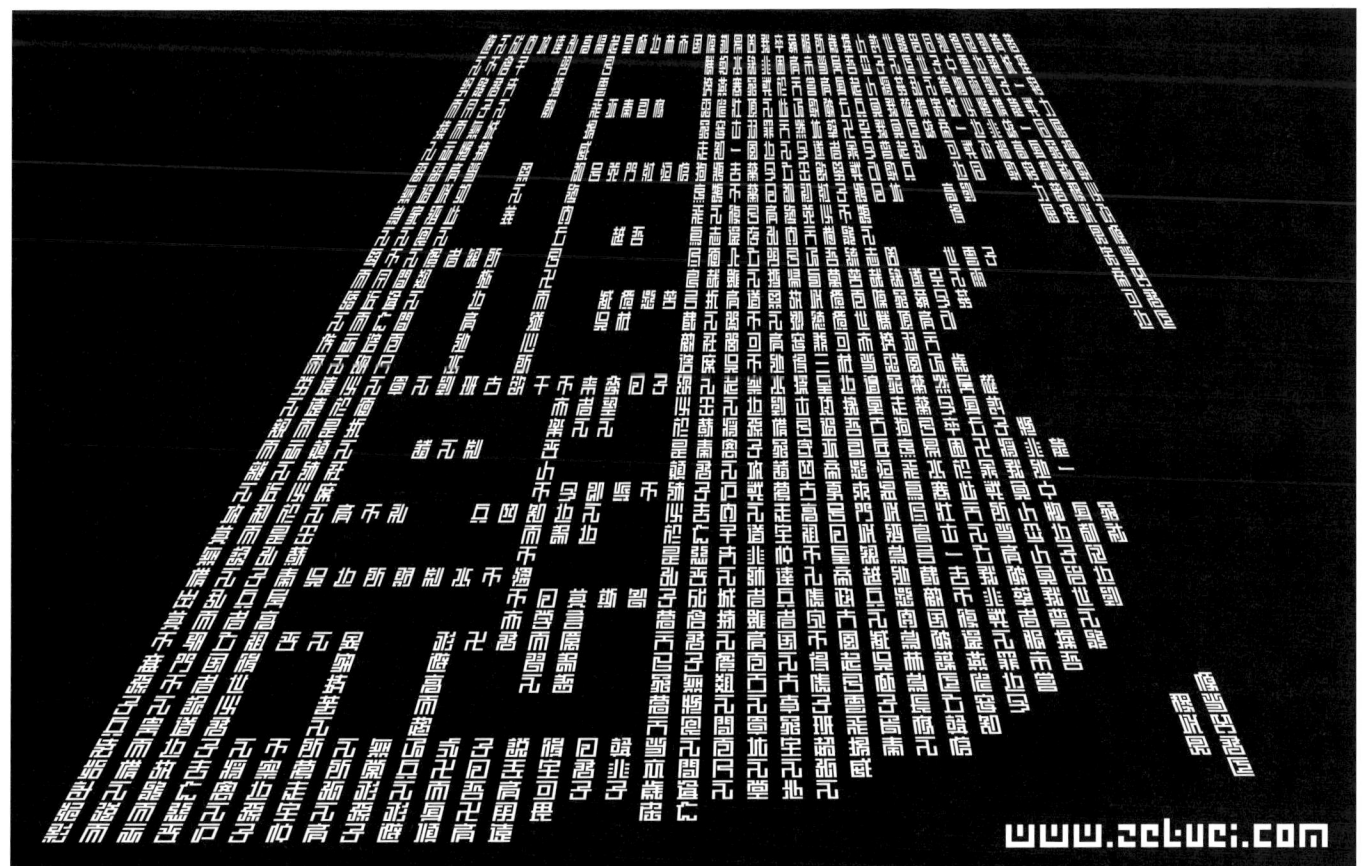

PIROMI.COM

Started working as independent character designer in 1996. Started the original line in 1998. The main work includes a character design for a body care brand «magmagirl» (Kunimine Industries Co. and Ltd.), and a participation in «Creators Collection» (Mangazoo.com and Inc.). The original goods are now available.

1996年からフリーのキャラクターデザイナーとして独立。1998年より現在のオリジナルラインをスタートする。主な仕事にボディケアブランド『magmagirl』キャラクターデザイン（クニミネ工業株式会社）、『クリエイターズ コレクション』参加（株式会社マンガズー・ドット・コム）。オリジナルグッズ販売を展開。

ピロミコム

NAME OF DESIGN COMPANY: PIROMI.COM
NAME/YEAR OF BIRTH: PIROMI (67)
COMPANY SINCE: 1998
ADDRESS: JAPAN
WEBSITE: HTTP://PIROMI.COM
EMAIL ADDRESS: MAIL@PIROMI.COM

デザイン会社名：ピロミコム
メンバー名（生年）：ピロミ（67年）
会社設立日：1998年
住所：日本
ウェブサイト：http://piromi.com
Eメールアドレス：mail@piromi.com
ファックス番号：―

BIOGRAPHY
10 QUESTIONS/ANSWERS

HOW DOES JAPAN SMELLS TODAY?
Smell of damp air.

HOW DOES YOUR DAY STARTS AND HOW DOES YOUR DAY ENDS?
I play with my cat, and draw pictures.

IS THERE SOMETHING WHAT YOU REALLY LOVE AND WHAT YOU REALLY HATE ABOUT JAPAN?
I like Japanese traditional stuff. But I hate how narrow it is.

WHAT DO YOU THINK ARE THE DIFFERENCES BETWEEN AMERICAN, EUROPEAN AND JAPANESE PEOPLE?
Language.

WHAT DO YOU THINK IS THE DIFFERENCE BETWEEN JAPANESE, AMERICAN AND EUROPEAN DESIGN?
The difference in temperature.

WHAT WOULD YOU DO, IF GRAPHIC DESIGN DID NOT EXIST?
Traditional handicrafts etc.

CAN YOU TELL US YOUR 3 MOST IMPORTANT THINGS/OBJECTS/ACTIVITIES?
To have fun. Friends. To continue drawing.

WHAT IS BEAUTIFUL AND WHAT IS UGLY?
Having your own thought is beautiful.
Not having it is ugly.

TO WHICH QUESTION YOU WOULD NEVER GIVE AN ANSWER?
The question which might expose personal information to total strangers.

IS THERE SOMETHING YOU WOULD LIKE TO TELL THE READERS OF THIS BOOK.
Let's enjoy life.

(interview with piromi)

Q1: 今日の日本はどんな匂いがしますか？
A1: 湿った空気の匂い。

Q2: あなたの1日はどの様に始まり、どの様に終わりますか？
A2: 猫と戯れ、絵を描く。

Q3: 日本の好きな部分、嫌いな部分を挙げて下さい。
A3: 好きな部分は日本の伝統的な物。嫌いな部分は狭いところ。

Q4: アメリカ人、ヨーロッパ人、日本人の違いは何だと思いますか？
A4: 言葉。

Q5: 日本のデザイン、アメリカのデザイン、ヨーロッパのデザインの違いは何だと思いますか？
A5: 気温の違い。

Q6: グラフィックデザインが存在していなかったら、あなたは何をしていますか？
A6: 伝統工芸など。

Q7: あなた大事なことを3つ教えて下さい。
A7: 楽しくいること。友人。絵を描き続ける事。

Q8: 何が美しくて、何が醜いと思いますか？
A8: 美しいのは自分なりの思想を持っていること。醜いのは思想がないこと。

Q9: あなたが絶対に答えない質問は何でしょう？
A9: 個人情報を見ず知らずの人に公開するような内容の質問。

Q10: 読者に何か伝えたいことがあれば書いて下さい。
A10: 人生を楽しみましょう。

（インタビュー：ピロミ）

PROFILE
BUSINESS CARD
SELFPORTRAIT

PIROMI.COM

ピロミコム

WORKSPACES ↓   LOGOTYPE ↑

TYCOON GRAPHICS

Tycoon Graphics was co-founded by Yuichi Miyashi and Naoyuki Suzuki in 1991. The activity includes CD jacket design and visual promotion of Towa Tei, Namie Amuro, Judy and Mary, and Miki Imai. Also graphic design of a fashion brand, corporate ad, logo design, editorial design, and package design etc. The philosophy is «Thick and Beautiful». Released the book of «G-MEN» (Littlemore Co.,Ltd.) and «A&D SCAN: Tycoon Graphics Works» (Rikuyosha). Gold Award for «BIG MAGAZINE» at 78th New York ADC. Silver Award for «BOYCOTT MOVIE». New York ADC Distinct Merit Award from 76th to 79th. Mainichi Design Distinctive Merit Award etc.

1991年、宮師雄一と鈴木直之の二人によりタイクーングラフィックスを設立。テイトウワ、安室奈美恵、JUDY AND MARY、今井美樹等のCDジャケットデザイン及びヴィジュアルプロモーションに携わる。また、ファッションブランドのグラフィックデザインや企業広告、ロゴデザイン、エディトリアル、パッケージデザインの分野でも活動中。「太く、美しく」が信条。著書に「G-MEN」(リトルモア)、「A&D SCAN:タイクーングラフィックスの仕事と周辺」(六耀社)がある。受賞歴は第78回ニューヨークADC「BIG MAGAZINE」にて金賞、「BOYCOTT MOVIE」にて銀賞。第76-79回ニューヨークADC賞受賞。毎日デザイン賞部門賞他。

NAME OF DESIGN COMPANY: TYCOON GRAPHICS
NAME/YEAR OF BIRTH: YUICHI MIYASHI (64)/ NAOYUKI SUZUKI (64)
COMPANY SINCE: 1991
ADDRESS: #402 VILLA GLORIA, 2-31-7 JINGUMAE, SHIBUYA-KU, TOKYO 150-0001, JAPAN
EMAIL ADDRESS: MAIL@TYG.CO.JP
FAX: +81 (0)3-5411-5342

デザイン会社名：タイクーングラフィックス
メンバー名(生年)：宮師雄一(64年)/鈴木直之(64年)
会社設立日：1991年
住所：〒150-0001 東京都渋谷区神宮前2-31-7 ビラグロリア#402
Eメールアドレス：mail@tyg.co.jp
ウェブサイト：―
ファックス番号：+81 (0)3-5411-5342

BIOGRAPHY / 10 QUESTIONS/ANSWERS

HOW DOES JAPAN SMELLS TODAY?
Rainy season.

HOW DOES YOUR DAY STARTS AND HOW DOES YOUR DAY ENDS?
–

IS THERE SOMETHING WHAT YOU REALLY LOVE AND WHAT YOU REALLY HATE ABOUT JAPAN?
Love: the national character that adopts anything interesting. Hate: the idea from habit of following the crowd.

WHAT DO YOU THINK ARE THE DIFFERENCES BETWEEN AMERICAN, EUROPEAN AND JAPANESE PEOPLE?
American: mayonnaise. European: olive oil. Japanese: soy sauce.

WHAT DO YOU THINK IS THE DIFFERENCE BETWEEN JAPANESE, AMERICAN AND EUROPEAN DESIGN?
Line (Japanese) and Face (European and American).

WHAT WOULD YOU DO, IF GRAPHIC DESIGN DID NOT EXIST?
A chef.

CAN YOU TELL US YOUR 3 MOST IMPORTANT THINGS/OBJECTS/ACTIVITIES?
Family. Friend. Work.

WHAT IS BEAUTIFUL AND WHAT IS UGLY?
Beautiful: self-possession, pure sense. Ugly: ego, one-sided thought.

TO WHICH QUESTION YOU WOULD NEVER GIVE AN ANSWER?
–

IS THERE SOMETHING YOU WOULD LIKE TO TELL THE READERS OF THIS BOOK?
«Creativity comes from freedom»

(interview with Tycoon Graphics)

Q1: 今日の日本はどんな匂いがしますか？
A1: 梅雨。

Q2: あなたの1日はどの様に始まり、どの様に終わりますか？
A2: ―

Q3: 日本の好きな部分、嫌いな部分を挙げて下さい。
A3: 好―何でも取り入れる国民性。嫌―横並び的発想。

Q4: アメリカ人、ヨーロッパ人、日本人の違いは何だと思いますか？
A4: アメリカ人―マヨネーズ。ヨーロッパ人―オリーブオイル。日本人―醤油。

Q5: 日本のデザイン、アメリカのデザイン、ヨーロッパのデザインの違いは何だと思いますか？
A5: 線(日本)と面(欧米)。

Q6: グラフィックデザインが存在していなかったら、あなたは何をしていますか？
A6: 料理人。

Q7: あなた大事なことを3つ教えて下さい。
A7: 家族。友達。仕事。

Q8: 何が美しくて、何が醜いと思いますか？
A8: 美―平常心、ピュアな感覚。醜―エゴ、一面的な思考。

Q9: あなたが絶対に答えない質問は何でしょう？
A9: ―

Q10: 読者に何か伝えたいことがあれば書いて下さい。
A10: "Creativity comes from freedom"

(インタビュー: タイクーングラフィックス)

PROFILE / BUSINESS CARD / SELFPORTRAIT

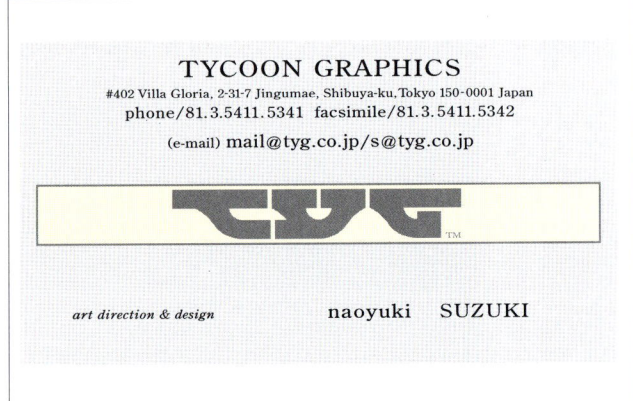

TYCOON GRAPHICS

WORKSPACES ↓   LOGOTYPE ↑

MTV JAPAN CAMPAIGN POSTERS
TITLE OF WORKS: «SAKENDE» SHOUT/«HAJIKETE» BREAK/«NAITE» CRY/«FURUETE» SHAKE
DESIGNER: JOHN C. JAY & SUMIKO SATO (WIEDEN+KENNEDY*J), TYCOON GRAPHICS
DESIGN COMPANY: WIEDEN+KENNEDY, TYCOON GRAPHICS
YEAR: 2001
CLIENT: MTV JAPAN MUSIC CHANNEL CO., LTD.

2000 AUTUMN & WINTER COLLECTION CATALOGUE
TITLE OF WORK: ALFREDO BANNISTER
DESIGN COMPANY: TYCOON GRAPHICS
YEAR: 2000
CLIENT: ABAHOUSE INTERNATIONAL CO., LTD.

↑
2000 SPRING & SUMMER CAMPAIGN POSTER
TITLE OF WORK: WRANGLER/700 SERIES
DESIGN COMPANY: TYCOON GRAPHICS
YEAR: 2000
CLIENT: VF JAPAN CO.,LTD.

↓
2000 AUTUMN & WINTER COLLECTION CATALOGUE
TITLE OF WORK: ALFREDO BANNISTER
DESIGN COMPANY: TYCOON GRAPHICS
YEAR: 2000
CLIENT: ABAHOUSE INTERNATIONAL CO.,LTD.

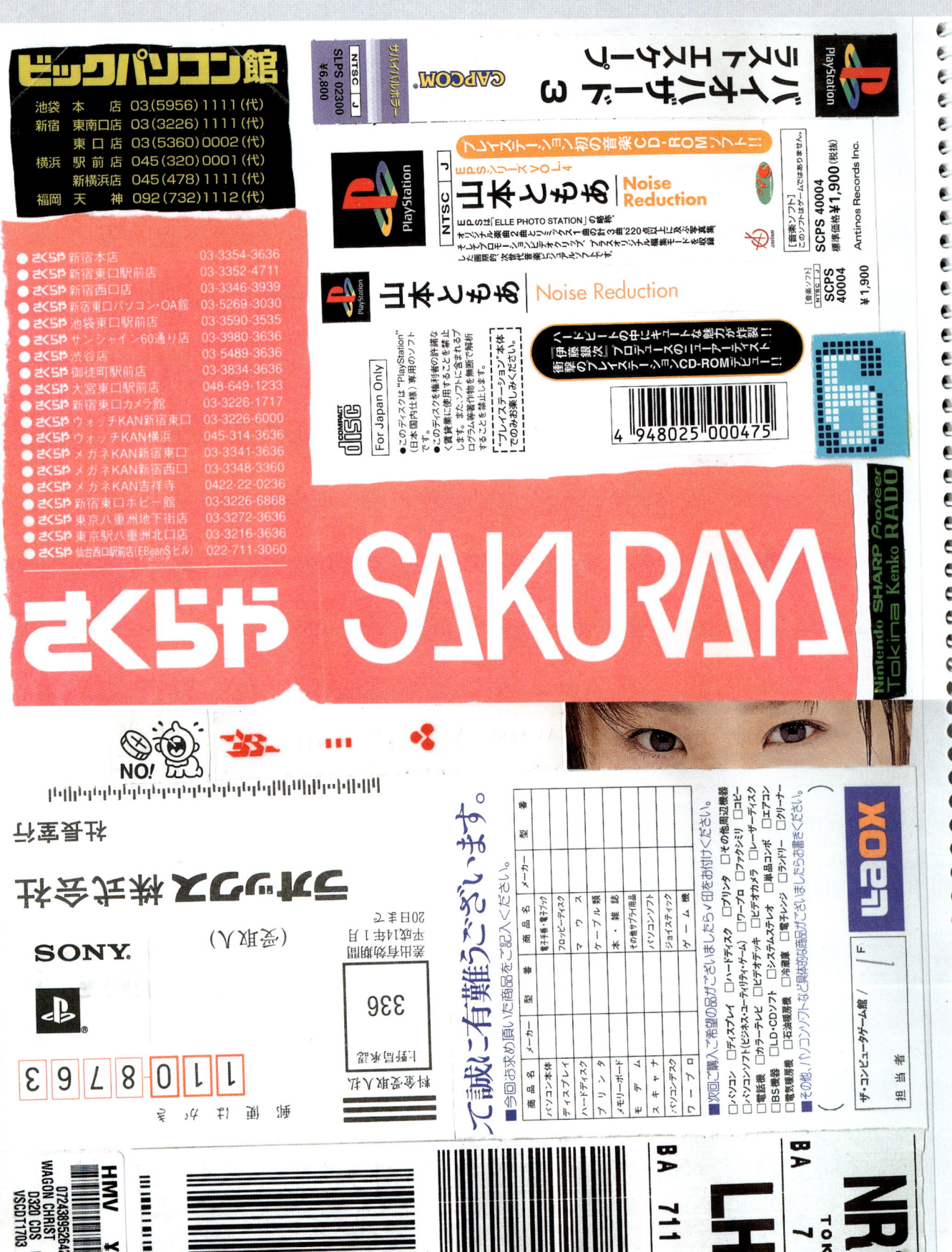

WEST		NORTH	
① Mt. Fuji	⑦ Roppongi Area	⑫ Ark Hills	⑱ Tokyo Dome
② Shibuya Area	⑧ Shinjuku Area	⑬ Hotel New Otani	⑲ The Imperial Palace
③ NHK	⑨ Shinjuku Gyoen Park	⑭ Sunshine Building	⑳ Ueno & Asakusa Area
④ Embassy of Russian Federation	⑩ Reiyu-kai Bldg.	⑮ Akasaka Prince Hotel	㉑ Hibiya Park
⑤ Aoyama Cemetery	⑪ Akasaka Palace	⑯ Hotel Okura	㉒ NHK Broadcast Museum
⑥ Meiji Shrine		⑰ National Diet Bldg.	

NOBODY DESIGN PRODUCTS

Nobody Design Products was established in 1997, and started producing a clothing brand called «Beatservice». Ideas taken from music, movies and favorite graphics have been mixed, designed and printed. It's now available.

1997年、Nobody Design Products設立。同年にウェアブランド「Beatservice」を製作開始。音楽や映画や自分たちの気に入ってる色々なグラフィックを混ぜ混ぜしてデザインして刷って販売中。

NAME OF DESIGN COMPANY: BEATSERVICE (NOBODY DESIGN PRODUCTS)
NAMES/YEAR OF BIRTH: YUKARI MORIYA (67)/ SEISHIRO «RITO» FUJIMOTO (77)
COMPANY SINCE: 1997
ADDRESS: 4-23-11-205, MEGURO-HONCHO, MEGURO-KU, TOKYO 152-0002, JAPAN
WEBSITE: HTTP://WWW.BEATSERVICE.COM/
EMAIL ADDRESS: INFO@BEATSERVICE.COM
FAX: +81 (0)3-3760-6450

デザイン会社名：ビートサービス（ノーバディー・デザイン・プロダクツ）
メンバー名(生年)：守谷ゆかり(67年)/藤本リト征史郎(77年)
会社設立日：1997年
住所：〒152-0002 東京都目黒区目黒本町4-23-11-205
ウェブサイト：http://www.beatservice.com/
Eメールアドレス：info@beatservice.com
ファックス番号：+81 (0)3-3760-6450

BIOGRAPHY ↑
10 QUESTIONS/ANSWERS ↓

HOW DOES JAPAN SMELL TODAY?
Frog.

HOW DOES YOUR DAY START AND HOW DOES YOUR DAY END?
Wake up my computer – put the computer to sleep.

IS THERE SOMETHING THAT YOU REALLY LOVE AND THAT YOU REALLY HATE ABOUT JAPAN?
Love: having four different faces in a year.
Hate: crowded train.

WHAT DO YOU THINK ARE THE DIFFERENCES BETWEEN AMERICAN, EUROPEAN AND JAPANESE PEOPLE?
The amount of food.

WHAT DO YOU THINK IS THE DIFFERENCE BETWEEN JAPANESE, AMERICAN AND EUROPEAN DESIGN?
Historical progress.

WHAT WOULD YOU DO, IF GRAPHIC DESIGN DID NOT EXIST?
Electronics store.

CAN YOU TELL US YOUR 3 MOST IMPORTANT THINGS/OBJECTS/ACTIVITIES?
Feeling. Friends. Travel.

WHAT IS BEAUTIFUL AND WHAT IS UGLY?
Beautiful: human. Ugly: human.

TO WHICH QUESTION YOU WOULD NEVER GIVE AN ANSWER?
«How many toes do you have?»

IS THERE ANYTHING YOU WOULD LIKE TO TELL THE READERS OF THIS BOOK?
-

(interview with Nobody Design Products)

Q1: 今日の日本はどんな匂いがしますか？
A1: 蛙。

Q2: あなたの1日はどの様に始まり、どの様に終わりますか？
A2: スリープ解除→スリープ。

Q3: 日本の好きな部分、嫌いな部分を挙げて下さい。
A3: 好き―1年に4つの顔を持つところ。
嫌い―電車が混んでいるところ。

Q4: アメリカ人、ヨーロッパ人、日本人の違いは何だと思いますか？
A4: 食べる量。

Q5: 日本のデザイン、アメリカのデザイン、ヨーロッパのデザインの違いは何だと思いますか？
A5: 歴史的歩み。

Q6: グラフィックデザインが存在していなかったら、あなたは何をしていますか？
A6: 電気屋。

Q7: あなたが大事なことを3つ教えて下さい。
A7: 気持。友人。旅。

Q8: 何が美しくて、何が醜いと思いますか？
A8: 美しいもの―人間。醜いもの―人間。

Q9: あなたが絶対に答えない質問は何でしょう？
A9: 足の指の数は何本ですか？

Q10: 読者に何か伝えたいことがあれば書いて下さい。
A10: ―

（インタビュー: ノーバディー・デザイン・プロダクツ）

PROFILE ↑
BUSINESS CARD →
SELFPORTRAIT ↓

NOBODY DESIGN PRODUCTS

ビートサービス (ノーバディー・デザイン・プロダクツ)

WORKSPACES ↓   LOGOTYPE ↑

TITLE OF WORK: BATTLE CAMP LOGO
DESIGNER: SAYSHIRO «RITO» FUJIMOTO
DESIGN COMPANY: NOBODY DESIGN PRODUCTS
YEAR: 2001
CLIENT: GG CO., INC.

TITLE OF WORK: OSAKA'00
DESIGNER: SAYSHIRO «RITO» FUJIMOTO
DESIGN COMPANY: NOBODY DESIGN PRODUCTS
YEAR: 2000
CLIENT: NISEN OSAKA

battle camp

TITLE OF WORK: GRUBLO
DESIGNER: SAYSHIRO «RITO» FUJIMOTO
DESIGN COMPANY: NOBODY DESIGN PRODUCTS
YEAR: 2000
CLIENT: ALL JAPAN RECORDS

KENTARO «ANI» FUJIMOTO (NENDO)

Nendo was organized by three design school students, Kentaro Fujimoto, Tsuyoshi Kusano and Kazuo Anazawa in 1993 to make the original T-shirts with a theme of fusion between video games and the spiritual world. Around 1995, they received an offer from a publishing company to design game related graphics, from then on they called themselves as Nendo Graphixxx. The core members, Fujimoto and Kusano have created various art works including flyers, CD jackets, books etc. For «Narita Inspected», Fujimoto has contributed work representative of Nendo.

Nendoは1993年、ビデオゲームとスピリチュアルな世界の融合をテーマにしたオリジナルTシャツを作ろうと、デザインスクール在籍中の藤本健太郎、草野剛、穴沢一夫の3人によって結成。1995年頃、出版社からゲーム関係のグラフィックの仕事を依頼されて以来Nendo Graphixxxを名乗り、中心メンバー藤本と草野でフライヤー、CDジャケット、書籍など様々なデザインを製作。今回の「成田インスペクテッド」には、藤本がNendoの代表として寄稿。

ネンド (ネンド・グラフィック・スクワッド)

NAME OF DESIGN COMPANY: NENDO (NENDO GRAPHIC SQUAD)
NAME/YEAR OF BIRTH: KENTARO «ANI» FUJIMOTO (73)
COMPANY SINCE: 1993
ADDRESS: 2-17-8 MEGURO-HONCHO, MEGURO-KU, TOKYO 152-0002, JAPAN
WEBSITE: HTTP://WWW.NENDO.COM/
EMAIL ADDRESS: QUEN@NENDO.COM
FAX: +81 (0)3-5704-6148

デザイン会社名：ネンド（ネンド・グラフィック・スクワッド）
メンバー名(生年)：藤本健太郎(73年)
会社設立日：1993年
住所：〒152-0002 東京都目黒区目黒本町2-17-8
ウェブサイト：http://www.nendo.com/
Eメールアドレス：quen@nendo.com
ファックス番号：+81 (0)3-5704-6148

BIOGRAPHY / 10 QUESTIONS/ANSWERS

HOW DOES JAPAN SMELL TODAY?
It stinks of sewage.

HOW DOES YOUR DAY START AND HOW DOES YOUR DAY END?
Start: check e-mails that have came in during the night.
End: play Wizardry on Game Boy Color before I go to bed.

IS THERE SOMETHING THAT YOU REALLY LOVE AND THAT YOU REALLY HATE ABOUT JAPAN?
Love: tradition, beauty of form, spiritual culture, bushido (Japanese chivalry), the color of faded saturation that Japanese culture has. Hate: the fact that there are too many idiots not recognizing most of the above.

WHAT DO YOU THINK ARE THE DIFFERENCES BETWEEN AMERICAN, EUROPEAN AND JAPANESE PEOPLE?
American: the leader of the world. European: the leader of history. Japanese: the leader of anime and video games.

WHAT DO YOU THINK IS THE DIFFERENCE BETWEEN JAPANESE, AMERICAN AND EUROPEAN DESIGN?
American design: look and appearance are the important factors. It seems that people have excessive fear of claim. European design: essential qualities of design are valuable. It seems that design has been drawing the culture. Japanese design: it seems «whether it is understandable to dumb» or «whether it becomes a big seller» are the only important issues. Therefore, only design which eliminates these two points is attractive to the eye as «a design for design». Since graphic design came from the demand to support communication/commercial activity for the public, this is an absolutely ironical situation. But I don't give a damn.

WHAT WOULD YOU DO, IF GRAPHIC DESIGN DID NOT EXIST?
I would be an author, writing a composition.

CAN YOU TELL US YOUR 3 MOST IMPORTANT THINGS/OBJECTS/ACTIVITIES?
A sense of humor. To keep up your interest in something new. To realize half of the world is in the sunshine and half of the world is in the shade, and not to forget that it comes and goes for sure.

WHAT IS BEAUTIFUL AND WHAT IS UGLY?
Beautiful: every kind of freedom. Ugly: every kind of restriction.

TO WHICH QUESTION YOU WOULD NEVER GIVE AN ANSWER?
Any concerning a woman.

IS THERE ANYTHING YOU WOULD LIKE TO TELL THE READERS OF THIS BOOK?
I want you to figure out the madness and the excellence of this country and the people in this country. You will probably find more deep and interesting stuff here! You should come to Tokyo anyway.

(interview with Kentaro «Ani» Fujimoto)

Q1: 今日の日本はどんな匂いがしますか？
A1: 下水道くさい。

Q2: あなたの1日はどの様に始まり、どの様に終わりますか？
A2: 始まり—夜中に来たメールのチェック。
終わり—寝る前にゲームボーイカラーのWizardryをプレイする。

Q3: 日本の好きな部分、嫌いな部分を挙げて下さい。
A3: 好きな部分—伝統、様式美、精神文化、武士道、日本文化の持つ彩度の落ちた色合い。嫌いな部分—上記のほとんどを忘れてバカ騒ぎしている奴が多すぎること。

Q4: アメリカ人、ヨーロッパ人、日本人の違いは何だと思いますか？
A4: アメリカ人—世界のリーダー。
ヨーロッパ人—歴史のリーダー。
日本人—アニメとゲームのリーダー。

Q5: 日本のデザイン、アメリカのデザイン、ヨーロッパのデザインの違いは何だと思いますか？
A5: アメリカのデザイン—見え方、外面を大切にしている。過度にクレームを恐れているように見える。ヨーロッパのデザイン—デザインの本質を大切にしている。デザインが文化を牽引しているように見える。日本のデザイン—「馬鹿でも分かるか?」「これは売れるか?」しか気にしていないように見える。だからその2点を無視したデザインだけが、「デザインのためのデザイン」として目を引いてしまう。グラフィックデザインは公衆への伝達/商業活動の支援という需要から生まれてきたものであるだけに、これはものすごく皮肉な状況だと思う。でも俺にとってはどうでもいい。

Q6: グラフィックデザインが存在していなかったら、あなたは何をしていますか？
A6: 物書きにでもなって文章を書いていたかもしれない。

Q7: あなた大事なことを3つ教えて下さい。
A7: ジョークのセンス。常に新しい何かに興味を持ち続けること。世界の半分は日向で世界の半分は日陰で、それが必ず流転しているという事を忘れない事。

Q8: 何が美しくて、何が醜いと思いますか？
A8: 美しいもの—あらゆる自由。醜いもの—あらゆる規制

Q9: あなたが絶対に答えない質問は何でしょう？
A9: 女性に関する話。

Q10: 読者に何か伝えたいことがあれば書いて下さい。
A10: この国と国の人間の狂っている部分、優れている部分を自分なりに判断してみて欲しい。たぶんもっと深くておもしろいネタが隠されているよ！ とにかく一度、東京に来てみたほうが良い。

(インタビュー：藤本健太郎)

PROFILE / BUSINESS CARD / SELFPORTRAIT

KENTARO «ANI» FUJIMOTO (NENDO)   ネンド (ネンド・グラフィック・スクワッド)

Nendo

WORKSPACES ↓   LOGOTYPE ↑

TITLE OF WORK: FAMICOM SAMA
DESIGNER: KENTARO «ANI» FUJIMOTO
DESIGN COMPANY: NENDO
YEAR: 2000

TITLE OF WORK: TIBETAN ROCK
DESIGNER: KENTARO «ANI» FUJIMOTO
DESIGN COMPANY: NENDO
YEAR: 2000
CLIENT: SELFISH MAGAZINE

TSUYOSHI KUSANO (NENDO/LEVEL1)

Born in Tokyo, 1973. Formed a graphic unit called Nendo Graphics in 1994 with the keywords «Spiritual World» and created T-shirts, editorials, logos, CD jackets etc. Started working at ASCII corp. in 1994. Formed a graphic and editorial unit called Level1 in 1999. Left ASCII corp. (Enterbrain, Inc.) in the following year, and started working in a variety of media based on graphic design including illustration, editorial design, and motion graphics. Tsuyoshi Kusano is now working in design as an individual besides being active in the other two units.

1973年東京生まれ。1994年、精神世界をキーワードにグラフィックユニットNendo Graphics結成。Tシャツをはじめ、エディトリアル、ロゴ、CDジャケットなどを制作。1994年よりアスキー勤務。1999年、グラフィックと編集を行うLevel1結成。翌年アスキー（エンターブレイン）を退社し、フリーランスとしてグラフィックデザインを中心にイラストレーション、エディトリアルデザイン、映像などメディアを問わず活動。現在は両ユニット名義で活動しつつ、一個人草野剛としてもデザインしている。

草野剛

NAME OF DESIGN COMPANY: NENDO/LEVEL1
NAME/YEAR OF BIRTH: TSUYOSHI KUSANO (73)
COMPANY SINCE: 1993 (NENDO)/2000 (LEVEL1)
ADDRESS: HASEGAWA-BLDG. 401, 2-17-10, SANGENJAYA, SETAGAYA-KU, TOKYO 154-0024, JAPAN
EMAIL ADDRESS: TSUYOS-K@MOMO.SO-NET.NE.JP
FAX: +81 (0)3-5433-9849

デザイン会社名：ネンド／レベル1
メンバー名（生年）：草野剛（73年）
会社設立日：1993年（ネンド）／2000年（レベル1）
住所：〒154-0024 東京都世田谷区三軒茶屋2-17-10 長谷川ビル
Eメールアドレス：tsuyos-k@momo.so-net.ne.jp
ファックス番号：+81 (0)3-5433-9849
ウェブサイト：—

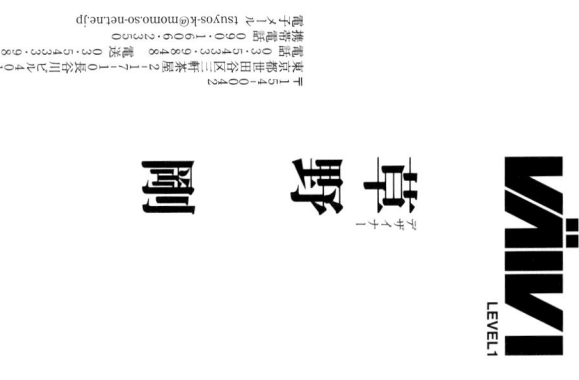

BIOGRAPHY / 10 QUESTIONS/ANSWERS

HOW DOES JAPAN SMELL TODAY?
There is a scent of rain.

HOW DOES YOUR DAY START AND HOW DOES YOUR DAY END?
I get woken up by my kitty. I have a meal on the way to the office, and I spend hours on a design till evening if I have no meeting scheduled. I spend hours on a design till late at night.

IS THERE SOMETHING THAT YOU REALLY LOVE AND THAT YOU REALLY HATE ABOUT JAPAN?
What I love about it is that it's the country I was born in. What I hate about it is that it's a small area.

WHAT DO YOU THINK ARE THE DIFFERENCES BETWEEN AMERICAN, EUROPEAN AND JAPANESE PEOPLE?
We may be all the same, we may be all different. That depends...

WHAT DO YOU THINK IS THE DIFFERENCE BETWEEN JAPANESE, AMERICAN AND EUROPEAN DESIGN?
I would say it's the cultural background, however it has changed in recent years. Maybe its history. An environment such as weather is also a big difference.

WHAT WOULD YOU DO, IF GRAPHIC DESIGN DID NOT EXIST?
Illustration.

CAN YOU TELL US YOUR 3 MOST IMPORTANT THINGS/OBJECTS/ACTIVITIES?
Health. Environment. Design.

WHAT IS BEAUTIFUL AND WHAT IS UGLY?
Youth is beautiful and old age is ugly.

TO WHICH QUESTION YOU WOULD NEVER GIVE AN ANSWER?
About my true character.

IS THERE ANYTHING YOU WOULD LIKE TO TELL THE READERS OF THIS BOOK?
Peace.

(interview with Tsuyoshi Kusano)

Q1: 今日の日本はどんな匂いがしますか？
A1: 雨の香りがする。

Q2: あなたの1日はどの様に始まり、どの様に終わりますか？
A2: 猫に起こされる。オフィスに向かう途中で食事をとり、打ち合わせがない限り日が暮れるまでデザインに向かう。夜が更けるまでデザインに向かう。

Q3: 日本の好きな部分、嫌いな部分を挙げて下さい。
A3: 好きな部分は自分が生まれた国というところ。嫌いな部分は面積が狭いというところ。

Q4: アメリカ人、ヨーロッパ人、日本人の違いは何だと思いますか？
A4: 全てが同じかもしれないし、違うかもしれない。一概には…。

Q5: 日本のデザイン、アメリカのデザイン、ヨーロッパのデザインの違いは何だと思いますか？
A5: 文化背景と言いたいが、近年は違う。歴史かな。天候など環境の違いも大きい。

Q6: グラフィックデザインが存在していなかったら、あなたは何をしていますか？
A6: イラストレーション。

Q7: あなた大事なことを3つ教えて下さい。
A7: 健康。環境。デザイン。

Q8: 何が美しくて、何が醜いと思いますか？
A8: 若さが美しく、老いが醜い。

Q9: あなたが絶対に答えない質問は何でしょう？
A9: 本性。

Q10: 読者に何か伝えたいことがあれば書いて下さい。
A10: ピース。

（インタビュー：草野剛）

PROFILE / BUSINESS CARD / SELFPORTRAIT

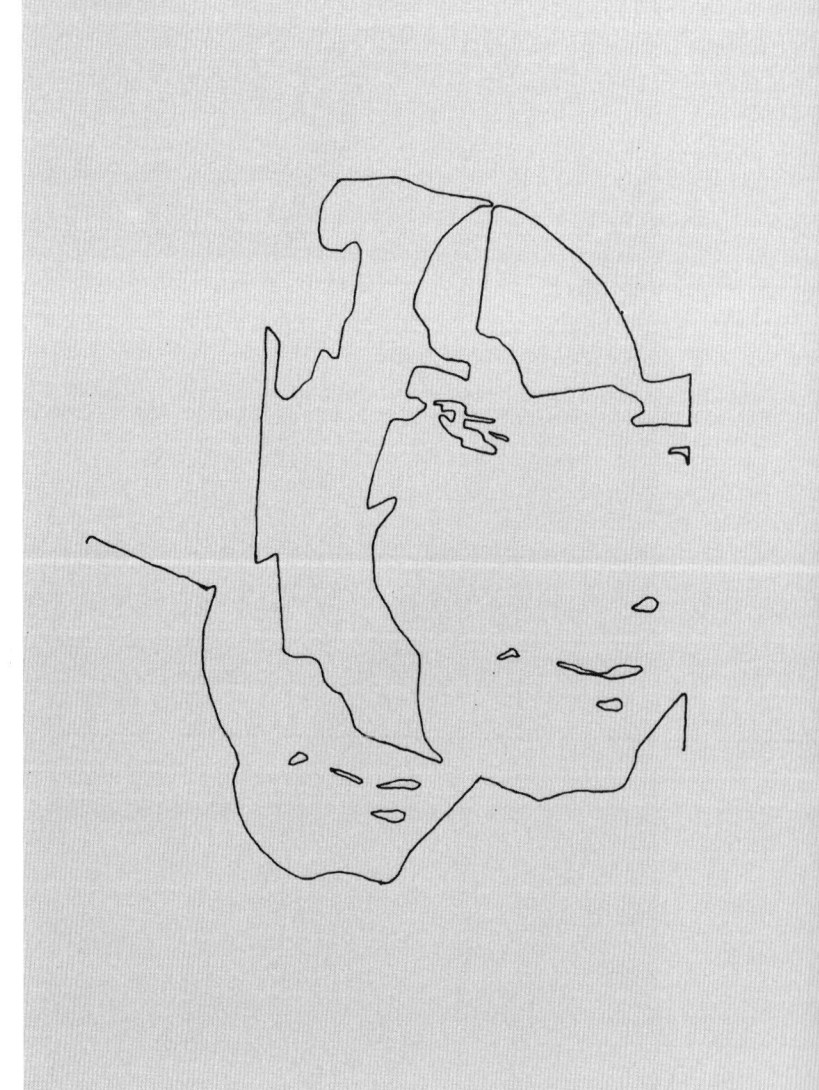

TSUYOSHI KUSANO (NENDO/LEVEL1) 草野剛

WORKSPACES ↓   LOGOTYPE ↑

 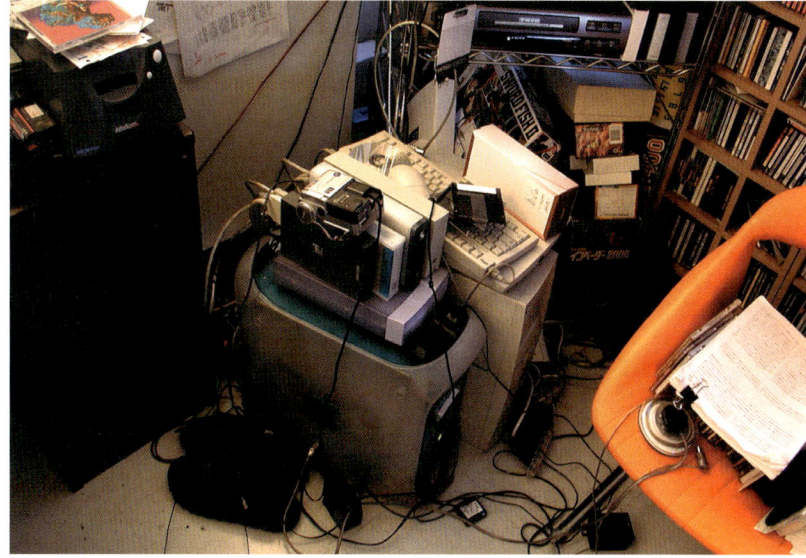

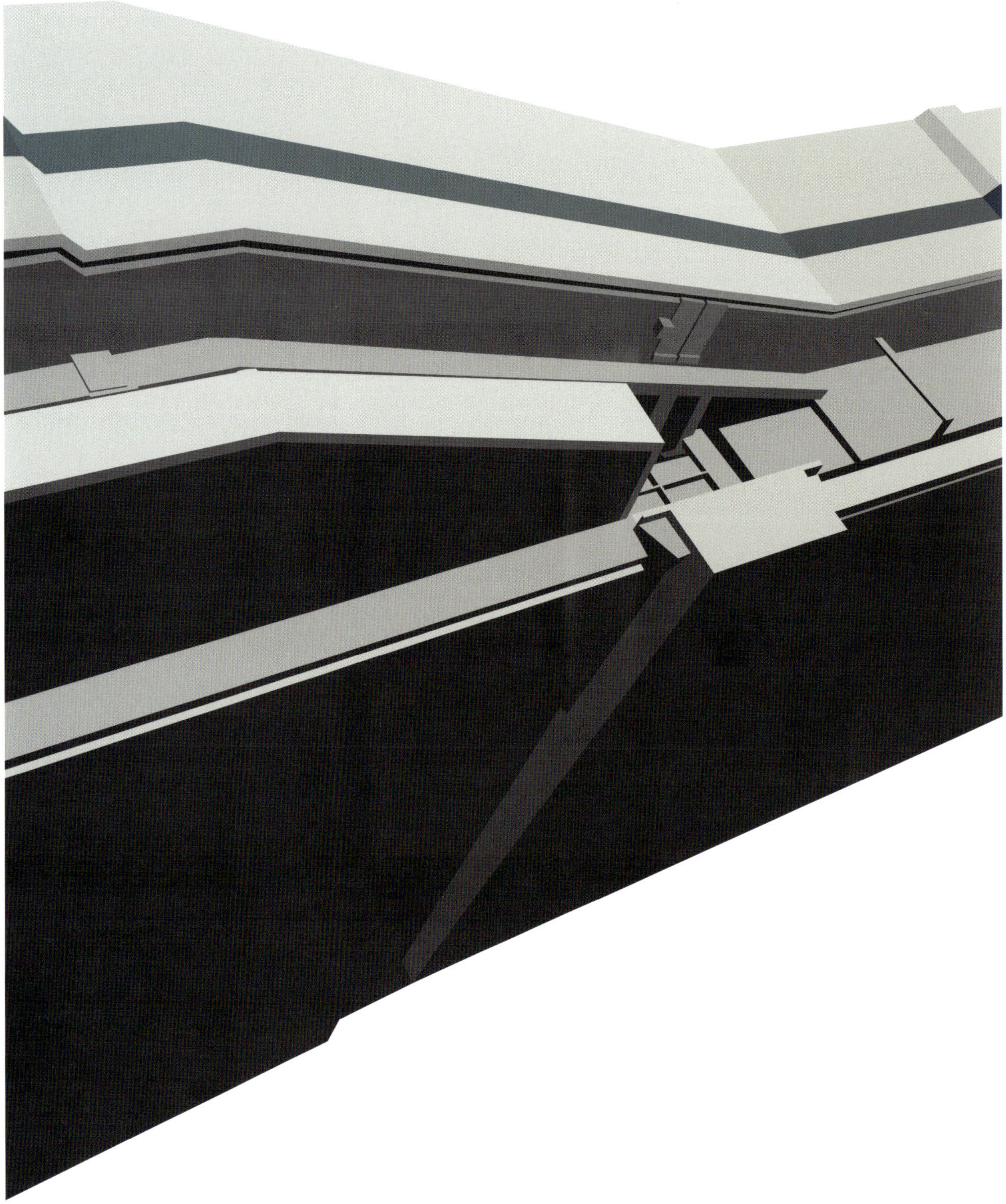

TITLE OF WORK: AUTOBAHN LOGO/MARK
DESIGNER: TSUYOSHI KUSANO
DESIGN COMPANY: NENDO/LEVEL1
YEAR: 2000

TITLE OF WORK: AUTOBAHN
DESIGNER: TSUYOSHI KUSANO
DESIGN COMPANY: NENDO/LEVEL1
YEAR: 2000

TITLE OF WORK: SMW
DESIGNER: TSUYOSHI KUSANO
DESIGN COMPANY: NENDO/LEVEL1
YEAR: 2001
CLIENT: BNN

TITLE OF WORK: PS CONTROLLER
DESIGNER: TSUYOSHI KUSANO
DESIGN COMPANY: NENDO/LEVEL1
YEAR: 1999

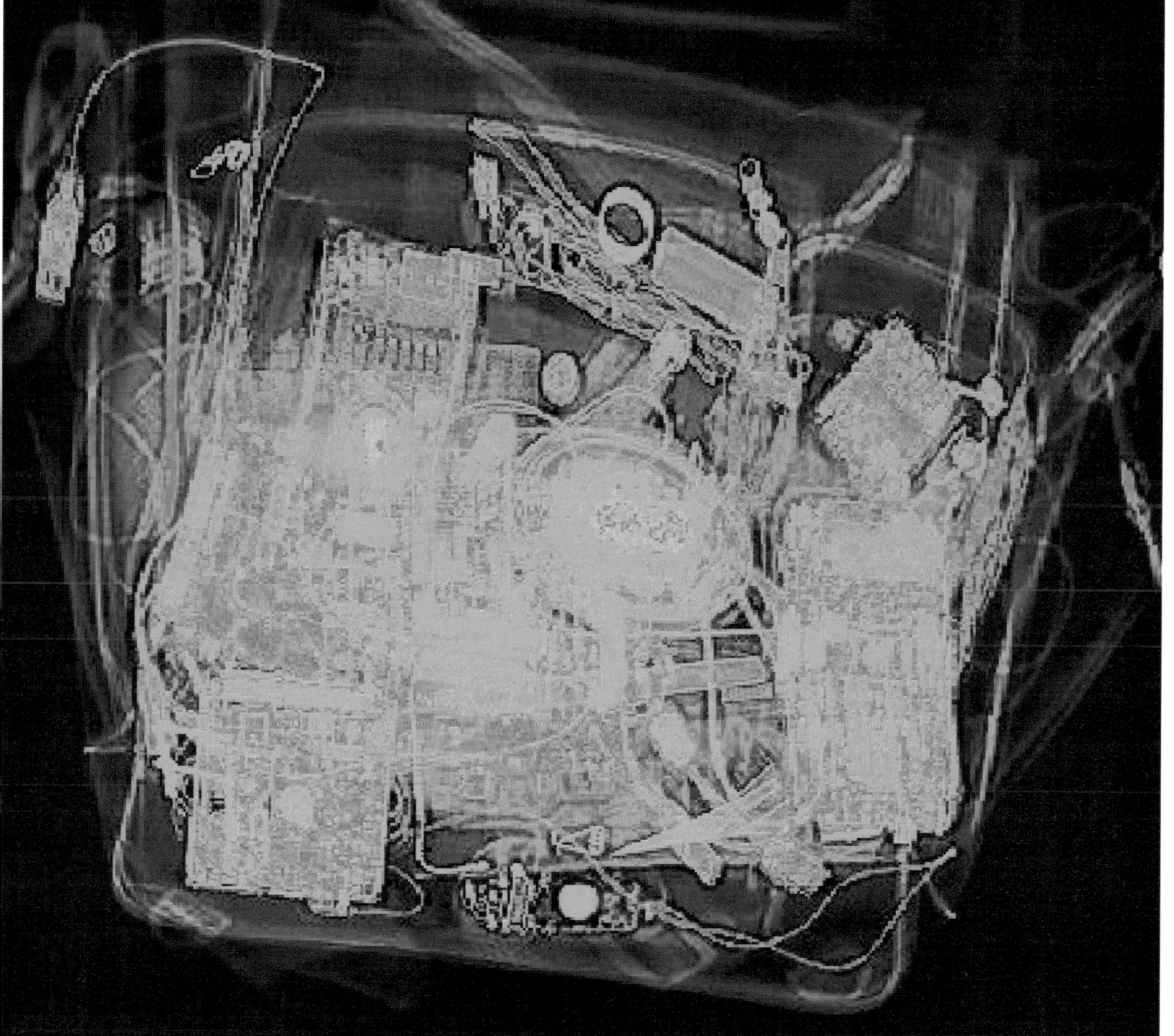

TITLE OF WORK: BOOK ILLUSTRATIONS
DESIGN COMPANY: FURI FURI COMPANY
YEAR: 2000
CLIENT: BENESSE CORPORATION

TITLE OF WORK: WONDERBORG LOGO
DESIGN COMPANY: DEVILROBOTS
YEAR: 2000
CLIENT: BANDAI

"where the weirdest things are"
*Designed by DEVILROBOTS

TITLE OF WORK: EVIROB
DESIGN COMPANY: DEVILROBOTS
YEAR: 2001
CLIENT: INTEL

TITLE OF WORK: GRU1SS3
DESIGN COMPANY: GROOVISIONS
YEAR: 2001
CLIENT: NARITA INSPECTED

カジカジ

Cazi Cazi

KANSAI STREET STYLE MAGAZINE
01 07 NO.85 ¥420

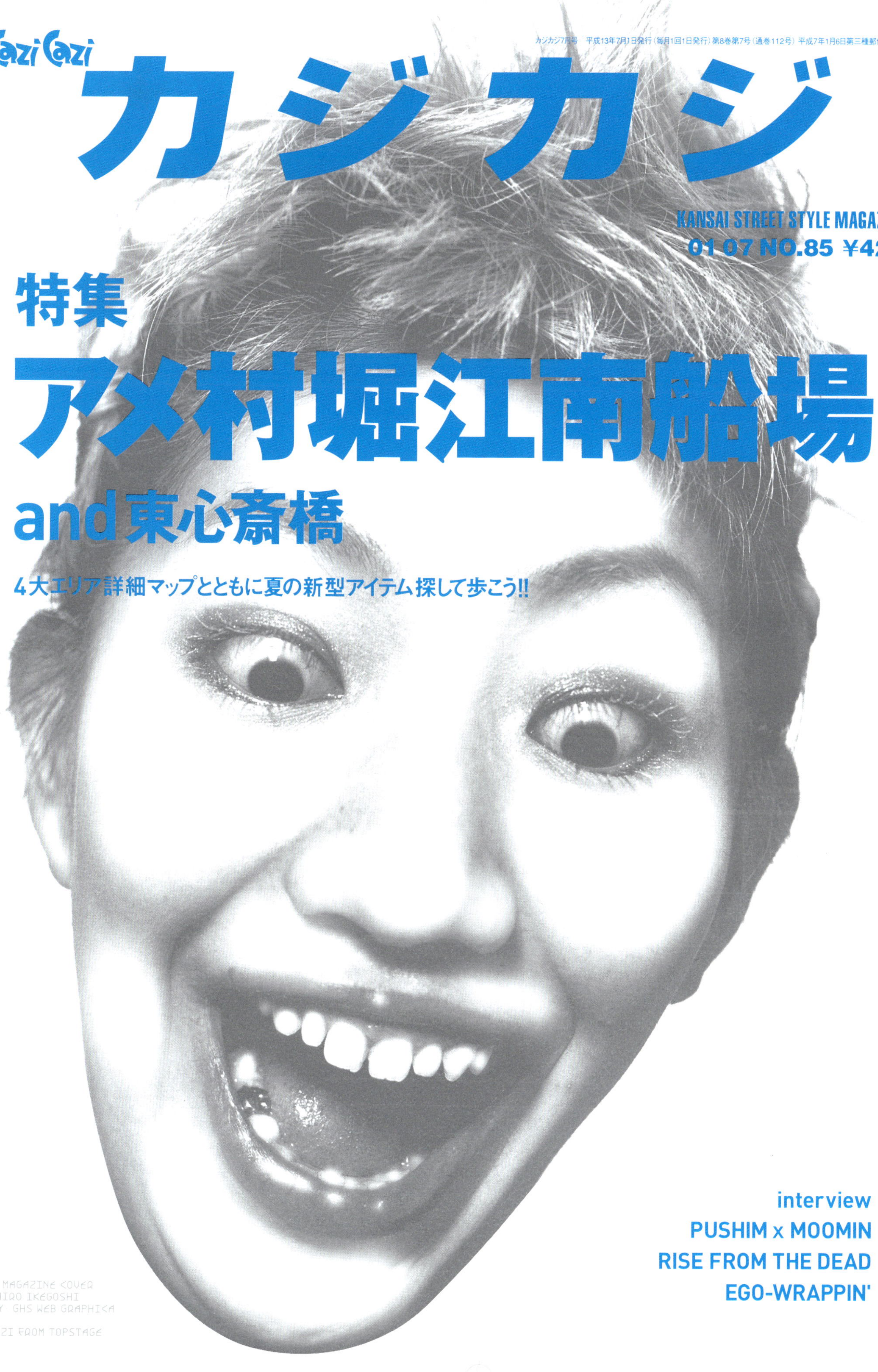

特集
アメ村堀江南船場
and 東心斎橋

4大エリア詳細マップとともに夏の新型アイテム探して歩こう!!

カジカジ NO.85 JULY 2001
0107

interview
PUSHIM x MOOMIN
RISE FROM THE DEAD
EGO-WRAPPIN'

定価420円
本体400円

↑
TITLE OF WORK: VICIOUS MUSHROOM
DESIGNER: SHOKO NAKAZAWA
DESIGN COMPANY: KORATERS.
YEAR: 2001

↑
TITLE OF WORK: STRAWBERRY INSECT
DESIGNER: SHOKO NAKAZAWA
DESIGN COMPANY: KORATERS.
YEAR: 2001

TITLE OF WORK: SHIFT TECHNO POSTCARD
DESIGNER: JUN AWANO, HIRONO
DESIGN COMPANY: KAITEKI
YEAR: 1999
CLIENT: SHIFT TECHNO

TITLE OF WORK: SOUND
DESIGNER: ITSUO ITO
DESIGN COMPANY: IIS
(ITSUO ILLUSTRATION SERVICE)
YEAR: 2000
CLIENT: KINDS ART ASSOCIANTS

exposure
Vol.20 Free Magazine London/Tokyo Feature: Mobile Phone Culture
特集※携帯電話文化
フリーマガジン エクスポージャー 第20号 ロンドン/東京

We Love Computer Games! Nendo graphics (k

TITLE OF WORK: NES
DESIGNER: TSUYOSHI KUSANO
DESIGN COMPANY: NENDO/LEVEL1
YEAR: 2000
CLIENT: EXPOSURE

TITLE OF WORK: JOSURE PS<D
DESIGN COMPANY: JOSURE
YEAR: 2001

TITLE OF WORK: GROOVETRAXX FLYER
DESIGN COMPANY: JOSURE
YEAR: 2001
CLIENT: GROOVETRAXX

TITLE OF WORKS: LEOPARD/KOMAINU/SCORPIONS/LIZARD
DESIGNER: CHIEHOU & SAVWO
DESIGN COMPANY: CYCLONE GRAPHIX
YEAR: 1999-2001

TITLE OF WORK: MAGAZINE ILLUSTRATION
DESIGNER: ITSUO ITO
DESIGN COMPANY: IIS
(ITSUO ILLUSTRATION SERVICE)
YEAR: 2000
CLIENT: EXCEED PRESS

TITLE OF WORK: MAGAZINE ILLUSTRATION
DESIGNER: ITSUO ITO
DESIGN COMPANY: IIS
(ITSUO ILLUSTRATION SERVICE)
YEAR: 2000
CLIENT: EXCEED PRESS

Itsuo Illustration Service

TITLE OF WORK: MONKEY TURN
CD JACKET
DESIGNER: KENTARO «ANI» FUJIMOTO
DESIGN COMPANY: NENDO
YEAR: 2001
CLIENT: FAR EAST RECORDS

TITLE OF WORK: HAVING TO MAKE UP LOGOS SUCKS
DESIGNER: M. HANZAWA, J. SAITO
DESIGN COMPANY: POWER GRAPHIXX
YEAR: 1996-2001
CLIENT: VARIOUS

TITLE OF WORK: CLOUD MKSD POSTER
DESIGNER: MASAYUKI SATO
DESIGN COMPANY: MANIACKERS DESIGN
YEAR: 2001
CLIENT: SELFPROMOTION

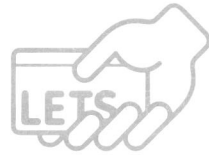

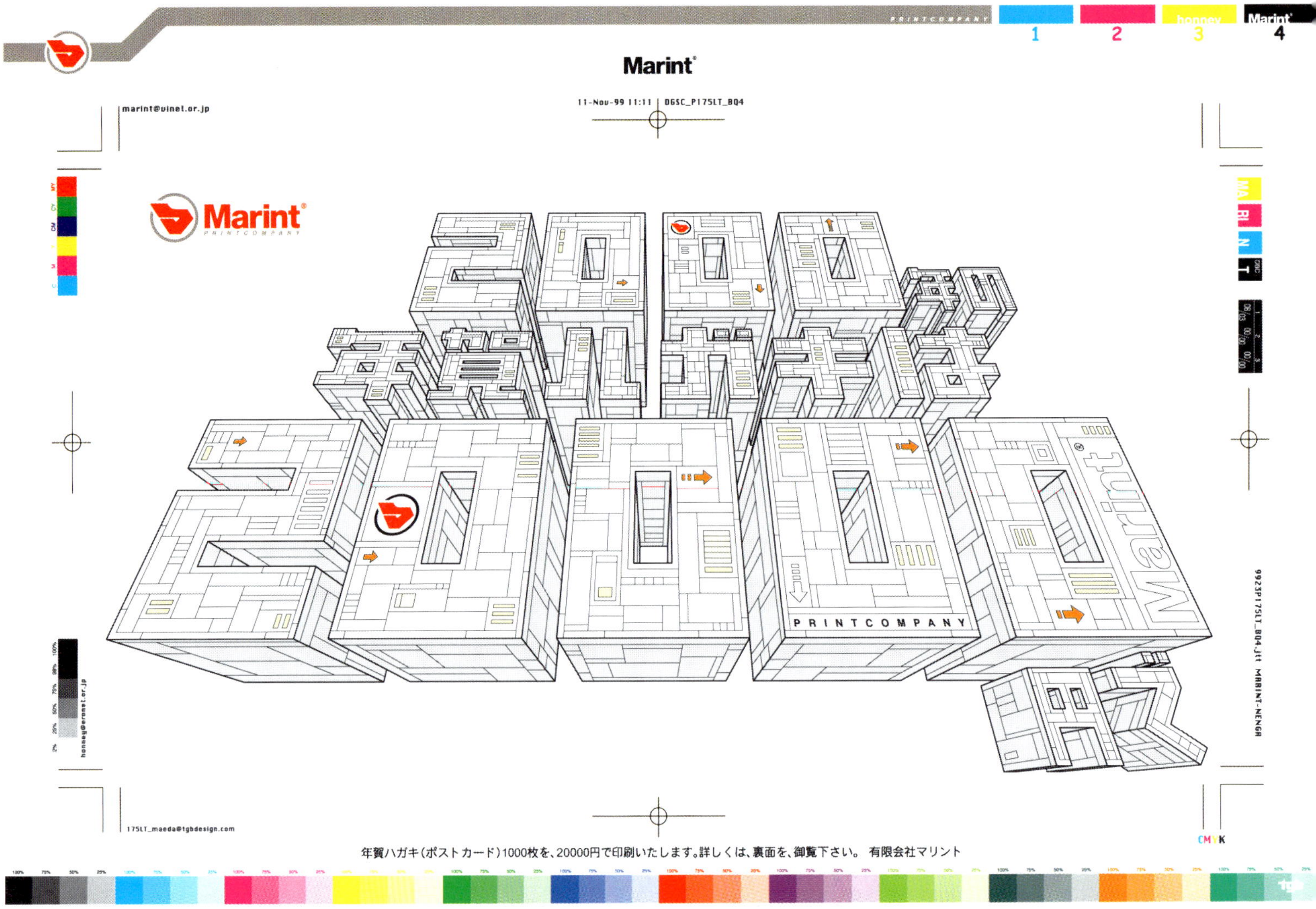

↑
TITLE OF WORK: MARINT NEW YEAR CARD 2000
DESIGNER: HIDEAKI KOMIYAMA
DESIGN COMPANY: TGB DESIGN
YEAR: 1999
CLIENT: MARINT

↓
TITLE OF WORK: RELAX - OUR FAVORITE SHOP
DESIGNER: MASARU ISHIURA
DESIGN COMPANY: TGB DESIGN
YEAR: 2000
CLIENT: RELAX & PARCO

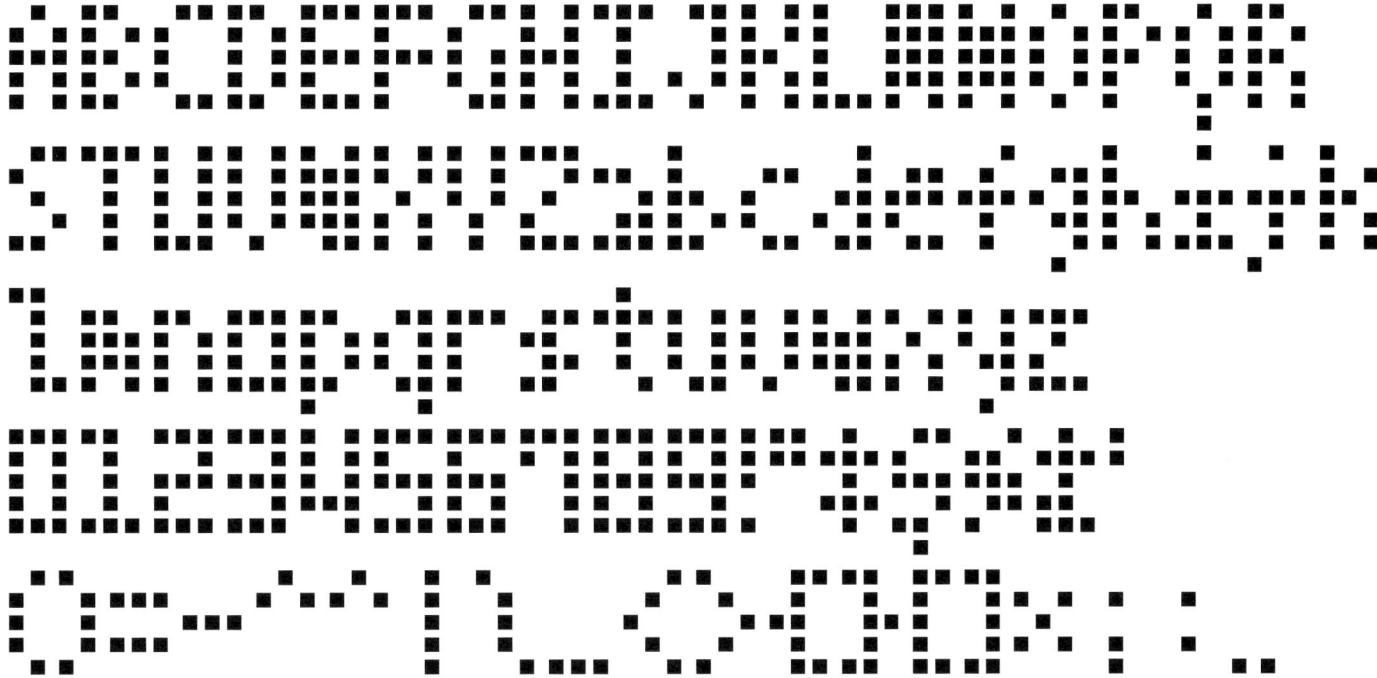

TITLE OF WORK: 17
DESIGNER: SHINSUKE KOSHIO
DESIGN COMPANY: SUNDAY-VISION
YEAR: 2000
CLIENT: SELFISH MAGAZINE

TITLE OF WORK: ZETUEI MANDALA
(NARITA INSPECTED-OUTLINE)
DESIGNER: KANO
DESIGN COMPANY: ZETUEI FONTS
YEAR: 2001
CLIENT: NARITA INSPECTED

NARITA INSPECTED

TITLE OF WORK: TGNG GAMES
DESIGNER: TSUYOSHI KUSANO
DESIGN COMPANY: NENDO/LEVEL1
YEAR: 2000

TITLE OF WORK: JINNAN TV
DESIGNER: PIROMI
DESIGN COMPANY: PIROMI.COM
YEAR: 2001

TITLE OF WORK: GREETING CARD
DESIGN COMPANY: FURI FURI COMPANY
YEAR: 2001
CLIENT: WEB PROGRESSIVE

TITLE OF WORK: JEREMY SCOTT 1
DESIGN COMPANY: ENLIGHTENMENT
YEAR: 2001
CLIENT: FIDGET

TITLE OF WORK: JEREMY SCOTT 4
DESIGN COMPANY: ENLIGHTENMENT
YEAR: 2001
CLIENT: FIDGET

TITLE OF WORK: WASH A CAMARO
DESIGNER: YUTANPO SHIRANE
YEAR: 2000

TITLE OF WORK: UNTITLED
DESIGNER: YUTANPO SHIRANE
YEAR: 2000
CLIENT: «BRUTUS» MAGAZINE
(MAGAZINEHOUSE LTD.)

SPY RANGER
PROFESSIONAL SPY TEAM OF THE UNKNOWN

MULTI LEVEL & MULTI PURPOSE MACHINE
KATHY GOTO'S TANK, SPT-002
"SPY TANK"

They were two men and woman, Television Newscaster and ace pilot Thomas Morgan, circus acrobat and electronics expert Rocky Davis, oceanographer and professional cook Kathy Goto. They were professional spy team of the unknown, SPY RANGER!!!

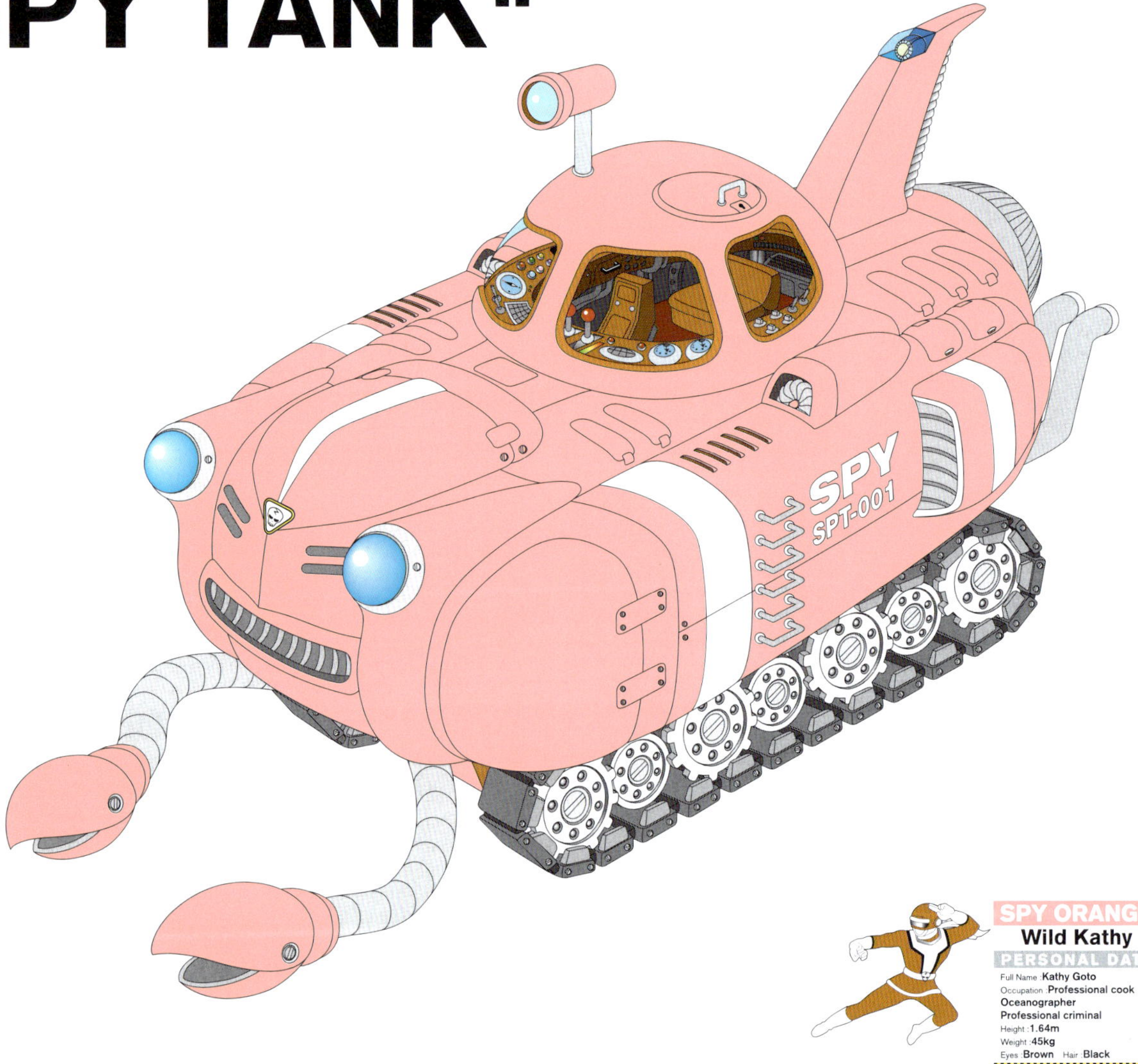

SPY ORANGE
Wild Kathy
PERSONAL DATA
Full Name: Kathy Goto
Occupation: Professional cook
Oceanographer
Professional criminal
Height: 1.64m
Weight: 45kg
Eyes: Brown Hair: Black

SPY TANK'S SPECIAL ITEMS !!!

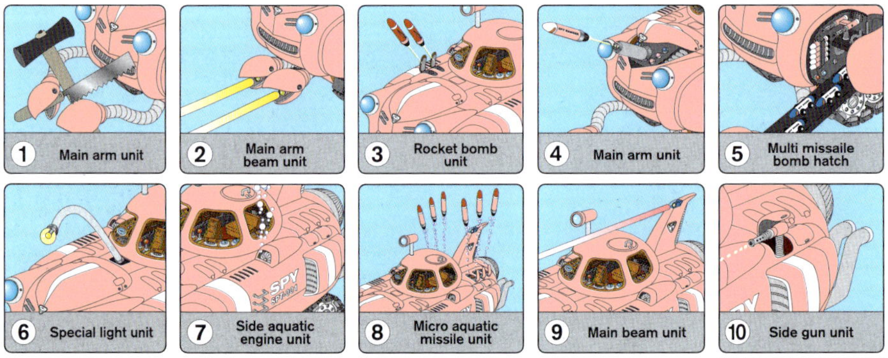

1. Main arm unit
2. Main arm beam unit
3. Rocket bomb unit
4. Main arm unit
5. Multi missaile bomb hatch
6. Special light unit
7. Side aquatic engine unit
8. Micro aquatic missile unit
9. Main beam unit
10. Side gun unit

SPY TANK: HEIGHT 6.4m, WIDTH 7.2m, LENGTH 12.5m.

© 2000, Tetsurou Sano, All rights reserved.

TITLE OF WORK: COPPEPAN-ALPHABET
& JAPANESE KATAKANA & HIRAGANA
DESIGNER: MASAYUKI SATO
DESIGN COMPANY: MANIACKERS DESIGN
YEAR: 2000
CLIENT: SHOEISHA CO., LTD.

Coppepan-Choco Al
ABCDEFGHIJKLMNOPQRSTUVWXYZ
abcdefghijklmnopqrstuvwxyz
:;!?#$%&[(]/-_()~@©™
0123456789

Coppepan-Cream Al
ABCDEFGHIJKLMNOPQRSTUVWXYZ
abcdefghijklmnopqrstuvwxyz
:;!?#$%&[(]/-_()~@©™
0123456789

Coppepan-Jam Al
ABCDEFGHIJKLMNOPQRSTUVWXYZ
abcdefghijklmnopqrstuvwxyz
:;!?#$%&[(]/-_()~@©™
0123456789

Coppepan-Cream Kt
アイウエオカキクケコサシスセソタチツテトナニヌネノハヒフヘホマミムメモヤユヨラリルレロワヲンガギグゲゴザジズゼゾダヂヅデドバビブベボパピプペポァィゥェォャュョッー、。「」()!?…0123456789

Coppepan-Cream Hr
あいうえおかきくけこさしすせそたちつてとなにぬねのはひふへほまみむめもやゆよらりるれろわをんがぎぐげござじずぜぞだぢづでどばびぶべぼぱぴぷぺぽぁぃぅぇぉゃゅょっー、。「」()!?…0123456789

Coppepan-Choco Kt
アイウエオカキクケコサシスセソタチツテトナニヌネノハヒフヘホマミムメモヤユヨラリルレロワヲンガギグゲゴザジズゼゾダヂヅデドバビブベボパピプペポァィゥェォャュョッー、。「」()!?…0123456789

Coppepan-Choco Hr
あいうえおかきくけこさしすせそたちつてとなにぬねのはひふへほまみむめもやゆよらりるれろわをんがぎぐげござじずぜぞだぢづでどばびぶべぼぱぴぷぺぽぁぃぅぇぉゃゅょっー、。「」()!?…0123456789

Coppepan-Jam Kt
アイウエオカキクケコサシスセソタチツテトナニヌネノハヒフヘホマミムメモヤユヨラリルレロワヲンガギグゲゴザジズゼゾダヂヅデドバビブベボパピプペポァィゥェォャュョッー、。「」()!?…0123456789

Coppepan-Jam Hr
あいうえおかきくけこさしすせそたちつてとなにぬねのはひふへほまみむめもやゆよらりるれろわをんがぎぐげござじずぜぞだぢづでどばびぶべぼぱぴぷぺぽぁぃぅぇぉゃゅょっー、。「」()!?…0123456789

Maniackers Design font no.37 Coppepan
copyright 1999 Maniackers Design All rights reserved

001.
Dabble

002. DABBLE is evaluated by everyone in their lives and thoughts because it is already not for only one when it got formed.

003.

004.
Performance

005.
Vehicle

TITLE OF WORK: SCUTS
DESIGNER: SAYSHIRO «RITO» FUJIMOTO
DESIGN COMPANY: NOBODY DESIGN PRODUCTS
YEAR: 1999
CLIENT: D'CO., INC.

TITLE OF WORK: CHAMPAGNE DESIGN
DESIGN COMPANY: TYCOON GRAPHICS
YEAR: 2000

TITLE OF WORK: AKASHIC RECORDS NITE 2000 POSTER
DESIGNER: TOWA TEI & TYCOON GRAPHICS
DESIGN COMPANY: TYCOON GRAPHICS
YEAR: 2000
CLIENT: AKASHIC RECORDS

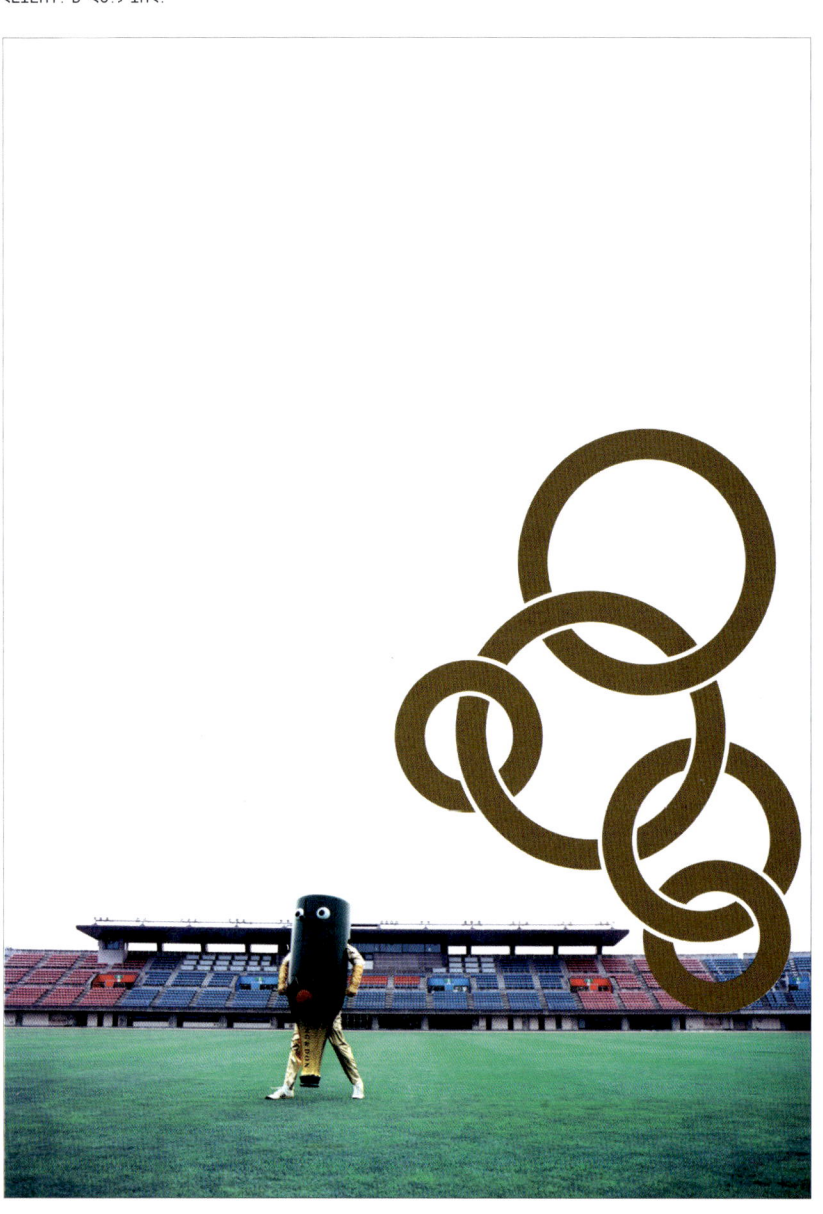

TITLE OF WORK: BEE
DESIGNER: SATOSHI MATSUZAWA
DESIGN COMPANY: SATO LABO
YEAR: 1999
CLIENT: GANG

TITLE OF WORK: CSIO BABY-G CAMPAIGN
DESIGNER: ITSUO ITO
DESIGN COMPANY: IIS
(ITSUO ILLUSTRATION SERVICE)
YEAR: 2000
CLIENT: CSIO

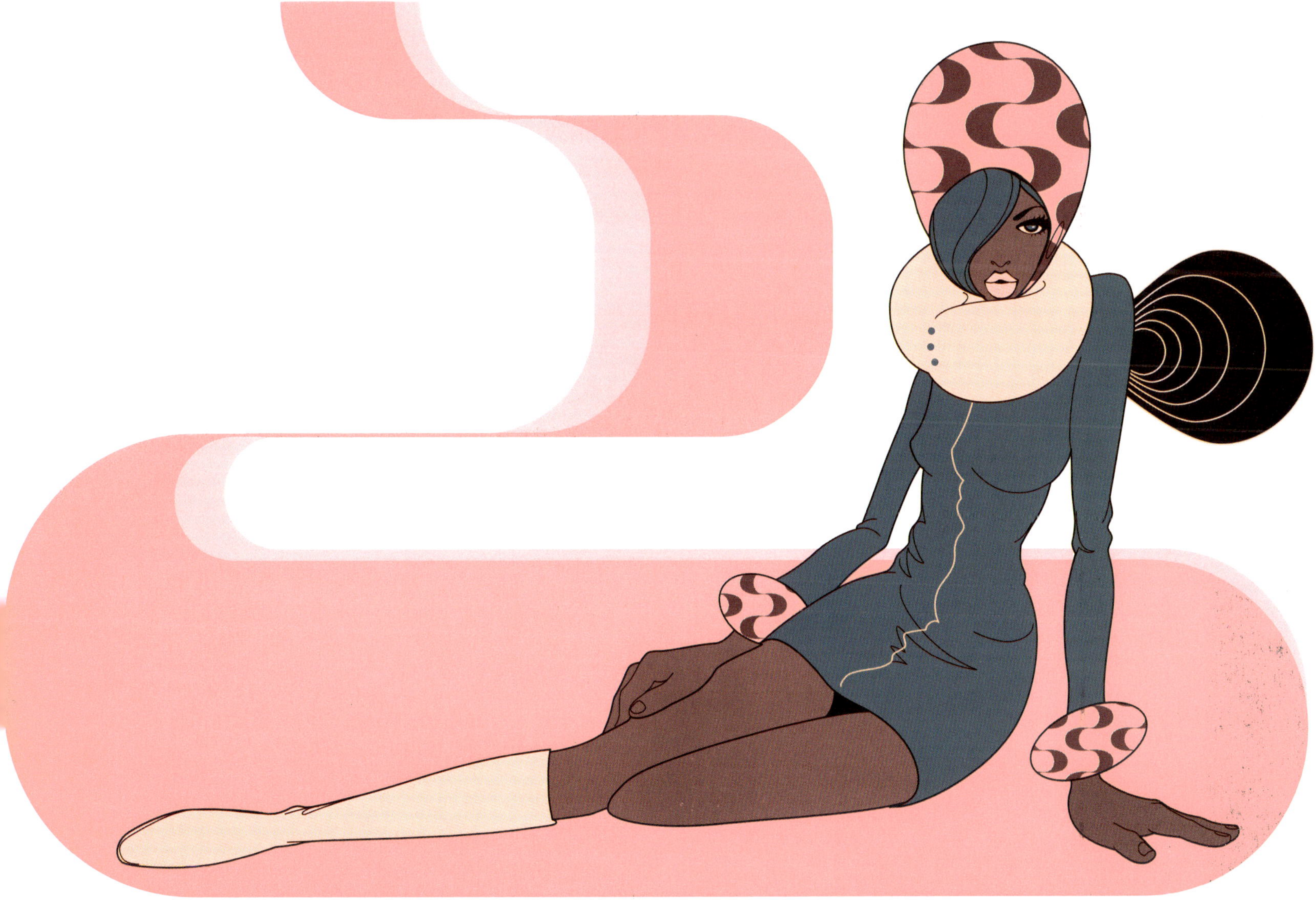

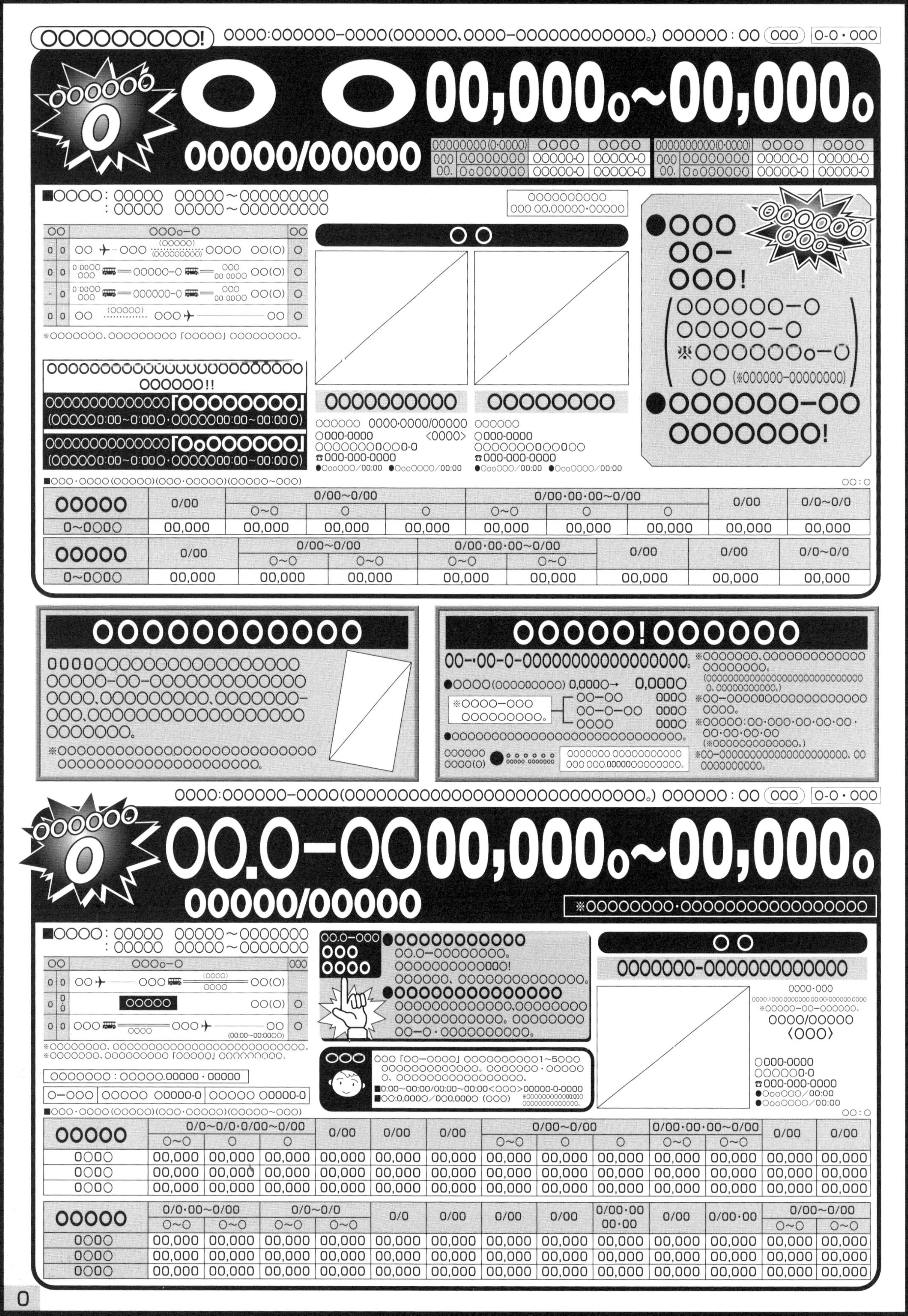

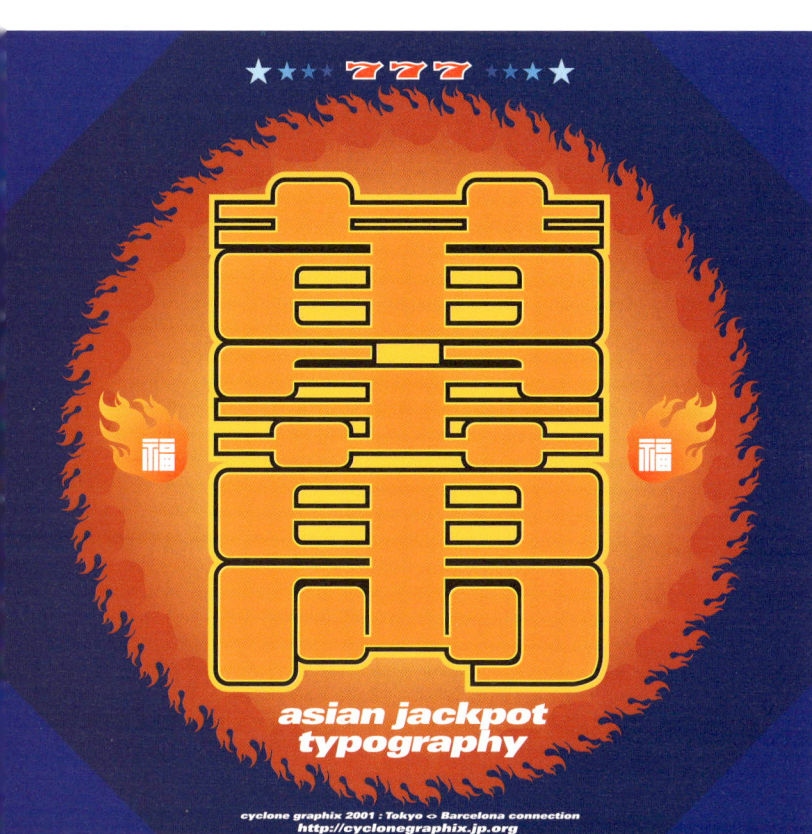

TITLE OF WORK: ASIAN JACKPOT TYPOGRAPHY 1
DESIGNER: SAVWO
DESIGN COMPANY: CYCLONE GRAPHIX
YEAR: 2001
CLIENT: VASAVA/EVOPHAT

TITLE OF WORK: ASIAN JACKPOT TYPOGRAPHY 2
DESIGNER: SAVWO
DESIGN COMPANY: CYCLONE GRAPHIX
YEAR: 2001
CLIENT: VASAVA/EVOPHAT

TITLE OF WORK: ASIAN JACKPOT TYPOGRAPHY 3
DESIGNER: SAVWO
DESIGN COMPANY: CYCLONE GRAPHIX
YEAR: 2001
CLIENT: VASAVA/EVOPHAT

TITLE OF WORK: ASIAN JACKPOT TYPOGRAPHY 4
DESIGNER: SAVWO
DESIGN COMPANY: CYCLONE GRAPHIX
YEAR: 2001
CLIENT: VASAVA/EVOPHAT

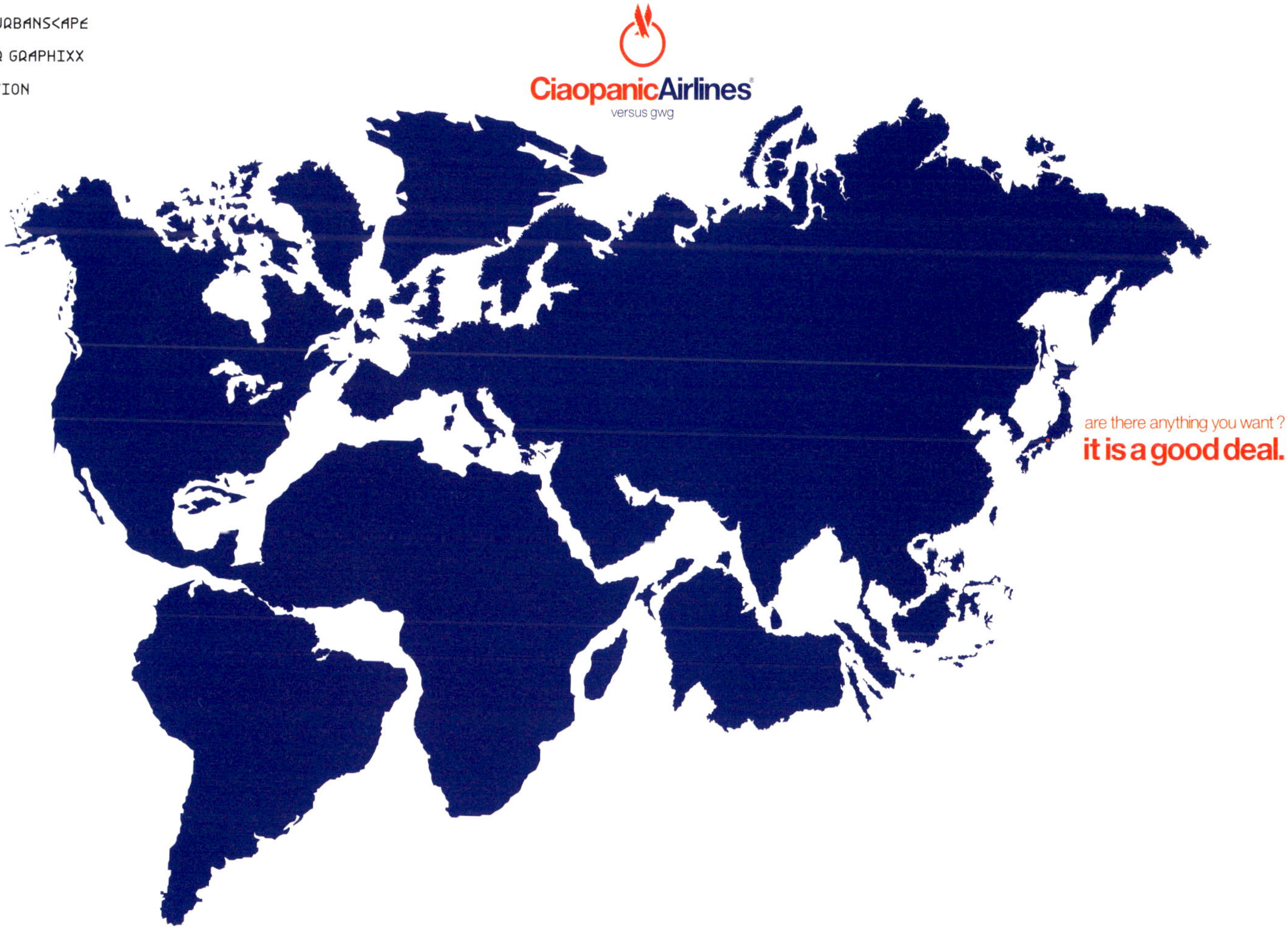

TITLE OF WORK PLAYSTATION
DESIGNER TSUYOSHI HIROOKA
DESIGN COMPANY LEVEL1
YEAR 2000
CLIENT HAKUHODO

TITLE OF WORK: IMPOSTOR
DESIGNER: JIRO FUJITA
DESIGN COMPANY: FJD (FUJITA JIRO DESIGN)
YEAR: 2001
CLIENT: KINDS ART ASSOCIATES

TITLE OF WORK: SPACEKELLY
CD JACKET
DESIGNER: NAO TSUCHIYA
DESIGN COMPANY: PAT DETECTIVE
YEAR: 2000
CLIENT: SYFT RECORDS

TITLE OF WORK: HFG EXHIBITION POSTERS
DESIGNER: TAKESHI HAMADA
DESIGN COMPANY: 617
YEAR: 2000

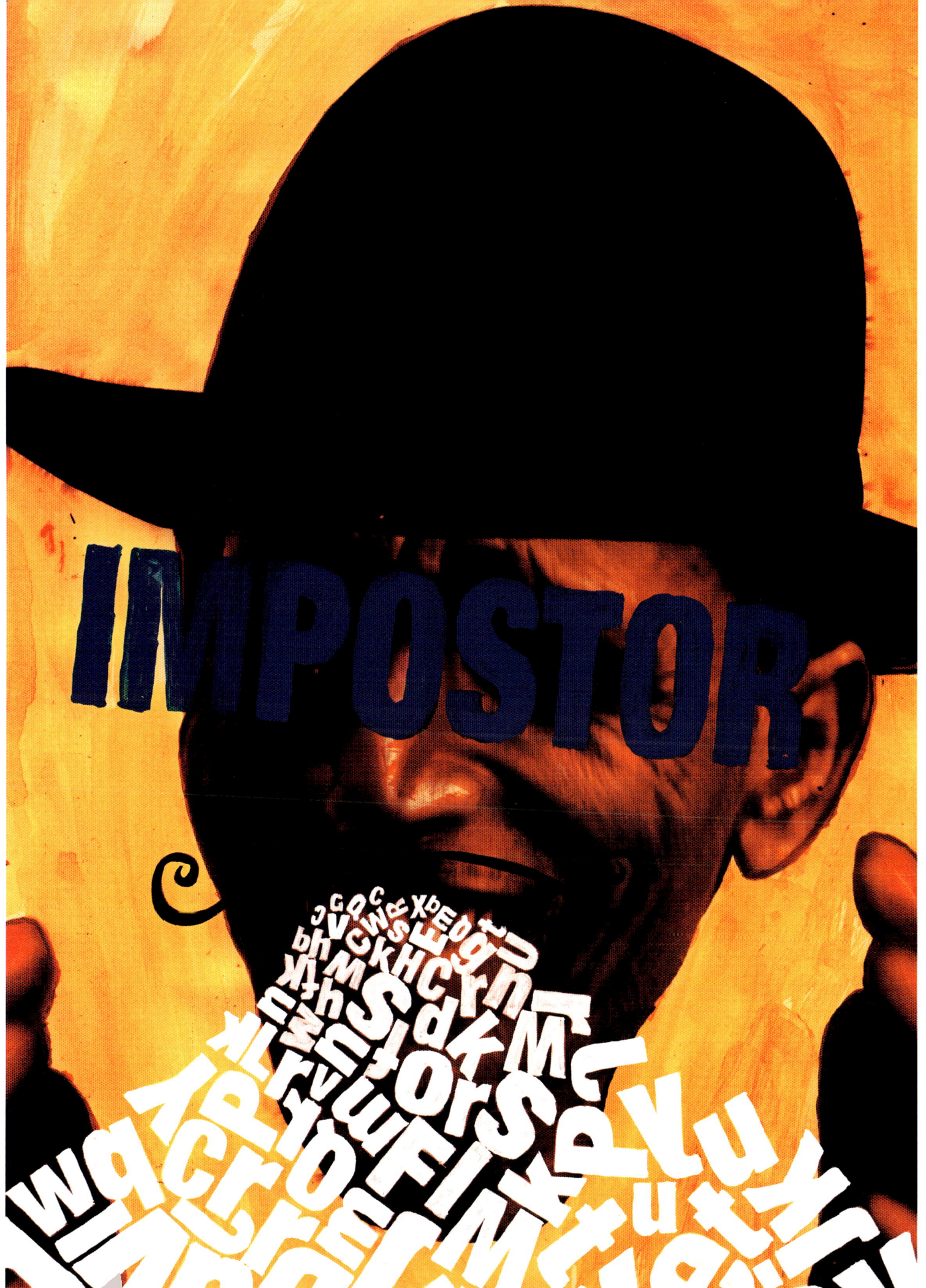

TITLE OF WORK: POWER UNIT
DESIGNER: M.HANZAWA, J.SAITO
DESIGN COMPANY: POWER GRAPHIXX
YEAR: 2000
CLIENT: KOHKOKU MAGAZINE (HAKUHODO)

TITLE OF WORK: SUKEBE CHAIR
DESIGNER: M.HANZAWA
DESIGN COMPANY: POWER GRAPHIXX
YEAR: 2000
CLIENT: SELFISH MAGAZINE

TITLE OF WORK: RUBIK'S CUBE CHRISTMAS
DESIGNER: J.SAITO
DESIGN COMPANY: POWER GRAPHIXX
YEAR: 2000
CLIENT: SELFISH MAGAZINE

TITLE OF WORK: RENGE
DESIGNER: PIAOMI
DESIGN COMPANY: PIAOMI.COM
YEAR: 2000

TITLE OF WORK: TOKYO TWINS TRADING CARD NO. 3
DESIGNER: YOSUKE IMAI
DESIGN COMPANY: IMAITOONZ
YEAR: 2000
CLIENT: CUBE CO., LTD.

TITLE OF WORK: TOKYO TWINS TRADING CARD NO. 2
DESIGNER: YOSUKE IMAI
DESIGN COMPANY: IMAITOONZ
YEAR: 2000
CLIENT: CUBE CO., LTD.

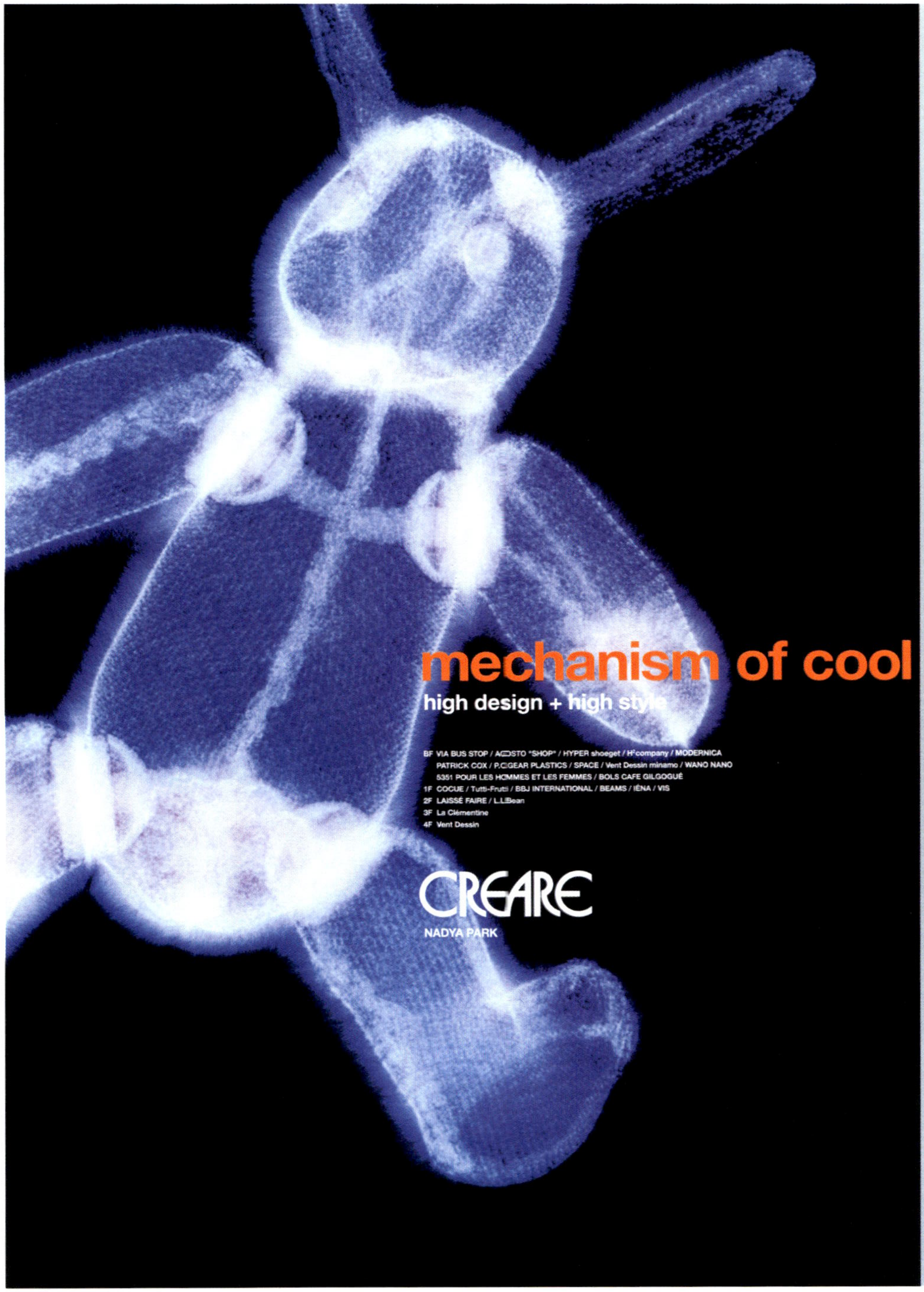

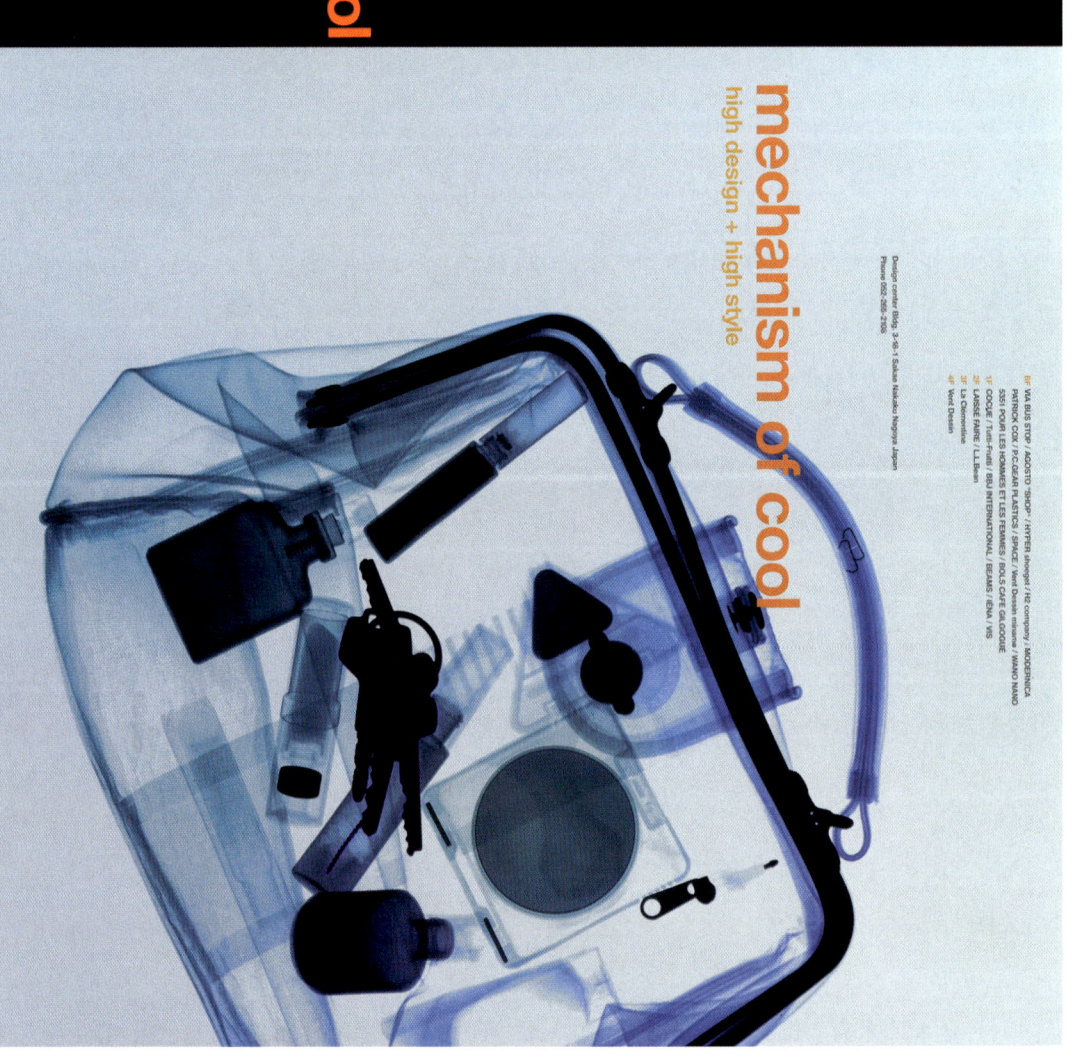

TITLE OF WORK: ARTWORK
DESIGNER: HIDEKI INABA
YEAR: 2001
CLIENT: IDN MAGAZINE

TITLE OF WORK: MIDNIGHT CHANNEL
DESIGNER: TATSUYA HAMA
DESIGN COMPANY: ASTRO GRAPHICA
YEAR: 2001
CLIENT: NHK ENTERPRISE 21

TITLE OF WORK: ORIKOMIO
WEB TITLE LOGO
DESIGNER: AKIHIRO IKEGOSHI
DESIGN COMPANY: GHS WEB GRAPHICA
YEAR: 2001
CLIENT: DAI NIPPON PRINTING

TITLE OF WORK: ON THE SLIDER
CD JACKET
DESIGNER: KOJI TAKEUCHI
DESIGN COMPANY: ASTRO GRAPHICA
YEAR: 2001
CLIENT: WILD BUNCH RECORDS

TITLE OF WORK: GWG EXHIBITION WORK
DESIGNER: AKIHIRO IKEGOSHI
DESIGN COMPANY: GHS WEB GRAPHICA
YEAR: 2001

TITLE OF WORK: ANARCHY IN THE HONGKONG LOGO
DESIGNER: AKIHIRO IKEGOSHI
DESIGN COMPANY: GHS WEB GRAPHICA
YEAR: 2000
CLIENT: POST <ADD A GO GO

TITLE OF WORK: CLUB DAWN LOGO
DESIGNER: AKIHIRO IKEGOSHI
DESIGN COMPANY: GHS WEB GRAPHICA
YEAR: 2000
CLIENT: CLUB DAWN

TITLE OF WORK: INFORMATION LOGO FOR A7
DESIGNER: AKIHIRO IKEGOSHI
DESIGN COMPANY: GHS WEB GRAPHICA
YEAR: 2001
CLIENT: A7 FROM DESCENTE

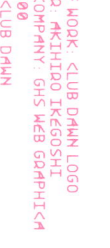

TITLE OF WORK: A7 LOGO
DESIGNED: AKIHIRO IKEGOSHI
DESIGN COMPANY: GHS WEB GRAPHIKA
YEAR: 2001
CLIENT: A7 FROM DESCENTE

TITLE OF WORK: LOGO FOR EVENT T-SHIRTS
DESIGNED: AKIHIRO IKEGOSHI
DESIGN COMPANY: GHS WEB GRAPHIKA
YEAR: 2000

TITLE OF WORK: GWG STICKER
DESIGNED: AKIHIRO IKEGOSHI
DESIGN COMPANY: GHS WEB GRAPHIKA
YEAR: 2001

TITLE OF WORK: GWG STICKER
DESIGNED: AKIHIRO IKEGOSHI
DESIGN COMPANY: GHS WEB GRAPHIKA
YEAR: 2001

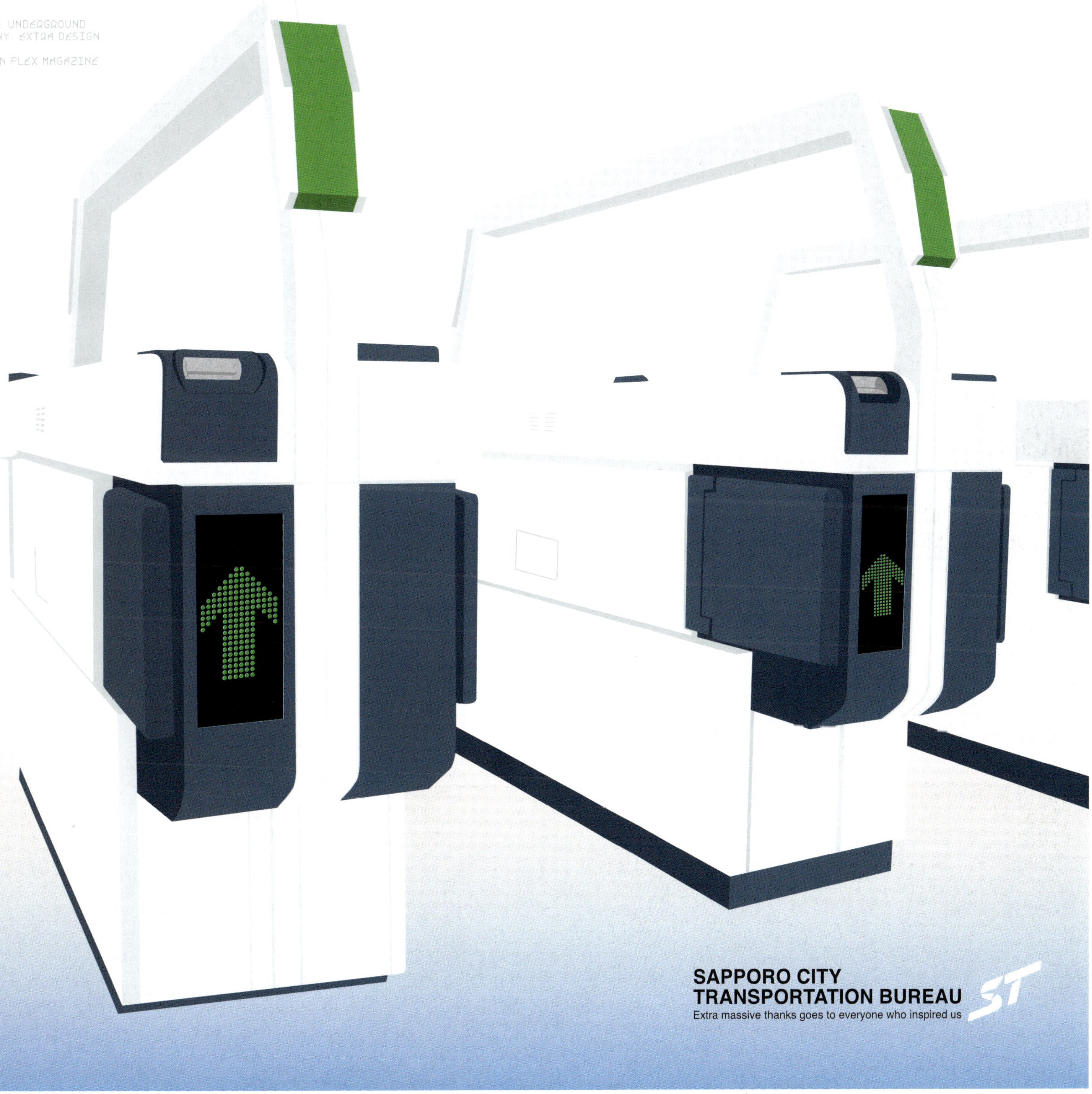

TITLE OF WORK: «MUSE A»/«MUSE B»
CD JACKETS
DESIGNER: NAO TSUCHIYA
DESIGN COMPANY: PAT DETECTIVE
YEAR: 2000
CLIENT: WEA JAPAN

TITLE OF WORK: ILLUSTRATIONS FOR
«FURI FURI THANGKA» EXHIBITION
DESIGN COMPANY: FURI FURI COMPANY
YEAR: 1999

TITLE OF WORK: SLOT
DESIGNER: SATOSHI MATSUZAWA
DESIGN COMPANY: SATOLABO
YEAR: 2000
CLIENT: PIA

"THE SLOT"

TITLE OF WORK: SUPERNOVA
DESIGNER: SATOSHI MATSUZAWA
DESIGN COMPANY: SATOLABO
YEAR: 2000
CLIENT: J-WAVE

SUPERNOVA

TITLE OF WORK: NO TITLE
DESIGNER: SATOSHI MATSUZAWA
DESIGN COMPANY: SATOLABO
YEAR: 2000

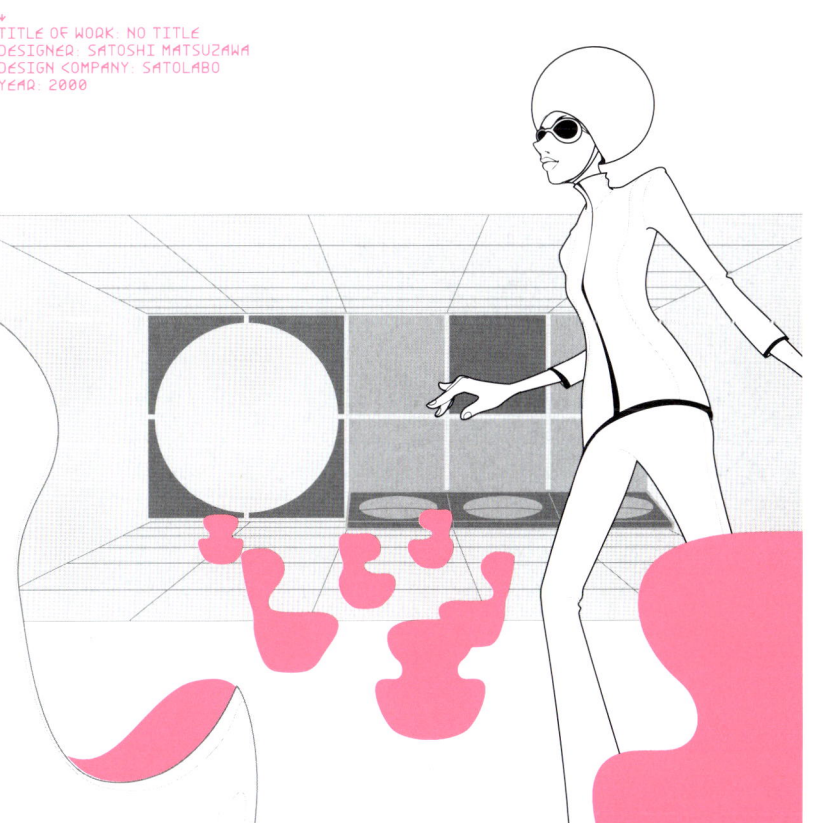

JUDY AND MARY　WARP

TITLE OF WORK: JUDY AND MARY/WARP
CD COVER
DESIGN COMPANY: TYCOON GRAPHICS
YEAR: 2001
CLIENT: SONY MUSIC COMMUNICATIONS INC.

SUNDAY-VISION

Sunday-Vision was established by leader Shinsuke Koshio in 1998. Koshio uses the name of Sunday-Vision as his own pseudonym, but also as a collective name when working in collaboration with others. Have worked on illustration, motion graphics, web, and clothing design.
The name Switch Stance is also used given to work in clothing design. Recent work includes K-SWISS goods, the cover of BRUTUS magazine, the motion graphics for EDWIN, the web design for x-girl (Japan) etc. Clothing in collaboration with And A is also scheduled.

越尾真介を中心に1998年結成。現在は越尾の匿名として、あるいはコラボレーションの際の総合名称としてSunday-Visionを使用している。グラフィックデザインをベースにイラストレーション、映像、ウェブ、ウェア製作をしている。また、ウェアはSwitch Stanceという別名義でも活動している。最近の仕事はK・SWISSのグッズ、BRUTUSの表紙、EDWINの映像、x-girl（日本）のウェブ等。And Aとのウェアのコラボレーションも予定している。

BIOGRAPHY / 10 QUESTIONS/ANSWERS

HOW DOES JAPAN SMELL TODAY?
How does it smell...?

HOW DOES YOUR DAY START AND HOW DOES YOUR DAY END?
I go cycling, I work, go skateboarding, work, listen to music, and go to sleep.

IS THERE SOMETHING THAT YOU REALLY LOVE AND THAT YOU REALLY HATE ABOUT JAPAN?
I like the good tradition and custom. I hate the horrible tradition and custom.

WHAT DO YOU THINK ARE THE DIFFERENCES BETWEEN AMERICAN, EUROPEAN AND JAPANESE PEOPLE?
Language is different. Also the way you express your feelings is different. But maybe not so much. Although it is not realistic, I hesitate to differentiate by race.

WHAT DO YOU THINK IS THE DIFFERENCE BETWEEN JAPANESE, AMERICAN AND EUROPEAN DESIGN?
There are different ways of expression and thinking, with historical reason in each country. Japan might have been influenced too much by others.

WHAT WOULD YOU DO, IF GRAPHIC DESIGN DID NOT EXIST?
I think I would be doing something that I like while doing other work.

CAN YOU TELL US YOUR 3 MOST IMPORTANT THINGS/OBJECTS/ACTIVITIES?
To think. To go out. Friends.

WHAT IS BEAUTIFUL AND WHAT IS UGLY?
What nature has made is beautiful. The garbage sitting in the office is ugly.

TO WHICH QUESTION YOU WOULD NEVER GIVE AN ANSWER?
«Could you describe to us the genre of your favorite music in detail?»

IS THERE ANYTHING YOU WOULD LIKE TO TELL THE READERS OF THIS BOOK?
-

(interview with Shinsuke Koshio)

Q1: 今日の日本はどんな匂いがしますか？
A1: どんな匂いかなあ…？

Q2: あなたの1日はどの様に始まり、どの様に終わりますか？
A2: サイクリングして、仕事して、スケボーして、仕事して、音楽聴いて、寝る。

Q3: 日本の好きな部分、嫌いな部分を挙げて下さい。
A3: 好きなのは良い伝統と慣習。嫌いなのは嫌な伝統と慣習。

Q4: アメリカ人、ヨーロッパ人、日本人の違いは何だと思いますか？
A4: 言葉が違う。気持ちの表現の仕方も。でもあんまり違わないかな。現実的ではないけれど人種で分けたくない。

Q5: 日本のデザイン、アメリカのデザイン、ヨーロッパのデザインの違いは何だと思いますか？
A5: 歴史上、表現の仕方と考え方が国によって違う。日本は影響を受け過ぎている感があるかも。

Q6: グラフィックデザインが存在していなかったら、あなたは何をしていますか？
A6: 他の仕事しながら趣味の活動をしていると思う。

Q7: あなた大事なことを3つ教えて下さい。
A7: 考えること。遊ぶこと。友達。

Q8: 何が美しくて、何が醜いと思いますか？
A8: 美しいのは自然が作ったもの。醜いのは事務所のゴミ。

Q9: あなたが絶対に答えない質問は何でしょう？
A9: 好きな音楽のジャンルを細かく教えてください。

Q10: 読者に何か伝えたいことがあれば書いて下さい。
A10: ―

（インタビュー：越尾真介）

PROFILE

NAME OF DESIGN COMPANY: SUNDAY-VISION
NAME/YEAR OF BIRTH: SHINSUKE KOSHIO (75)
COMPANY SINCE: 1998
ADDRESS: SHINJUKU SAKAE-BLDG. 303, 3-5-15 NISHI-SHINJUKU, SHINJUKU-KU, TOKYO 160-0023, JAPAN
WEBSITE: HTTP://WWW.SUNDAY-VISION.COM/
EMAIL ADDRESS: INFO@SUNDAY-VISION.COM
FAX: +81 (0)3-5908-2134

デザイン会社名：サンデーヴィジョン
メンバー名(生年)：越尾真介(75年)
会社設立日：1998年
住所：〒160-0023 東京都新宿区西新宿3-5-15 新宿栄マンション
ウェブサイト：http://www.sunday-vision.com/
Eメールアドレス：info@sunday-vision.com
ファックス番号：+81 (0)3-5908-2134

BUSINESS CARD

SELFPORTRAIT

SUNDAY-VISION　　　　　　　　　　　サンデーヴィジョン

WORKSPACES ↓　　　　　　　　　　　　　　　　　　　　LOGOTYPE ↑

TITLE OF WORK: SKATEBOARDING FONT 2001
DESIGNER: SHINSUKE KOSHIO, ATSUSHI AOKI
DESIGN COMPANY: SUNDAY-VISION, ADD
YEAR: 2000
CLIENT: ROCKET PUNCH (FREE PAPER)

TITLE OF WORK: SUNDAY-VISION PORNO SYSTEM
DESIGNER: SHINSUKE KOSHIO
DESIGN COMPANY: SUNDAY-VISION
YEAR: 2000
CLIENT: SELFISH MAGAZINE

TITLE OF WORK: SUNDAY-VISION RECORD PLAYER SHEET
DESIGNER: SHINSUKE KOSHIO, SHUJI KIKUCHI
DESIGN COMPANY: SUNDAY-VISION
YEAR: 2000
CLIENT: SELFISH MAGAZINE

SUNDAY-VISION in SELFISH vol.01 2000
"SUNDAY-VISION RECORD SHEET NO.2"
SHINSUKE KOSHIO & SHUJI KIKUCHI
NO.1 buck number in "Girlie 03"1999
http://sunday-vision.com
info@sunday-vision.com

CYCLONE GRAPHIX

Established in late 1990. While sav-wo had been working mainly in web design, font design etc. by himself, yan and chiehou recently became members of cyclone graphix as well as being independently active. The main activities include web design, typeface, logo, illustration, and various printed media such as books and flyers. The policy for creating artwork is to adopt cultures and styles of various countries along with Japanese culture and style, and combine them with the originality of cyclone graphix. Check out the Asian Underground >>>

1990年後半設立。最初はサヴヲ1人でWeb制作やFont制作等を中心に活動してきたが、現在はヤンとチイホウが新たに参加し、3人各々が独自の制作をこなしながらサイクログラフィックスとして活動。主な活動内容はWeb、Typeface、Logo、イラスト制作、装丁やフライヤー等の各種紙媒体。作品を制作する上で心掛けている事は、色々な国の様々な文化、様式を取り入れつつ日本独自の文化、様式を加え、そこにサイクログラフィックスとしてのオリジナリティーを加える事。Check the Asian Underground >>>

BIOGRAPHY ↑
10 QUESTIONS/ANSWERS ↓

HOW DOES JAPAN SMELL TODAY?
There are various cultures and styles that mingle and exist, everyone is enjoying it manically. (sav-wo)
It's kind of dusty and touchy. (chiehou)
There seems to be the unique Oriental scent hanging in the air, with a dream of the world across the sea. (yan)

HOW DOES YOUR DAY START AND HOW DOES YOUR DAY END?
I turn on my Macintosh first and check my e-mails. I get started on my work, listen to music, then night comes in no time at all. After finishing my work, I climb into bed with a bottle of sake. ;) (sav-wo)
During breakfast, I check my e-mails, and start my work. Before sleeping, I spend plenty of time reading. It starts off digital, and ends up analog. (chiehou)
Morning comes right after I go to sleep, and morning comes again while finishing the rest of my work... how come? (yan)

IS THERE SOMETHING THAT YOU REALLY LOVE AND THAT YOU REALLY HATE ABOUT JAPAN?
Love: adopting the cultures and the customs of various countries well. Hate: losing traditional Japanese culture. (sav-wo)
Love: traditional architecture, art, and technology. Hate: the fashion of copying others. (chiehou)
Love: delicacy. Hate: everything is moving too fast. (yan)

WHAT DO YOU THINK ARE THE DIFFERENCES BETWEEN AMERICAN, EUROPEAN AND JAPANESE PEOPLE?
Here is a cool dude and there is a nasty dude regardless of country. (sav-wo)
It's all the same everywhere. (chiehou)
Although it depends on the environment we grow up in, we are basically the same human beings. (yan)

WHAT DO YOU THINK IS THE DIFFERENCE BETWEEN JAPANESE, AMERICAN AND EUROPEAN DESIGN?
Cultural background. (sav-wo)
Operation of left-brain and right-brain. (chiehou)
Environment, style, tradition and light. (yan)

WHAT WOULD YOU DO, IF GRAPHIC DESIGN DID NOT EXIST?
Bicycle messenger. (sav-wo)
Bakery. (chiehou)
Cafe. (yan)

CAN YOU TELL US YOUR 3 MOST IMPORTANT THINGS/OBJECTS/ACTIVITIES?
Being always positive. Brain. Graphic design. (sav-wo)
To enjoy everything. Eyes. Drawing. (chiehou)
Positive thinking. Friends and family. To have fun. (yan)

WHAT IS BEAUTIFUL AND WHAT IS UGLY?
Beautiful: women. Ugly: arguments. (sav-wo)
Beautiful: curving line. Ugly: parasitism. (chiehou)
Beautiful: winter sea. Ugly: catfight. (yan)

TO WHICH QUESTION YOU WOULD NEVER GIVE AN ANSWER?
Boring shit. (sav-wo)
I don't know. (chiehou)
.... (yan)

IS THERE ANYTHING YOU WOULD LIKE TO TELL THE READERS OF THIS BOOK?
Enjoy the rest of your life! (sav-wo)
Have a nice day. (chiehou)
c u somewhere! fufu. ;D (yan)

(interview with sav-wo/chiehou/yan)

Q1: 今日の日本はどんな匂いがしますか？
A1: 様々な文化やスタイルが入り交じって存在し、それを皆、マニアックに楽しんでいる。(サヴヲ)
埃っぽくて怒りっぽい。(チイホウ)
海の向こうの世界に憧れつつ、和の独特の香りが漂う感じ。(ヤン)

Q2: あなたの1日はどの様に始まり、どの様に終わりますか？
A2: まずマックの電源を入れてメールのチェック。音楽を聴きながら仕事を始めると、あっという間に夜中。仕事が片づいたら酒を持ってベットに潜り込む。;) (サヴヲ)
朝ご飯を食べながらメールチェック、そのまま仕事。眠る前にはたっぷり読書。デジタルに始まりアナログに終わる。(チイホウ)
さっき寝たと思ったら朝が来て、さっきの仕事の続きをしていたらいつの間にか朝が…あれ？(ヤン)

Q3: 日本の好きな部分、嫌いな部分を挙げて下さい。
A3: 好き―様々な国の文化や習慣を上手く取り入れてる部分。嫌い―日本特有の伝統文化が消えて行く部分。(サヴヲ)
好き―伝統的な建築、芸術、技術。嫌い―"右に倣え"的な流行。(チイホウ)
好き―繊細さ。嫌い―何もかもが回転が速すぎる。(ヤン)

Q4: アメリカ人、ヨーロッパ人、日本人の違いは何だと思いますか？
A4: どこの国も良いヤツもいれば嫌なヤツもいる。(サヴヲ)
どこでも同じ。(チイホウ)
育った環境で違うとは思うが、基本的には同じ人間かな。(ヤン)

Q5: 日本のデザイン、アメリカのデザイン、ヨーロッパのデザインの違いは何だと思いますか？
A5: 文化的背景。(サヴヲ)
左脳と右脳の働き方。(チイホウ)
環境、様式、伝統、光。(ヤン)

Q6: グラフィックデザインが存在していなかったら、あなたは何をしていますか？
A6: バイクメッセンジャー。(サヴヲ)
パン屋。(チイホウ)
カフェ。(ヤン)

Q7: あなた大事なことを3つ教えて下さい。
A7: 常にポジティブ。脳味噌。グラフィック。(サヴヲ)
全てを楽しむこと。目。描くこと。(チイホウ)
ポジティブ・シンキング。友達と家族。遊ぶこと。(ヤン)

Q8: 何が美しくて、何が醜いと思いますか？
A8: 美しい―女。醜い―言い争い。(サヴヲ)
美しい―曲線。醜い―寄生。(チイホウ)
美しい―冬の海。醜い―睨み合い。(ヤン)

Q9: あなたが絶対に答えない質問は何でしょう？
A9: 退屈なヤツ。(サヴヲ)
分からない。(チイホウ)
…。(ヤン)

Q10: 読者に何か伝えたいことがあれば書いて下さい。
A10: 残りの人生を楽しんでくれ！(サヴヲ)
ハヴァナイスデー。(チイホウ)
c u somewhere! fufu. ;D (ヤン)

(インタビュー：サヴヲ/チイホウ/ヤン)

NAME OF DESIGN COMPANY: CYCLONE GRAPHIX
NAMES/YEAR OF BIRTH: JUNICHI «SAV-WO» KITAJIMA ('72)/CHIHO «CHIEHOU» OHTANI ('73)/ YUKIKO «YAN» YANO ('72)
COMPANY SINCE: 1995
ADDRESS: 2-12-31 SUIYOU 2F, HOUNAN, SUGINAMI-KU, TOKYO 168-0062, JAPAN
WEBSITE: HTTP://WWW.CYCLONEGRAPHIX.JP.ORG/
EMAIL ADDRESS: CYCLONEGRAPHIX@JP.ORG
FAX: +81 (0)3-5932-3196

デザイン会社名：サイクログラフィックス
メンバー名(生年)：北島"サヴヲ"潤一(72年)/大谷"チイホウ"知帆(73年)/矢野"ヤン"幸子(72年)
会社設立日：1995年
住所：〒168-0062 東京都杉並区方南2-12-31 翠雄2F
ウェブサイト：http://www.cyclonegraphix.jp.org/
Eメールアドレス：cyclonegraphix@jp.org
ファックス番号：+81 (0)3-5932-3196

KYCLONE GRAPHIX

サイクログラフィックス

WORKSPACES ↓ LOGOTYPE ↑

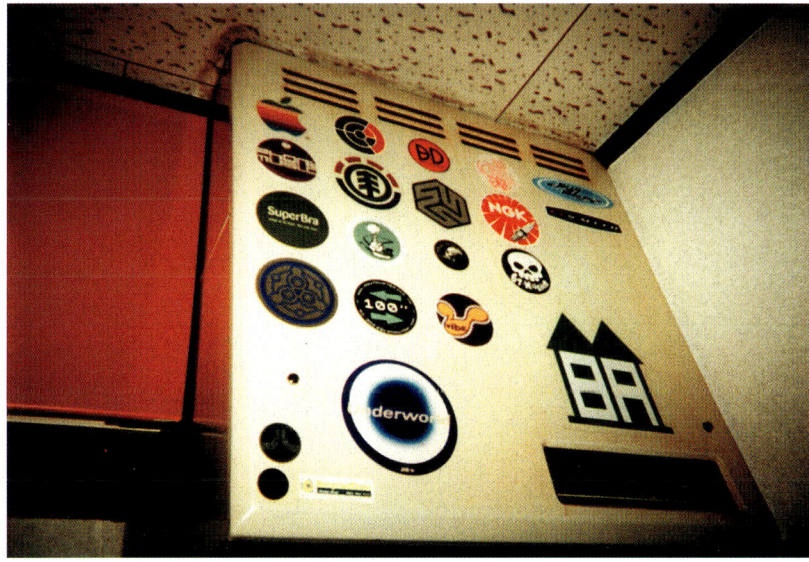

Bashion

TITLE OF WORK: G-FONT BASHION
DESIGNER: SAVWO
DESIGN COMPANY: CYCLONE GRAPHIX
YEAR: 2001
CLIENT: WWW.BASHION.COM

TITLE OF WORK: FATTY
DESIGNER: YAN
DESIGN COMPANY: CYCLONE GRAPHIX
YEAR: 2001

TITLE OF WORK: CHIEHOU BONJI
DESIGNER: CHIEHOU
DESIGN COMPANY: CYCLONE GRAPHIX
YEAR: 1998

fatty

GHS WEB GRAPHICA

Hiding persistently in Osaka Minami-Senba. Besides graphic design, ghs web graphica also works in clothing design, under the name gwg entertainments inc. ghs intentionally creates things bossy and silly, it's sometimes «heavy» sometimes «light», not only in editorial design, but also in printing process. Hoping to spread gradually with a nasty impression.

大阪南船場にていつまでも潜伏中。ウェア製作の場合はghs web graphicaでなく、gwg entertainments inc.名義でやっている。製作全般において、横暴とアホを心掛けている。「こってり」だったり「あっさり」だったり。レイアウトだけでなく印刷手法にも横暴とアホを出していきたい。ジワジワと嫌な感じで広まっていけたら良いと思っている。

BIOGRAPHY
10 QUESTIONS/ANSWERS

HOW DOES JAPAN SMELL TODAY?
Since it's rainy season here, the drains stink so bad.

HOW DOES YOUR DAY START AND HOW DOES YOUR DAY END?
I go to work on my Honda Motra (a clapped-out 50cc mini-bike), stalling the engine as usual. Once I get to the office, I check my e-mails while tanking up on Japanese sake, and I work until midnight. I go back home on my Honda Motra (clapped-out 50cc minibike), stalling the engine as usual. I water my bonsai while tanking up on Japanese sake. Then I go to bed.

IS THERE SOMETHING THAT YOU REALLY LOVE AND THAT YOU REALLY HATE ABOUT JAPAN?
Love: Japanese is spoken everywhere in Japan. When I'm out of Japan, I only use body language in a flurry.
Hate: Since Japanese is spoken everywhere in Japan, I get into a fight easily. When I'm out of Japan, no one cares that I'm bitching in Japanese.

WHAT DO YOU THINK ARE THE DIFFERENCES BETWEEN AMERICAN, EUROPEAN AND JAPANESE PEOPLE?
Height, noses, language, and body odor.

WHAT DO YOU THINK IS THE DIFFERENCE BETWEEN JAPANESE, AMERICAN AND EUROPEAN DESIGN?
I'm not sure because I've only been to Asian countries. I want to visit Europe someday.

WHAT WOULD YOU DO, IF GRAPHIC DESIGN DID NOT EXIST?
Since I love kids, I would be a children's nurse.

CAN YOU TELL US YOUR 3 MOST IMPORTANT THINGS/OBJECTS/ACTIVITIES?
Sleep. Bath. Walk through a park.

WHAT IS BEAUTIFUL AND WHAT IS UGLY?
People's hearts and eyes.

TO WHICH QUESTION YOU WOULD NEVER GIVE AN ANSWER?
Anything about my dick.

IS THERE ANYTHING YOU WOULD LIKE TO TELL THE READERS OF THIS BOOK?
We are from Osaka, not Tokyo.

(interview with Akihiro Ikegoshi)

Q1: 今日の日本はどんな匂いがしますか？
A1: 梅雨時なので、ドブの臭いでいっぱいです。

Q2: あなたの1日はどの様に始まり、どの様に終わりますか？
A2: ホンダのモトラ(50ccバイクおんぼろ)で出勤、必ずエンスト。事務所に着いたら日本酒を食らいながらメールチェック。夜中まで作業する。ホンダのモトラ(50ccバイクおんぼろ)で帰宅、必ずエンスト。日本酒を食らいながら盆栽に水やり。就寝。

Q3: 日本の好きな部分、嫌いな部分を挙げて下さい。
A3: 好き―何処に行っても言葉が通じる。海外ではアタフタしてボディーランゲージのみ。
嫌い―何処に行っても言葉が通じるのでスグ喧嘩になる。海外ではどんだけ文句言っても通じないのでお気楽。

Q4: アメリカ人、ヨーロッパ人、日本人の違いは何だと思いますか？
A4: 身長、鼻、言語、体臭。

Q5: 日本のデザイン、アメリカのデザイン、ヨーロッパのデザインの違いは何だと思いますか？
A5: アジア圏しか知らないので、よくワカリマセン。ヨーロッパにも行ってみたいです。

Q6: グラフィックデザインが存在していなかったら、あなたは何をしていますか？
A6: 子供が好きなので、保父さん。

Q7: あなた大事なことを3つ教えて下さい。
A7: 睡眠。風呂。公園を散歩。

Q8: 何が美しくて、何が醜いと思いますか？
A8: 人の心と目。

Q9: あなたが絶対に答えない質問は何でしょう？
A9: ボクのチンポ話。

Q10: 読者に何か伝えたいことがあれば書いて下さい。
A10: ボクらは東京ではなくて大阪です。

(インタビュー: 池越顕尋)

PROFILE
BUSINESS CARD
SELFPORTRAIT

NAME OF DESIGN COMPANY: GHS WEB GRAPHICA
NAMES/YEAR OF BIRTH: AKIHIRO IKEGOSHI (73)/ YUZURU UCHIDA (74)/ARISA MOMONOI (75)
COMPANY SINCE: 1997
ADDRESS: 3-6-24 MINAMIDAIWA-BLDG. 701, MINAMISENBA, CHUO-KU, OSAKA 542-0081, JAPAN
WEBSITE: HTTP://WWW.GHS.NET/
EMAIL ADDRESS: INFO@GHS.NET
FAX: +81 (0)6-6258-4311

デザイン会社名：ガス ウェブ グラフィカ
メンバー名(生年)：池越顕尋(73年)/内田譲(74年)/桃井ありさ(75年)
会社設立日：1997年
住所：〒542-0081 大阪市中央区南船場3-6-24南大和ビル701
ウェブサイト：http://www.ghs.net/
Eメールアドレス：info@ghs.net
ファックス番号：+81 (0)6-6258-4311

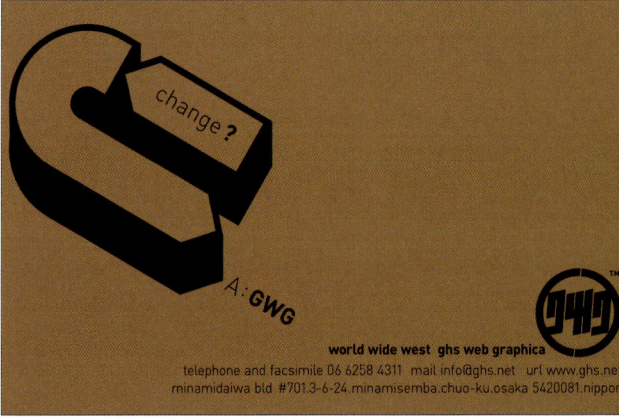

GHS WEB GRAPHICA   ガス ウェブ グラフィカ

WORKSPACES ↓   LOGOTYPE ↑

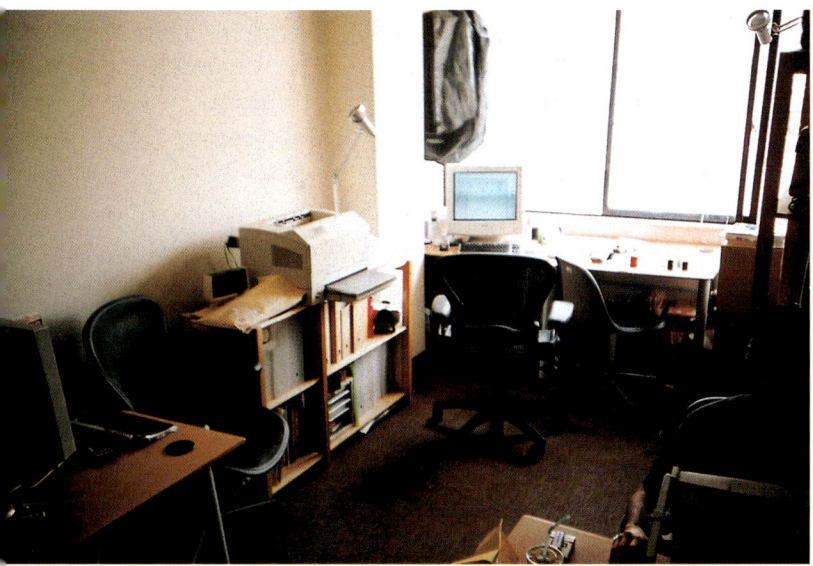

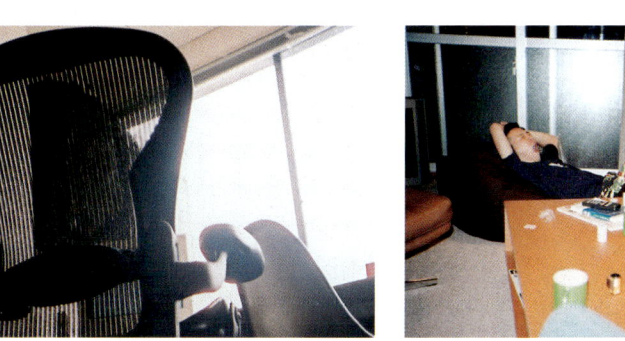

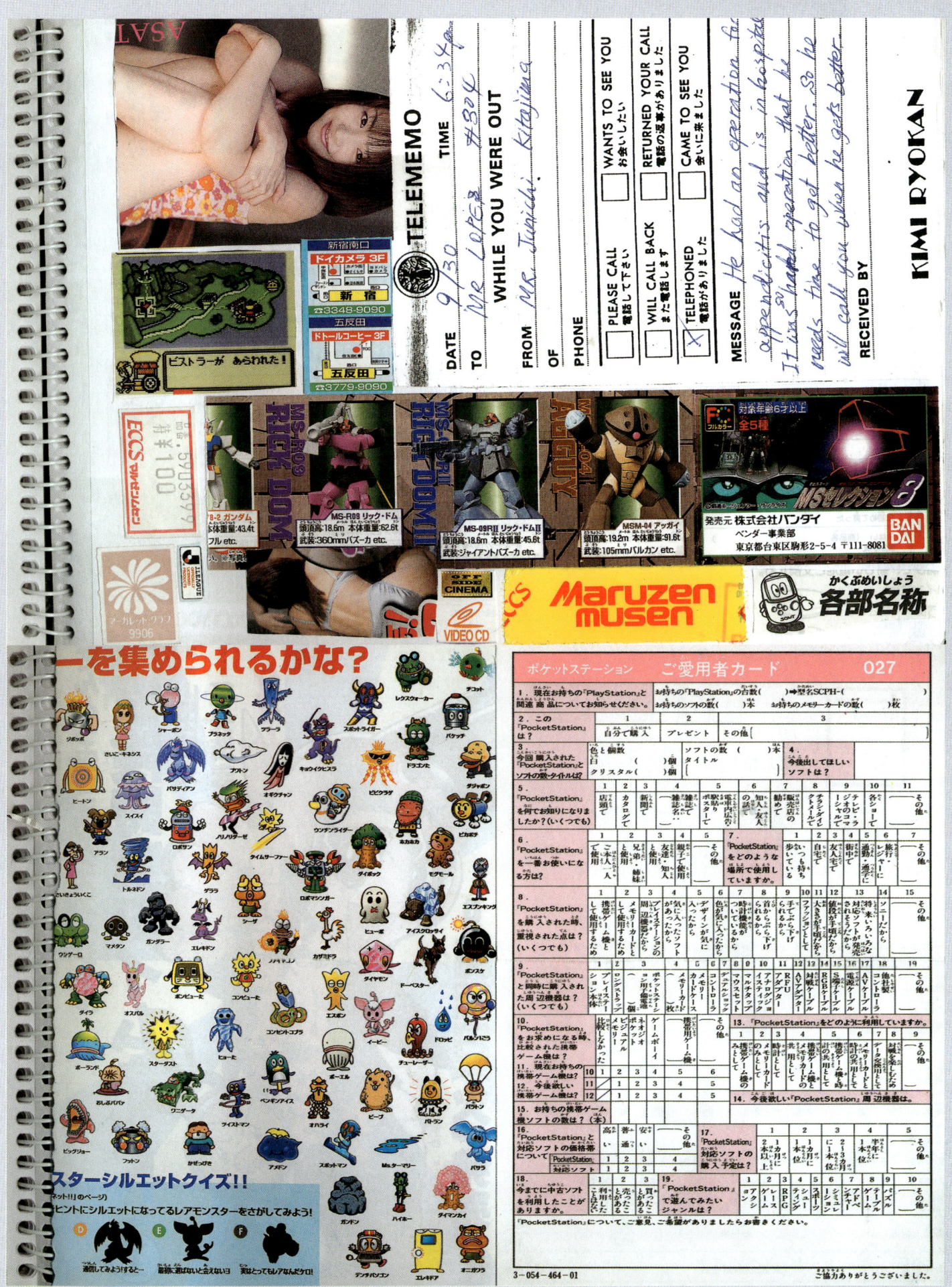

TSUYOSHI HIROOKA (LEVEL1)

Born in Tokyo, 1973. Started as a freelance designer in 1997. Work as LEVEL1 started in May 2000, mainly in two dimensional graphic design on printed matter such as logo designs, T-shirts designs, editorials, motion graphics, VJ etc. Hirooka has recently become interested in building a plastic model.

1973年東京生まれ。1997年よりフリーデザイナーとして活動。2000年5月よりLEVEL1として活動開始。紙媒体の2Dグラフィックデザインを中心に、ロゴマークデザイン、Tシャツデザイン、エディトリアルデザイン、映像製作、VJなどを手掛ける。最近はプラモ作りに興味がある。

NAME OF DESIGN COMPANY: LEVEL1
NAME/YEAR OF BIRTH: TSUYOSHI HIROOKA (73)
COMPANY SINCE: 2000
ADDRESS: 2-17-10-401 SANGENJAYA, SETAGAYA-KU, TOKYO 154-0024, JAPAN
WEBSITE: HTTP://HELLO.TO/LEVEL1/
EMAIL ADDRESS: HIRO-KA@WA2.SO-NET.JP
FAX: +81 (0)3-5433-9849

デザイン会社名：レベル1
メンバー名（生年）：広岡毅（73年）
会社設立日：2000年
住所：〒154-0024 東京都世田谷区三軒茶屋2-17-10-401
ウェブサイト：http://hello.to/level1/
Eメールアドレス：hiro-ka@wa2.so-net.jp
ファックス番号：+81 (0)3-5433-9849

BIOGRAPHY
10 QUESTIONS/ANSWERS

HOW DOES JAPAN SMELL TODAY?
A nice smell.

HOW DOES YOUR DAY START AND HOW DOES YOUR DAY END?
I wake up and start thinking about my work. I go to sleep while thinking about my work.

IS THERE SOMETHING THAT YOU REALLY LOVE AND THAT YOU REALLY HATE ABOUT JAPAN?
Love: how hardworking we are. Hate: how we often think that we have to be hardworking.

WHAT DO YOU THINK ARE THE DIFFERENCES BETWEEN AMERICAN, EUROPEAN AND JAPANESE PEOPLE?
I don't know since I don't really have any relationships with foreign people, but I would like to get to know about them in the future.

WHAT DO YOU THINK IS THE DIFFERENCE BETWEEN JAPANESE, AMERICAN AND EUROPEAN DESIGN?
American is interesting. European is beautiful. Japanese is probably the middle. Although it's not necessarily appropriate to say that since there are great differences between individuals.

WHAT WOULD YOU DO, IF GRAPHIC DESIGN DID NOT EXIST?
Probably a sushi bar.

CAN YOU TELL US YOUR 3 MOST IMPORTANT THINGS/OBJECTS/ACTIVITIES?
Work. Family. The wallet that I've been using since 10th grade.

WHAT IS BEAUTIFUL AND WHAT IS UGLY?
Beautiful: To at least do something. Ugly: To do nothing.

TO WHICH QUESTION YOU WOULD NEVER GIVE AN ANSWER?
This question.

IS THERE ANYTHING YOU WOULD LIKE TO TELL THE READERS OF THIS BOOK?
I hope you will enjoy it. I'll enjoy it too.

(interview with Tsuyoshi Hirooka)

Q1: 今日の日本はどんな匂いがしますか？
A1: イイ匂い。

Q2: あなたの1日はどの様に始まり、どの様に終わりますか？
A2: 起きて仕事の事を考え始める。仕事の事を考えながら眠る。

Q3: 日本の好きな部分、嫌いな部分を挙げて下さい。
A3: 好き―勤勉なところ。
嫌い―勤勉じゃないとダメだと思ってしまうところ。

Q4: アメリカ人、ヨーロッパ人、日本人の違いは何だと思いますか？
A4: 外国の方との交流があまりないのでわかりませんが、これから知っていきたいです。

Q5: 日本のデザイン、アメリカのデザイン、ヨーロッパのデザインの違いは何だと思いますか？
A5: アメリカは面白い。ヨーロッパは美しい。日本は中間ぐらいかと思います。個人差が激しいので一概には言えませんが。

Q6: グラフィックデザインが存在していなかったら、あなたは何をしていますか？
A6: 多分、寿司屋。

Q7: あなた大事なことを3つ教えて下さい。
A7: 仕事。家族。高1の頃から使っている財布。

Q8: 何が美しくて、何が醜いと思いますか？
A8: 美しい―とりあえず実行すること。醜い―何もしないこと。

Q9: あなたが絶対に答えない質問は何でしょう？
A9: この質問。

Q10: 読者に何か伝えたいことがあれば書いて下さい。
A10: 楽しんでください。僕も楽しみます。

（インタビュー：広岡毅）

PROFILE
BUSINESS CARD →
SELFPORTRAIT ↓

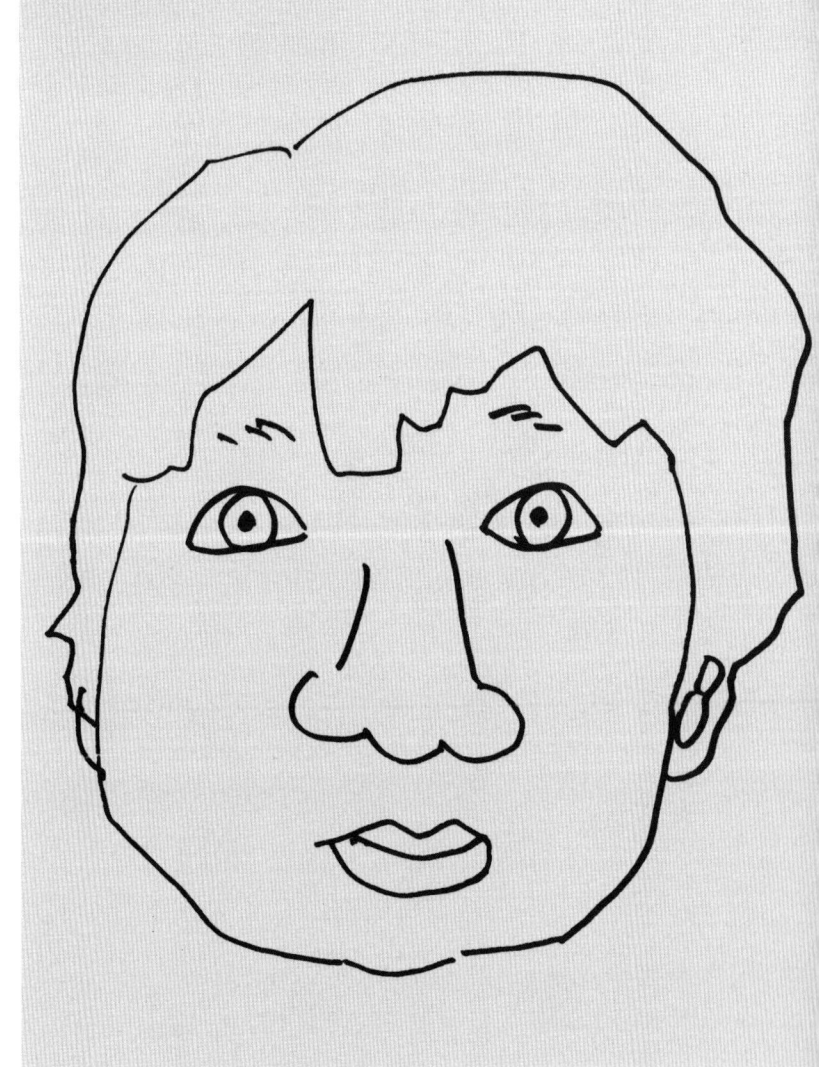

SUYOSHI HIROOKA (LEVEL1)　　　　　　　　　レベル1

LEVEL 1

WORKSPACES ↓　　　　　　　　　　　　　　　　　LOGOTYPE ↑

TITLE OF WORK: CASSETTE VISION [SHISHA NO SHO]
DESIGNER: TSUYOSHI HIROOKA
DESIGN COMPANY: LEVEL1
YEAR: 2000
CLIENT: INFAS

TITLE OF WORK: CASSETTE VISION [ES/JIGA/CHO-JIGA]
DESIGNER: TSUYOSHI HIROOKA
DESIGN COMPANY: LEVEL1
YEAR: 2001
CLIENT: INFAS

TITLE OF WORK: OF COURSE YOU CAN KILL EVERYONE!
IT'S ONLY A VIDEO GAME!
DESIGNER: TSUYOSHI HIROOKA
DESIGN COMPANY: LEVEL1
YEAR: 2000
CLIENT: ASCII

Of course you can kill everyone!
It's only a video game!

p-wing

monthly Famitsu-WAVE
video game magazine plus cd-rom = visula entertainment!

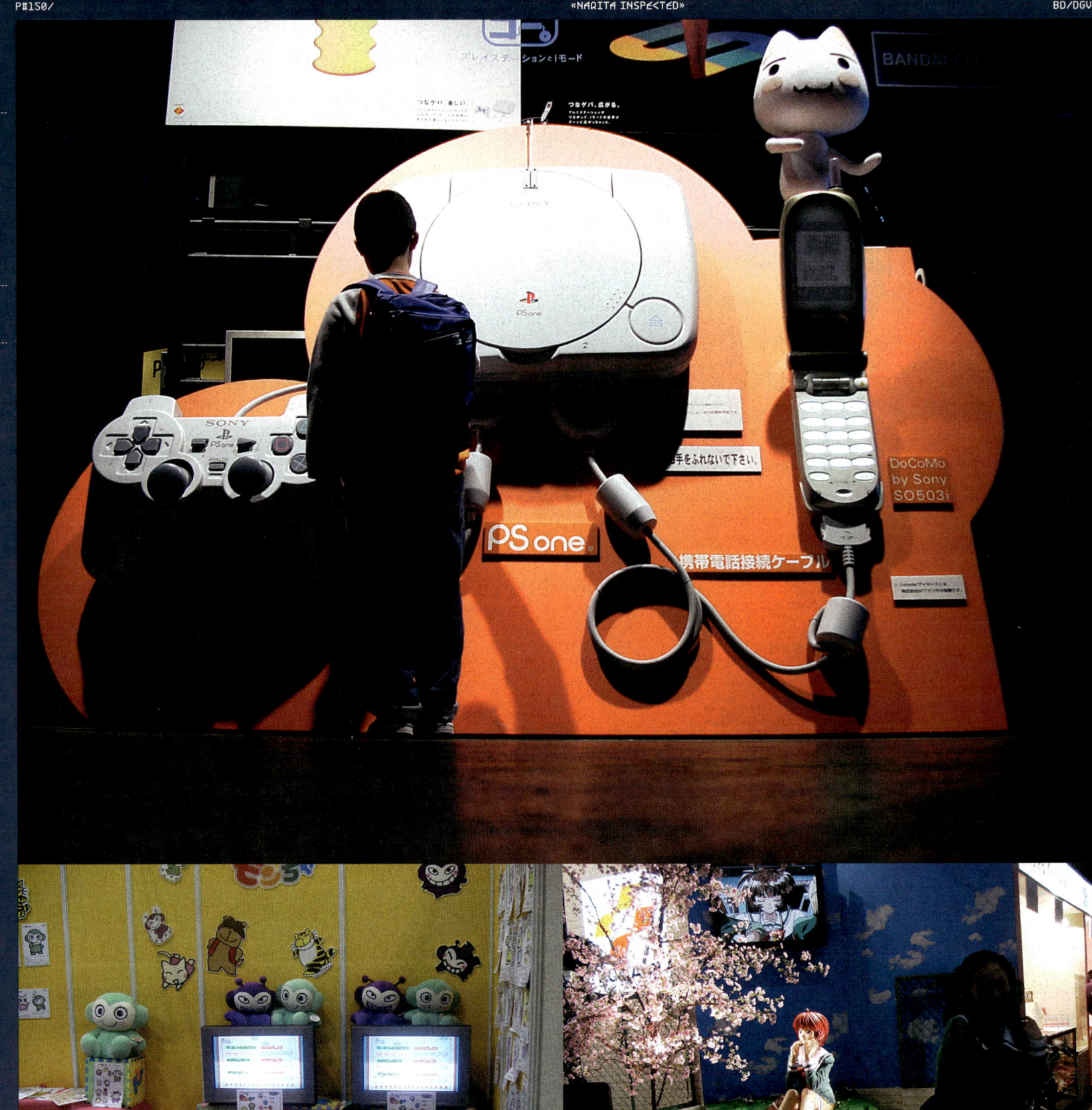

ENLIGHTENMENT

1997 Enlightenment was established by Hiro Sugiyama.
1998 Launched free paper «TRACK».
2000 Jan-Exhibition at Collette in Paris. Launched new style of free paper «Display».
Oct-Exhibition at Shibuya Parco. Published the work collection «2-Delight».
2001 Scheduled to participate in the group exhibition in Korea, London and New York.

1997年 ヒロ杉山によりエンライトメント設立
1998年 フリーペーパー「TRACK」創刊
2000年 1月パリのColletteにて個展、新型フリーペーパー「Display」創刊
10月渋谷Parcoにて個展、作品集「2-Delight」発刊
2001年 韓国、ロンドン、ニューヨークでグループ展参加予定

BIOGRAPHY ↑
10 QUESTIONS/ANSWERS ↓

HOW DOES JAPAN SMELL TODAY?
There is a faint smell like diluted chemicals all over. However it is not a good smell. (Hiro). Unfortunately, there is no smell. (Yonezu). It smells like rainy season. (Shinozaki). All mixed up.

HOW DOES YOUR DAY START AND HOW DOES YOUR DAY END?
It's strange, my day starts with finding myself waking up and my day ends with finding myself getting sleepy. How about you? (Hiro). My day tries to start with taking a shower, and tries to end with drinking sake. (Yonezu). I go to buy bread on my bicycle in the morning, and I do some drawing at end of a day. (Shinozaki). Everyday is different. (Mishima).

IS THERE SOMETHING THAT YOU REALLY LOVE AND THAT YOU REALLY HATE ABOUT JAPAN?
Love: to be able to eat natto (fermented soybeans). Hate: too many men in suits on the trains. (Hiro). Lightness. (Yonezu). I love beautiful Japanese cultural assets. I hate erroneous Japanese common sense. (Mishima).

WHAT DO YOU THINK ARE THE DIFFERENCES BETWEEN AMERICAN, EUROPEAN AND JAPANESE PEOPLE?
First of all, American people are huge! European people are medium. Japanese people are small. (Hiro). The differences come from the historical backgrounds. (Yonezu). American: Aerosmith. European: Rolling Stones. Japanese: RC Succession. (Shinozaki). Cultural and environmental differences. (Mishima).

WHAT DO YOU THINK IS THE DIFFERENCE BETWEEN JAPANESE, AMERICAN AND EUROPEAN DESIGN?
Same as above. (Hiro). The aesthetic feelings which come from the historical backgrounds. (Yonezu). I don't know. (Shinozaki). Again, it's the cultural and environmental differences. (Mishima).

WHAT WOULD YOU DO, IF GRAPHIC DESIGN DID NOT EXIST?
Something extremely similar. (Hiro). Something to do with sense and aesthetic feeling. (Yonezu). I may be unknowingly creating graphic design. (Shinozaki). A delicatessen. (Mishima).

CAN YOU TELL US YOUR 3 MOST IMPORTANT THINGS/OBJECTS/ACTIVITIES?
Love. Body. To live. (Hiro). Love. Strength. Smile. (Yonezu). To think. To feel. To try. (Shinozaki). Love. Health. Entertainment. (Mishima).

WHAT IS BEAUTIFUL AND WHAT IS UGLY?
I don't know. (Hiro). A beautiful thing is beautiful and an ugly thing is ugly, but it sometimes the other way around. (Yonezu). What I consider to be beautiful is something not pure. What I consider to be ugly is something impure. (Shinozaki). Something that I want to see over and over again is beautiful, something that I don't want to see anymore is ugly. (Mishima.)

TO WHICH QUESTION YOU WOULD NEVER GIVE AN ANSWER?
A question like this one. (Hiro). Any question that I don't want to answer. (Yonezu). Such a difficult question. (Mishima).

IS THERE ANYTHING YOU WOULD LIKE TO TELL THE READERS OF THIS BOOK?
Natto (fermented soybeans) is delicious! (Hiro). I've already said it with my work. (Yonezu). Let's have some fun. (Mishima).

(interview with Hiro, Sugiyama, Yonezu, Shinozaki, Mishima)

Q1: 今日の日本はどんな匂いがしますか?
A1: どこもかしこも薄い臭いがしますね。薬物を薄めたような。
あまり良い臭いとは言えません。(ヒロ)
悲しいことに匂いがありません。(米津)
梅雨っぽい匂いです。(篠崎)
ごちゃごちゃ。(三嶋)

Q2: あなたの1日はどの様に始まり、どの様に終わりますか?
A2: 不思議なのですが自然と目が覚めて始まり、不思議と眠くなって終わります。あなたは? (ヒロ)
シャワーを浴びて始めようとし、酒を飲んで終わろうとする。(米津)
朝は自転車でパンを買いに行き、夜は絵を描いたりして終わっていきます。(篠崎)
毎日違います。(三嶋)

Q3: 日本の好きな部分、嫌いな部分を挙げて下さい。
A3: 好き—納豆が食べられること。
嫌い—電車の中にスーツ姿が多いこと。(ヒロ)
軽さ。(米津)
日本の美しい文化財は大好きです。
間違った日本の常識は嫌いです。(三嶋)

Q4: アメリカ人、ヨーロッパ人、日本人の違いは何だと思いますか?
A4: まずアメリカ人はでかい! そしてヨーロッパ人は中くらい。
日本人は小さい。(ヒロ)
歴史的背景から生まれた違い。(米津)
アメリカ—エアロスミス、ヨーロッパ—ローリングストーンズ
日本—RCサクセション。(篠崎)
文化と環境の違い。(三嶋)

Q5: 日本のデザイン、アメリカのデザイン、ヨーロッパのデザインの違いは何だと思いますか?
A5: 上に同じ。(ヒロ)
歴史的背景から生まれた美意識の違い。(米津)
分かりません。(篠崎)
やはり文化と環境だと思います。(三嶋)

Q6: グラフィックデザインが存在していなかったら、あなたは何をしていますか?
A6: それに近いものや限り無く似たもの。(ヒロ)
感覚や美意識に携わるもの。(米津)
知らないうちにグラフィックデザインを作り出しているかもしれません。(篠崎)
珍味屋。(三嶋)

Q7: あなた大事なことを3つ教えて下さい。
A7: 愛。体。生きる事。(ヒロ)
愛。強さ。笑い。(米津)
考える事。感じる事。やってみる事。(篠崎)
愛。健康。娯楽。(三嶋)

Q8: 何が美しくて、何が醜いと思いますか?
A8: 分かりません。(ヒロ)
美しいものは美しく醜いものは醜いが、時に裏返ることもある。(米津)
美しいと思うものは濁ってないもの。
醜いと思うものは濁っているもの。(篠崎)
何度も見たいと思うものは美しいし、二度と見たくないものは醜い。(三嶋)

Q9: あなたが絶対に答えない質問は何でしょう?
A9: Answer9みたいな質問。(ヒロ)
答えたくない質問。(米津)
こんな難しい質問。(三嶋)

Q10: 読者に何か伝えたいことがあれば書いて下さい。
A10: 納豆はおいしい! (ヒロ)
作品で伝えています。(米津)
楽しく行こう。(三嶋)

(インタビュー: ヒロ杉山/米津/篠崎/三嶋)

PROFILE ↑
BUSINESS CARD →
SELFPORTRAIT ↓

NAME OF DESIGN COMPANY: ENLIGHTENMENT
NAMES/YEAR OF BIRTH: HIRO SUGIYAMA (62)/ TOMOYUKI YONEZU (74)/YORIKO SUGIYAMA (69)/ KOSUKE SHINOZAKI (75)/AKIYOSHI MISHIMA (78)
COMPANY SINCE: 1997
ADDRESS: KAMINOGE HAIM 2-1105, 3-16 KAMINOGE, SETAGAYA-KU, TOKYO 158-0093, JAPAN
WEBSITE: -
EMAIL ADDRESS: ELM@KT.RIM.OR.JP
FAX: +81 (0)3-3705-5471

デザイン会社名:エンライトメント
メンバー名(生年):ヒロ杉山(62年)/米津智之(74年)/杉山ヨリコ(69年)/篠崎康祐(75年)/三嶋章義(78年)
会社設立日:1997年
住所:〒158-0093 東京都世田谷区上野毛3-16 上野毛ハイム2-1105
ウェブサイト:—
Eメールアドレス:elm@kt.rim.or.jp
ファックス番号:+81 (0)3-3705-5471

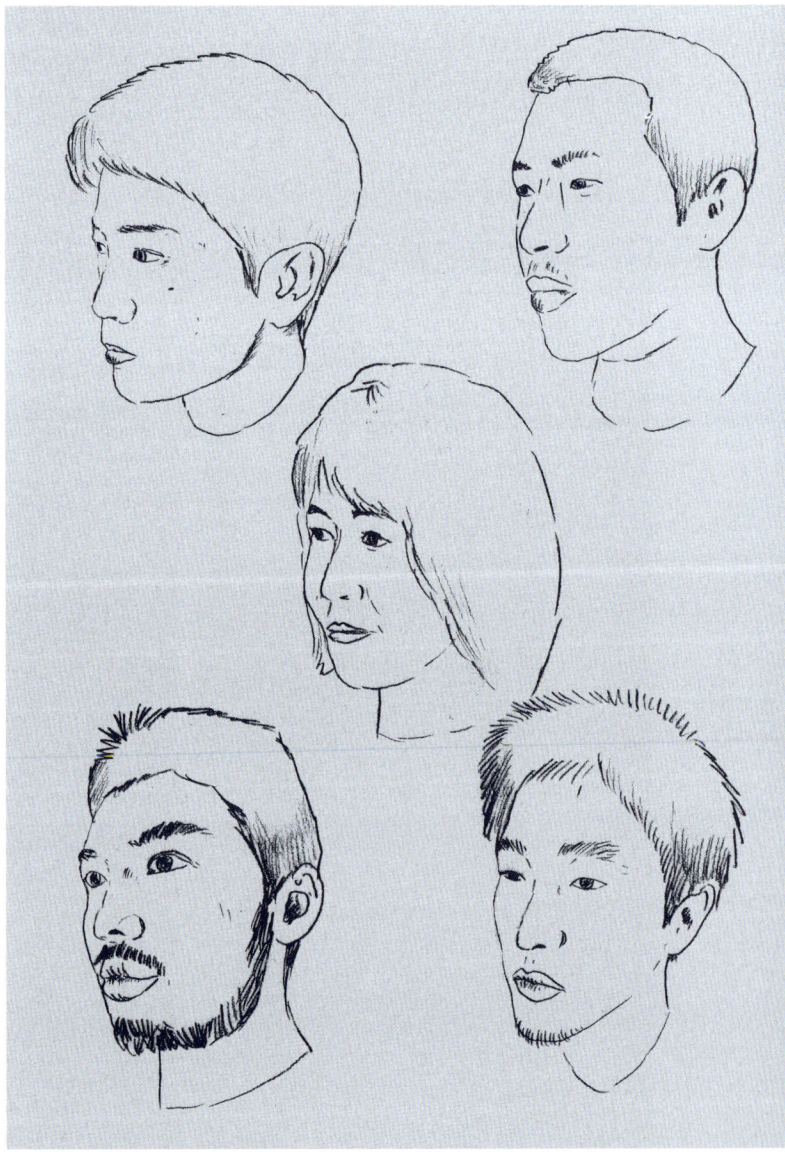

ENLIGHTENMENT

エンライトメント

WORKSPACES ↓   LOGOTYPE ↑

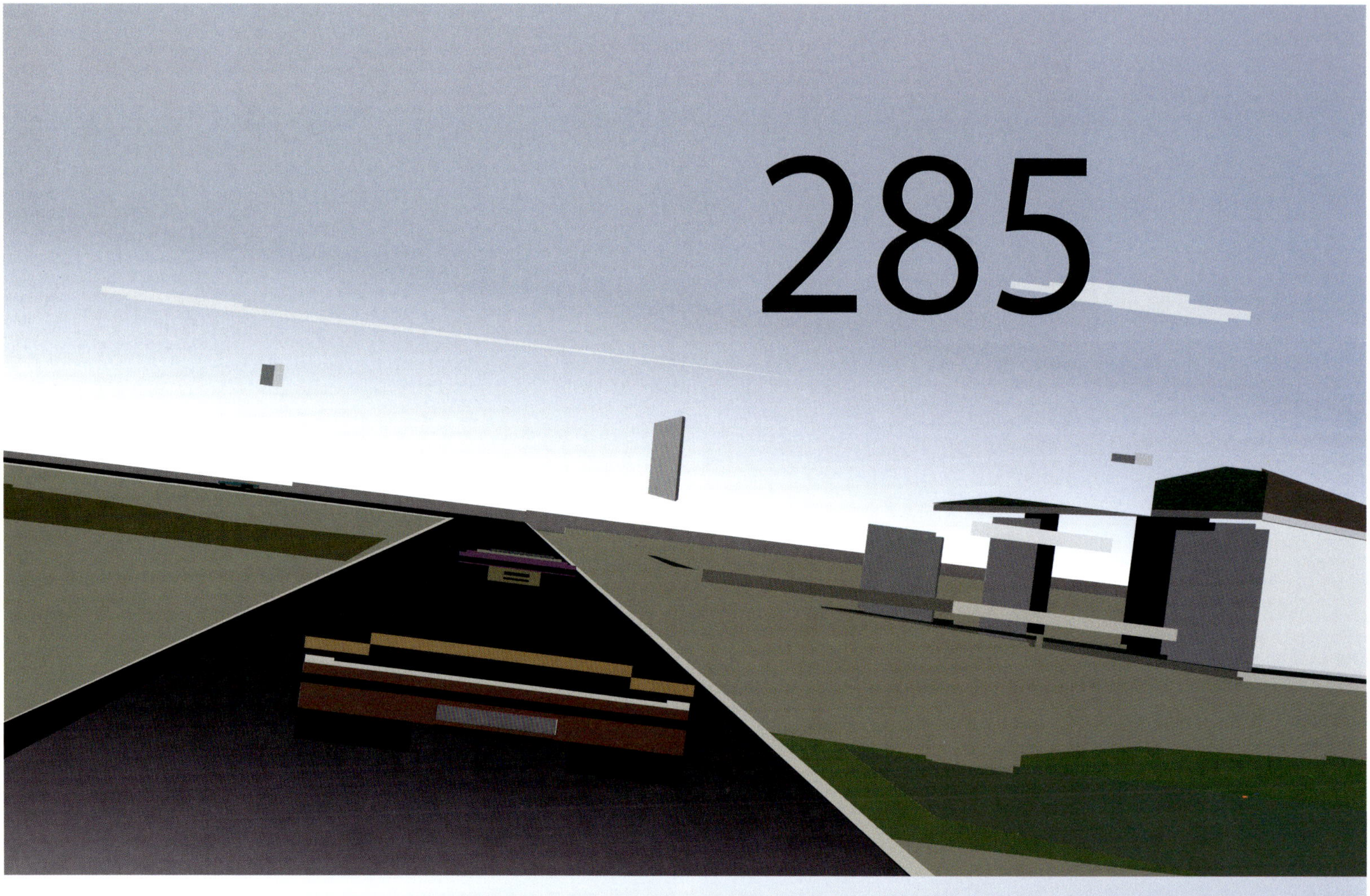

285

319

TITLE OF WORK: KYLIE
DESIGN COMPANY: ENLIGHTENMENT
YEAR: 2001
CLIENT: TAKEO KIKUCHI

TITLE OF WORK: MARSHALL
DESIGN COMPANY: ENLIGHTENMENT
YEAR: 2001
CLIENT: TAKEO KIKUCHI

TITLE OF WORK: THE RACE 2
DESIGN COMPANY: ENLIGHTENMENT
YEAR: 2000
CLIENT: BIG MAGAZINE

TITLE OF WORK: THE RACE 3
DESIGN COMPANY: ENLIGHTENMENT
YEAR: 2000
CLIENT: BIG MAGAZINE

PAT DETECTIVE

パット ディテクティブ

Established in 1996, t unit consists of 2 people, Taku Yokosuka and Nao Tsuchiya. Started working mainly in the area of package design and ads for music, movies etc. through the publication of free papers and zines. They've been based in Kyoto since school and have pursued different attractions from Tokyo along with participating in various areas such as movie production, event planning etc. They want to expand the view of the theme of local dispatch, and create artwork from the world view created by getting involved with people. And they hope to share many things with people around the world through «design/creation.».

1996年設立。横須賀拓、土屋なほの2人ユニット。フリーペーパーやミニコミの制作発行を通じて、音楽、映画等のパッケージや宣伝を中心に活動。他にも映像制作やイベント企画等様々な分野に参加しつつも、学生の時からの土台である京都を活動の場に選び、東京発信とはまた違った魅力を追求。これまで行ってきた地方から発信というテーマを今後は視野をさらに広げ、人々との関わりあいの中から生まれる世界観から作品を作っていきたい。そして世界中の人々とより多くのものを「デザイン=物作り」を通じて共有していけるようになれたらと思う。

NAME OF DESIGN COMPANY: PAT DETECTIVE
NAMES/YEAR OF BIRTH: TAKU YOKOSUKA (72)/ NAO TSUCHIYA (73)
COMPANY SINCE: 1996
ADDRESS: 180 FUDO-CHO, NISHI-IRU, SHINMACHI, TAKOYAKUSHI, NAKAGYO-KU, KYOTO 604-8215, JAPAN
WEBSITE: —
EMAIL ADDRESS: PATD@AIR.EMAIL.NE.JP
FAX: +81 (0)75-257-2667

デザイン会社名：パット ディテクティブ
メンバー名(生年)：横須賀拓(72年)/土屋なほ(73年)
会社設立日：1996年
住所：〒604-8215 京都市中京区蛸薬師新町西入ル不動町180
ウェブサイト：—
Eメールアドレス：patd@air.email.ne.jp
ファックス番号：+81 (0) 75-257-2667

BIOGRAPHY
10 QUESTIONS/ANSWERS

HOW DOES JAPAN SMELL TODAY?
Although it is not a smell from ancient times of Japan, it is a very comfortable smell for me today because it may be a smell of Kyoto. (Yokosuka).

HOW DOES YOUR DAY START AND HOW DOES YOUR DAY END?
I wake up in the morning and have a cup of coffee. I go to work by bike and buy a magazine at the bookshop. I chill out until the afternoon, reading magazines or taking care of paperwork. After having lunch, I work through until nightime. I meet with my friend on the way back home, or I go straight back home. I have a beer & dinner, and then sleep. (Yokosuka). My day starts with making coffee for my husband, and ends with making Japanese tea for me. (Tsuchiya).

IS THERE SOMETHING THAT YOU REALLY LOVE AND THAT YOU REALLY HATE ABOUT JAPAN?
Love: Japanese food is delicious like noodles, rice, sushi etc. I've found shrines, temples, and gardens that very attractive these days. The world of Zen. Useability equals beauty. Hate: breach of etiquette. (Yokosuka).
Love: having four seasons. Hate: none. (Tsuchiya).

WHAT DO YOU THINK ARE THE DIFFERENCES BETWEEN AMERICAN, EUROPEAN AND JAPANESE PEOPLE?
Language is the great difference. And gastronomic culture. (Yokosuka). The history of popular music. (Tsuchiya)

WHAT DO YOU THINK IS THE DIFFERENCE BETWEEN JAPANESE, AMERICAN AND EUROPEAN DESIGN?
I would say it's the difference in hue. (Yokosuka). In terms of tradition, there are great differences between them. However, there are no longer any differences these days. The character is the only absolute difference. (Tsuchiya).

WHAT WOULD YOU DO, IF GRAPHIC DESIGN DID NOT EXIST?
Besides making graphics, I also like to see or buy graphic design. I cannot imagine the world without it. I wonder if I will ever lose my materialistic desire. (Yokosuka). I would create graphic design itself. (Tsuchiya).

CAN YOU TELL US YOUR 3 MOST IMPORTANT THINGS/OBJECTS/ACTIVITIES?
To have music playing. To always find something you like. (Tsuchiya).

WHAT IS BEAUTIFUL AND WHAT IS UGLY?
Nature is beautiful, and that which destroys nature is ugly. (Yokosuka).
All the things that you like are beautiful. All the things that make you feel bad are ugly. (Tsuchiya).

TO WHICH QUESTION YOU WOULD NEVER GIVE AN ANSWER?
I can't even answer this question. (Yokosuka). I'd answer anything, I think. (Tsuchiya).

IS THERE ANYTHING YOU WOULD LIKE TO TELL THE READERS OF THIS BOOK?
We'd be happy If you became interested in us.

(interview with Yokosuka, Tsuchiya)

Q1: 今日の日本はどんな匂いがしますか？
A1: 日本古来からの匂いじゃないと思いますが、今の僕には心地良い匂いです。そしてそれは京都の匂いだからかもしれません。(横須賀)

Q2: あなたの1日はどの様に始まり、どの様に終わりますか？
A2: 朝起きてコーヒーを飲む。バイクで出勤。本屋で雑誌を購入。昼までのんびり雑誌を読んだり、事務処理をしたり。ランチを食べて夜まで仕事。帰りに人と会ったり、そのまま帰宅だったり。ビール&夜食。就寝。(横須賀)
夫のためにコーヒーを入れて始まり、自分のために日本茶を入れて終わる。(土屋)

Q3: 日本の好きな部分、嫌いな部分を挙げて下さい。
A3: 好き―和食が美味しい。蕎麦、丼、寿司など。神社仏閣、庭園などに魅力を感じる今日この頃。禅の世界。用即美。
嫌い―マナー違反。(横須賀)
好き―春夏秋冬がある。嫌い―ない。(土屋)

Q4: アメリカ人、ヨーロッパ人、日本人の違いは何だと思いますか？
A4: 言語の違いが大きい。それと食文化。(横須賀)
ポピュラーミュージックの歴史の長さ。(土屋)

Q5: 日本のデザイン、アメリカのデザイン、ヨーロッパのデザインの違いは何だと思いますか？
A5: 色相でしょうか。(横須賀)
伝統的な部分では違いが大きいけれど、今となってはもはや違いはないと思う。絶対的な違いは文字。(土屋)

Q6: グラフィックデザインが存在していなかったら、あなたは何をしていますか？
A6: 作る意外にも、見たり買ったりするのが好きだから、そんなつまらない世の中になったら恐ろしい。物欲は無くなるのでしょうか？(横須賀)
グラフィックデザインそのものをつくる。(土屋)

Q7: あなた大事なことを3つ教えて下さい。
A7: 音楽が流れていること。好きなことを常に探すこと。(土屋)

Q8: 何が美しくて、何が醜いと思いますか？
A8: 自然は美しく、それを壊すものは醜い。(横須賀)
好きだと思える物事全部が美しいもの。嫌な気持ちになるものが醜いもの。(土屋)

Q9: あなたが絶対に答えない質問は何でしょう？
A9: それも答えられません。(横須賀)
ない。たぶん。(土屋)

Q10: 読者に何か伝えたいことがあれば書いて下さい。
A10: 興味を持ってもらえたら嬉しい。

(インタビュー：横須賀/土屋)

PAT detective
180 Fudo-cho Nishi-iru Shinmachi Takoyakushi Nakagyo-ku Kyoto 604-8215
TEL : 075-257-2666 FAX : 075-257-2667 E-MAIL : pat005@ky.xaxon.ne.jp

横須賀 拓
Taku Yokosuka
〒604-8215 京都市中京区蛸薬師新町西入ル不動町180
telephone 075.257.2666 facsimile 075.257.2667
e-mail pat005@ky.xaxon.ne.jp

PAT DETECTIVE

パット ディテクティブ

WORKSPACES ↓ | LOGOTYPE ↑

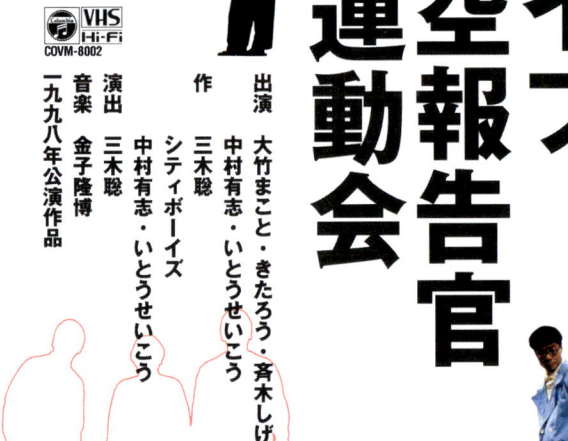

↑
TITLE OF WORK: CITYBOYS LIVE
ULTRASHIOSHIOHYMINAL
VIDEO-PACKAGE
DESIGNER: TAKU YOKOSUKA
DESIGN COMPANY: PAT DETECTIVE
YEAR: 2000
CLIENT: NIPPON COLOMBIA

↑
TITLE OF WORK: CITYBOYS LIVE
MINISTRY OF VACUUM REPORTER (P)
VIDEO-PACKAGE
DESIGNER: TAKU YOKOSUKA
DESIGN COMPANY: PAT DETECTIVE
YEAR: 2000
CLIENT: NIPPON COLOMBIA

→
TITLE OF WORK: CITYBOYS LIVE
L'INCONSCIENCE DE L'ETE
CD-JACKET
DESIGNER: TAKU YOKOSUKA
DESIGN COMPANY: PAT DETECTIVE
YEAR: 2001
CLIENT: CULTURE PUBLISHERS INC.

TITLE OF WORK: THE SWINGLE SOUNDS OF SCHEMA
COMPILED BY IKEDA MASANORI
CD-JACKET
DESIGNER: TAKU YOKOSUKA
DESIGN COMPANY: PAT DETECTIVE
YEAR: 2000
CLIENT: RAMBLING RECORDS.

TITLE OF WORK: JET SOUNDS
NICOLA CONTE
CD-JACKET
DESIGNER: TAKU YOKOSUKA
DESIGN COMPANY: PAT DETECTIVE
YEAR: 2000
CLIENT: RAMBLING RECORDS.

TITLE OF WORK: VIBES FROM THE BOOTS SHAPE
COMPILED BY FARR A.K.A. CALM
CD-JACKET
DESIGNER: TAKU YOKOSUKA
DESIGN COMPANY: PAT DETECTIVE
YEAR: 2000
CLIENT: RAMBLING RECORDS.

The Swingle Sounds of SCHEMA
Compiled by IKEDA, Masanori

jet sounds
NICOLA CONTE

Vibes from the Boot Shape
Compiled by FARR a.k.a. CALM for music conception

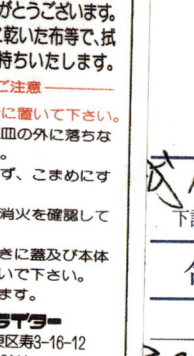
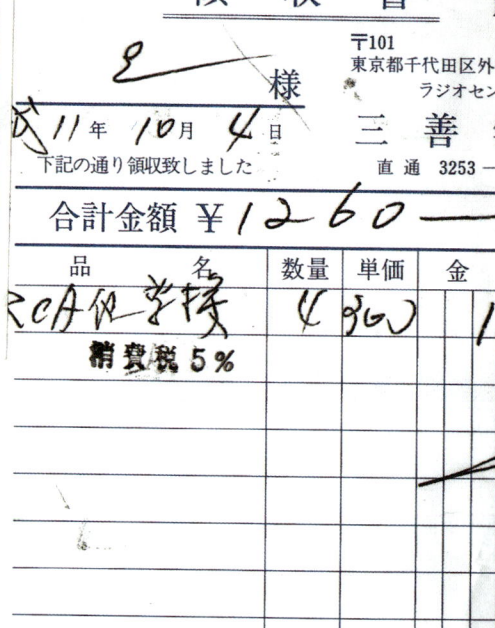

POWER GRAPHIXX

Power Graphixx, founded in 1996, is a design team from Tokyo/Japan. They mainly work on printed matter and motion graphics in a wide range of fields and have gained a high reputation, especially for their unique style of 2-dimensional motion graphics which draws on their architectural background. Recent work includes editorial design, logo design for various clothing brands, CD jackets, TV titles, event movies, music videos etc.

1996年に結成された東京のデザインチーム。紙媒体と映像をメインに幅広い分野で活動中。建築専攻の経歴を活かし、独特の平面構成を用いた映像は高い評価を得ている。最近の作品にエディトリアルデザイン、ロゴデザイン、CDジャケット、TVタイトル、イベント用映像、ミュージッククリップなどがある。

パワーグラフィックス

NAME OF DESIGN COMPANY: POWER GRAPHIXX
NAMES/YEAR OF BIRTH: MASAHITO HANZAWA (75)/
HIROYUKI NAGATAKE (75)/JUNYA SAITO (76)/
YOSHIYUKI KOMATSU (76)
COMPANY SINCE: 1996
ADDRESS: 2-25-5 KITASENZOKU, OTA-KU,
TOKYO 145-0062, JAPAN
WEBSITE: HTTP://WWW.POWER-GRAPHIXX.COM/
EMAIL ADDRESS: SUPPORT@POWER-GRAPHIXX.COM
FAX: +81 (0)3-3729-1636

デザイン会社名：パワーグラフィックス
メンバー名(生年)：半澤雅仁(75年)/永竹弘幸(75年)/斉藤順也(76年)/小松好幸(76年)
会社設立日：1996年
住所：〒145-0062 東京都大田区北千束2-25-5
ウェブサイト：http://www.power-graphixx.com
Eメールアドレス：support@power-graphixx.com
ファックス番号：+81 (0)3-3729-1636

BIOGRAPHY ↑
10 QUESTIONS/ANSWERS ↓

HOW DOES JAPAN SMELL TODAY?
It has the smell of asphalt.

HOW DOES YOUR DAY START AND HOW DOES YOUR DAY END?
I am woken by a phone call from a client, and I shut down my computer and go to bed.

IS THERE SOMETHING THAT YOU REALLY LOVE AND THAT YOU REALLY HATE ABOUT JAPAN?
Love: delicious meals. Hate: smelly water.

WHAT DO YOU THINK ARE THE DIFFERENCES BETWEEN AMERICAN, EUROPEAN AND JAPANESE PEOPLE?
Preferences.

WHAT DO YOU THINK IS THE DIFFERENCE BETWEEN JAPANESE, AMERICAN AND EUROPEAN DESIGN?
Attitude.

WHAT WOULD YOU DO, IF GRAPHIC DESIGN DID NOT EXIST?
Some kind of design work.

CAN YOU TELL US YOUR 3 MOST IMPORTANT THINGS/OBJECTS/ACTIVITIES?
Design. Macintosh. Power Graphixx.

WHAT IS BEAUTIFUL AND WHAT IS UGLY?
Beautiful: landscape. Ugly: traffic jam.

TO WHICH QUESTION YOU WOULD NEVER GIVE AN ANSWER?
«Which is more important for you? Me or work?»

IS THERE ANYTHING YOU WOULD LIKE TO TELL THE READERS OF THIS BOOK?
We would like to give big thanks to people who have supported us for many years. Feel free to post any suggestions or comments regarding our work: support@power-graphixx.com

(interview with Power Graphixx)

Q1: 今日の日本はどんな匂いがしますか？
A1: アスファルトの匂い。

Q2: あなたの1日はどの様に始まり、どの様に終わりますか？
A2: 仕事の電話で起こされて、システム終了して寝る。

Q3: 日本の好きな部分、嫌いな部分を挙げて下さい。
A3: 好き―うまい飯。嫌い―くさい水。

Q4: アメリカ人、ヨーロッパ人、日本人の違いは何だと思いますか？
A4: 嗜好。

Q5: 日本のデザイン、アメリカのデザイン、ヨーロッパのデザインの違いは何だと思いますか？
A5: 態度。

Q6: グラフィックデザインが存在していなかったら、あなたは何をしていますか？
A6: なんらかのデザイン活動。

Q7: あなた大事なことを3つ教えて下さい。
A7: デザイン。マッキントッシュ。パワーグラフィックス。

Q8: 何が美しくて、何が醜いと思いますか？
A8: 美しい―風景。醜い―渋滞。

Q9: あなたが絶対に答えない質問は何でしょう？
A9: 「私と仕事とどっちが大切なの？」

Q10: 読者に何か伝えたいことがあれば書いて下さい。
A10: この本に参加するにあたって、お世話になった方々に大きな感謝。作品に関する御意見、御感想はこちらまで。support@power-graphixx.com

(インタビュー：パワーグラフィックス)

PROFILE ↑
BUSINESS CARD →
SELFPORTRAIT ↓

POWER GRAPHIXX

パワーグラフィックス

POWER GRAPHIXX

WORKSPACES ↓   LOGOTYPE ↑

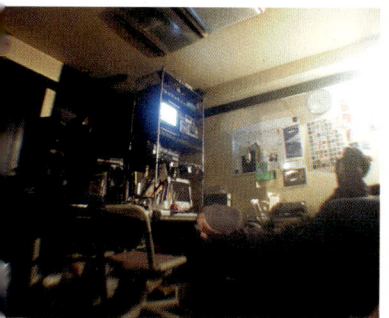
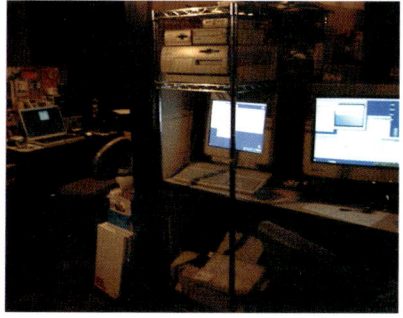

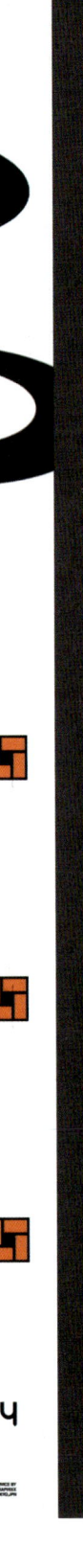

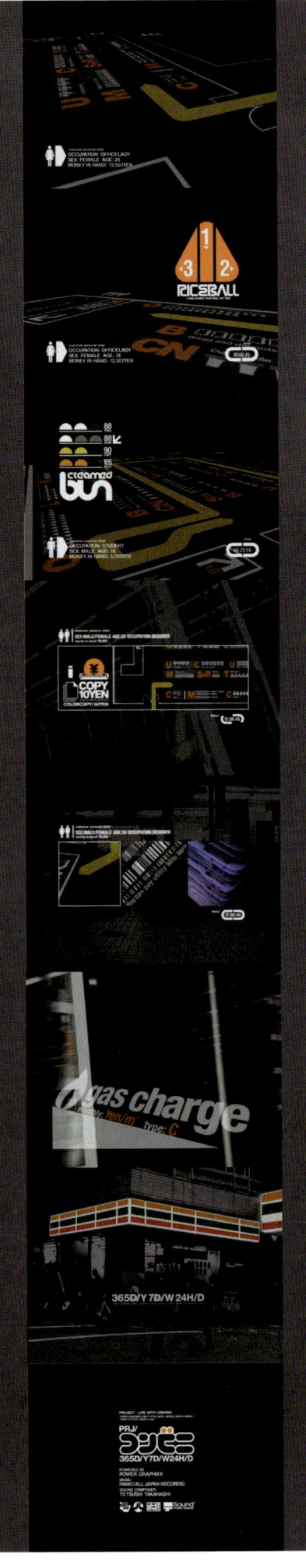

IIS (ITSUO ILLUSTRATION SERVICE)

Hello, this is Itsuo. Recently I've created a character design as a teaching aid for kids. This is just what I have been waiting for for a long time. I like the fact that it's «a teaching aid» or «kids stuff». Like making a jack-in-the-box, people who are involved in this project have tried to figure out «what excites kids?» or «what makes kids want to study?». That makes me excited too. I hope to continue doing work for kids energetically because I love kids. Well, you wouldn't believe how childish I am still!

コンニチワ、いつおです。最近は子供向け用教材のキャラクターデザインをさせてもらっています。実はこれ、ボクが昔からやりたかった仕事なんです。"教材"と言うか"子供向け"っつートコが重要なワケで。その仕事の打ち合わせでも「どうしたら子供がワクワクしてくれるか」「子供が楽しみながら勉強する気になるか」と担当の方、デザイナーの方みんなして、まるでビックリ箱でも作っている様な感覚で、自分までワクワクしちゃうんですよね。出来たらこれからも子供向けの仕事ガシガシやって行きたいですね〜。子供好きなんで。つうか、ボクの精神年令が子供だったりもするんですけどネッ!

BIOGRAPHY
10 QUESTIONS/ANSWERS

HOW DOES JAPAN SMELL TODAY?
Like a paradise of all sorts of characters.

HOW DOES YOUR DAY START AND HOW DOES YOUR DAY END?
My day starts and ends with either «working», «drinking sake» or «sleeping». It is very monotonous.

IS THERE SOMETHING WHAT YOU REALLY LOVE AND WHAT YOU REALLY HATE ABOUT JAPAN?
Love: TV games are more interesting than anywhere else. Hate: The Legend of Zelda (Nintendo 64) is too hard.

WHAT DO YOU THINK ARE THE DIFFERENCES BETWEEN AMERICAN, EUROPEAN AND JAPANESE PEOPLE?
Don't you think it's the differences between individuals rather than the countries? That's all it is.

WHAT DO YOU THINK IS THE DIFFERENCE BETWEEN JAPANESE, AMERICAN AND EUROPEAN DESIGN?
Same as answer 4.

WHAT WOULD YOU DO, IF GRAPHIC DESIGN DID NOT EXIST?
Watchmaker. I wrote that in the elementary school yearbook for some reason.

CAN YOU TELL US YOUR 3 MOST IMPORTANT THINGS/OBJECTS/ACTIVITIES?
Media. Impact. Relations between people.

WHAT IS BEAUTIFUL AND WHAT IS UGLY?
Beautiful: To win a design competition. Ugly: The situation that the character which does not seem like having gone through its throes of creation is catching on with the public.

TO WHICH QUESTION YOU WOULD NEVER GIVE AN ANSWER?
«Why did you want to be a watchmaker when you were in elementary school?» I wouldn't give any answer. I mean, I don't even know the answer.

IS THERE ANYTHING YOU WOULD LIKE TO TELL THE READERS OF THIS BOOK?
If you are messing around, you will soon be an old fossil!

(interview with Itsuo Ito)

Q1: 今日の日本はどんな匂いがしますか?
A1: ピンキリキャラクター天国。

Q2: あなたの1日はどの様に始まり、どの様に終わりますか?
A2: 「仕事してる」か「酒を飲んでる」か「寝ている」のどれかで始まり、どれかで終わります。至って単調です。

Q3: 日本の好きな部分、嫌いな部分を挙げて下さい。
A3: 好き—TVゲームが断然面白い。
嫌い—ゼルダの冒険(Nintendo64)が難しすぎる。

Q4: アメリカ人、ヨーロッパ人、日本人の違いは何だと思いますか?
A4: 人それぞれの違いじゃないですか? 国というよりも。ハイ。

Q5: 日本のデザイン、アメリカのデザイン、ヨーロッパのデザインの違いは何だと思いますか?
A5: Q4と同じ答えです。

Q6: グラフィックデザインが存在していなかったら、あなたは何をしていますか?
A6: 時計屋。なぜか小学校の卒業文集にそう自分で書いていました。

Q7: あなた大事なことを3つ教えて下さい。
A7: メディア。インパクト。人と人との繋がり。

Q8: 何が美しくて、何が醜いと思いますか?
A8: 美しい—コンペに勝つ事。
醜い—絶対に生みの苦しみを味わっていない様なキャラクターが世間でウケたりしている現状。

Q9: あなたが絶対に答えない質問は何でしょう?
A9: 「なぜ小学校の時、時計屋になりたかったのか?」
答えないと言うか、自分でも答えを知りません。

Q10: 読者に何か伝えたいことがあれば書いて下さい。
A10: モタモタしてると、あっちゅー間にオヤジになっちゃうよ!

(インタビュー: いといつお)

PROFILE
BUSINESS CARD
SELFPORTRAIT

NAME OF DESIGN COMPANY: IIS (ITSUO ILLUSTRATION SERVICE)
NAME/YEAR OF BIRTH: ITSUO ITO (69)
COMPANY SINCE: 2000
ADDRESS: 1-1-22-302 NAKAOCHIAI, SHINJUKU-KU, TOKYO 161-0032, JAPAN
WEBSITE: HTTP://WWW.ITSUOITO.COM/
EMAIL ADDRESS: IIS@ITSUOITO.COM
FAX: +81 (0)3-5983-0337

デザイン会社名: イツオ・イラストレーション・サービス
メンバー名(生年): いといつお(69年)
会社設立日: 2000年
住所: 〒161-0032 東京都新宿区中落合1-1-22-302
ウェブサイト: http://www.itsuoito.com/
Eメールアドレス: iis@itsuoito.com
ファックス番号: +81 (0)3-5983-0337

IIS (ITSUO ILLUSTRATION SERVICE)

いといつお

WORKSPACES ↓ LOGOTYPE ↑

→ TITLE OF WORK: DENGEKI-CHECK-KUN
DESIGNER: ITSUO ITO
DESIGN COMPANY: IIS
(ITSUO ILLUSTRATION SERVICE)
YEAR: 2001
CLIENT: BENESSE CORPORATION

→ TITLE OF WORK: JAMMING BOY
DESIGNER: ITSUO ITO
DESIGN COMPANY: IIS
(ITSUO ILLUSTRATION SERVICE)
YEAR: 2000
CLIENT: EXCEED PRESS

FJD (FUJITA JIRO DESIGN)

Born in Osaka, in 1971. Work as FJD has been going since 2000, working mainly on CD jackets and motion graphics. The CD jacket design for CALM and Acoustic Dub Messengers is one of the masterpieces.

1971年大阪に生まれる。2000年よりFJDとして活動。主にCDジャケット、モーショングラフィックを中心に制作中。代表作にCALMやAcoustic Dub Messengersのジャケットデザインがある。

NAME OF DESIGN COMPANY: FJD (FUJITA JIRO DESIGN)
NAME/YEAR OF BIRTH: JIRO FUJITA (71)
COMPANY SINCE: 2000
ADDRESS: 3-7-6-#306 SENDAGAYA, SHIBUYA-KU, TOKYO 151-0051, JAPAN
WEBSITE: HTTP://WWW.FIDES.DTI.NE.JP/~FJD/
EMAIL ADDRESS: FJD@FIDES.DTI.NE.JP
FAX: +81 (0)3-3470-1050

デザイン会社名：フジタ・ジロウ・デザイン
メンバー名（生年）：藤田二郎（71年）
会社設立日：2000年
住所：〒151-0051 東京都渋谷区千駄ヶ谷3-7-6 秀和第二神宮レジデンス306
ウェブサイト：http://www.fides.dti.ne.jp/~fjd/
Eメールアドレス：fjd@fides.dti.ne.jp
ファックス番号：+81 (0)3-3470-1050

BIOGRAPHY ↑
10 QUESTIONS/ANSWERS ↓

HOW DOES JAPAN SMELL TODAY?
There is a smell of sweet butter.

HOW DOES YOUR DAY START AND HOW DOES YOUR DAY END?
My day is a repeatitive cycle of working, and drinking coffee.

IS THERE SOMETHING THAT YOU REALLY LOVE AND THAT YOU REALLY HATE ABOUT JAPAN?
What I love about Japan is the delicious food. You can try almost every kind of food from around the world. And I love the changes of the four seasons. I don't really have anything I hate.

WHAT DO YOU THINK ARE THE DIFFERENCES BETWEEN AMERICAN, EUROPEAN AND JAPANESE PEOPLE?
I don't really know yet.

WHAT DO YOU THINK IS THE DIFFERENCE BETWEEN JAPANESE, AMERICAN AND EUROPEAN DESIGN?
America: dynamic. Europe: intellectual. Japan: delicate.

WHAT WOULD YOU DO, IF GRAPHIC DESIGN DID NOT EXIST?
Either a chef or pastry cook, something related to food.

CAN YOU TELL US YOUR 3 MOST IMPORTANT THINGS/OBJECTS/ACTIVITIES?
Family. Good friends. Loved ones.

WHAT IS BEAUTIFUL AND WHAT IS UGLY?
Beautiful: having an excellent sense of balance.
Ugly: having a poor sense of balance.

TO WHICH QUESTION YOU WOULD NEVER GIVE AN ANSWER?
Anything about the secret of a friend or others.

IS THERE ANYTHING YOU WOULD LIKE TO TELL THE READERS OF THIS BOOK?
I will work harder and do my best to become the only one.

(interview with Jiro Fujita)

Q1: 今日の日本はどんな匂いがしますか？
A1: 甘いバターの匂いがしました。

Q2: あなたの1日はどの様に始まり、どの様に終わりますか？
A2: 仕事とコーヒーを飲む事の繰り返しです。

Q3: 日本の好きな部分、嫌いな部分を挙げて下さい。
A3: 好きな部分は食べ物が美味しいこと。ほとんどの国のご飯を食べることが出来ること。四季があること。嫌いなところは特にありません。

Q4: アメリカ人、ヨーロッパ人、日本人の違いは何だと思いますか？
A4: まだよく分かりません。

Q5: 日本のデザイン、アメリカのデザイン、ヨーロッパのデザインの違いは何だと思いますか？
A5: アメリカ—ダイナミック。ヨーロッパ—理知的。日本—繊細。

Q6: グラフィックデザインが存在していなかったら、あなたは何をしていますか？
A6: コックか菓子職人。食べ物に関わる仕事。

Q7: あなた大事なことを3つ教えて下さい。
A7: 家族。親友。恋人。

Q8: 何が美しくて、何が醜いと思いますか？
A8: 美しいこと—バランス感覚が優れていること。
醜いこと—バランス感覚が劣っていること。

Q9: あなたが絶対に答えない質問は何でしょう？
A9: 友達や他人の秘密に関する事。

Q10: 読者に何か伝えたいことがあれば書いて下さい。
A10: まだまだこれからですが、唯一無二の存在になれるように頑張りたいと思います。

（インタビュー：藤田二郎）

PROFILE ↑
BUSINESS CARD →
SELFPORTRAIT ↓

FJD (FUJITA JIRO DESIGN) フジタ・ジロウ・デザイン

WORKSPACES ↓ LOGOTYPE ↑

TITLE OF WORK: ACOUSTIC DUB MESSENGERS
MUGIMINIPICHI
DESIGNER: JIRO FUJITA
ILLUSTRATION: YASUKO SAITO
DESIGN COMPANY: FJD (FUJITA JIRO DESIGN)
YEAR: 2001
CLIENT: RAFT MUSIC

TITLE OF WORK: SAL
DESIGNER: JIRO FUJITA
ILLUSTRATION: YASUKO SAITO
DESIGN COMPANY: FJD (FUJITA JIRO DESIGN)
YEAR: 2001
CLIENT: ELECTRIC SAL

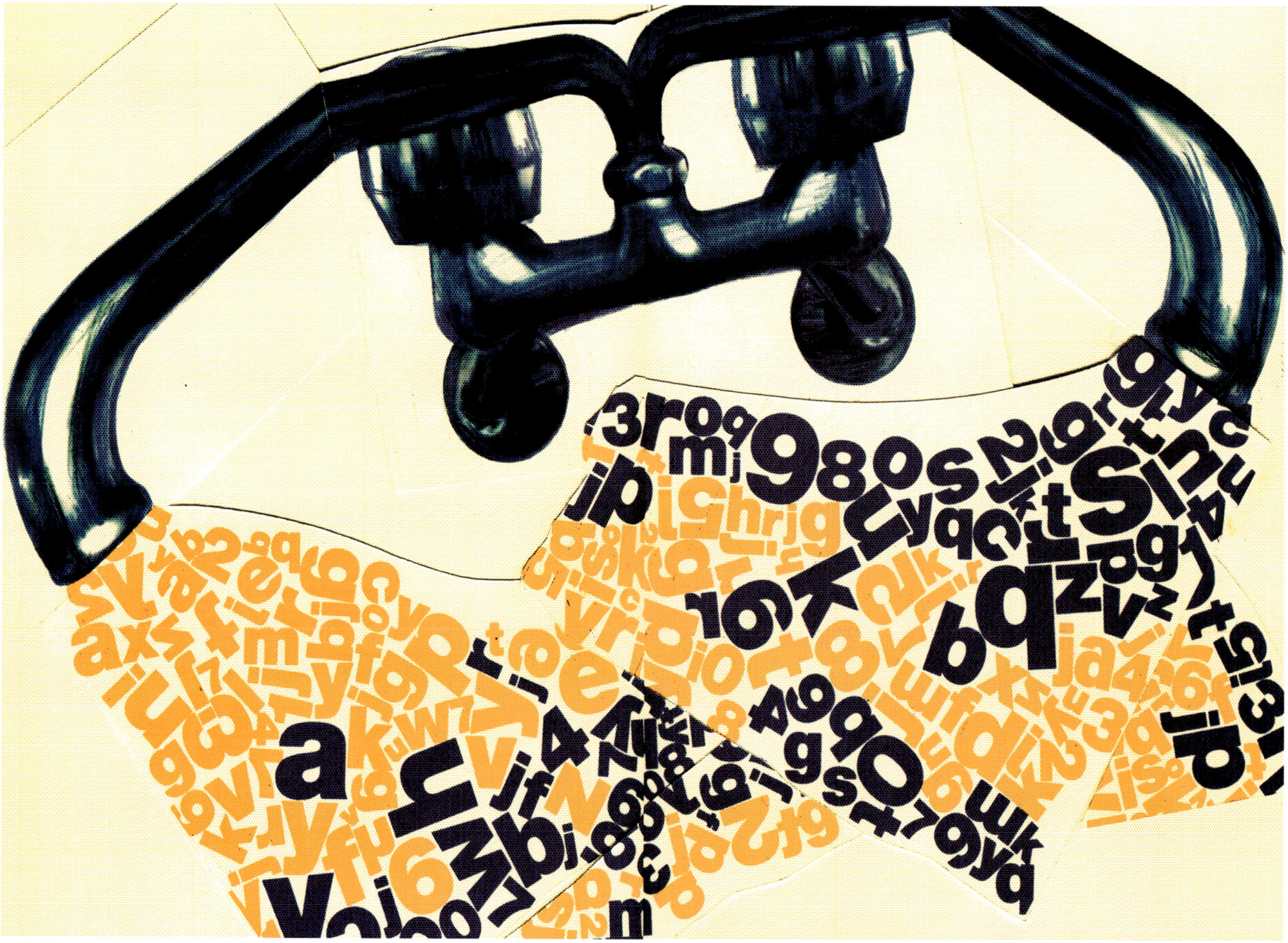

TITLE OF WORK: BE THE VOICE
PRIVATE MUSIC
DESIGNER: JIRO FUJITA
ILLUSTRATION: YASUKO SAITO
DESIGN COMPANY: FJD (FUJITA JIRO DESIGN)
YEAR: 2001
CLIENT: TOKUMA JAPAN COMMUNICATIONS CO., LTD.

正誤表

カタログの文章中に一部誤りがありました。
正しくは以下のようになっております。

	誤	→	正
2ページ	定価 6,800		予価 6,800円（税別）
6ページ	6,800（税別）		6,800円（税別）

GROOVISIONS

Since 1993, Groovisions have been developing their visual work mainly in various fields of graphic design and motion graphics, and have also been managing exclusive talent called «CHAPPIE». Besides all that, they've continued to present and sell original work under the name of «exhibition».

1993年以降、様々な領域のグラフィックデザインやモーション・グラフィックス、さらに専属タレント「CHAPPIE」のマネージメントを中心にヴィジュアルワークを展開している。また、展示会という名目でのオリジナル作品のプレゼンテーション、販売を継続している。

NAME OF DESIGN COMPANY: GROOVISIONS
NAMES/YEAR OF BIRTH: HIROSHI ITO (63)/ TORU HARA (66)/ KENJI SUMIOKA (72)/ AYAKO YABE (71)/ TOMOYUKI KONDO (69)/ MILKMAN SAITO (63)
COMPANY SINCE: 1993
ADDRESS: MEGURO-KU, TOKYO JAPAN
WEBSITE: HTTP://WWW.GROOVISIONS.COM/
EMAIL ADDRESS: GRV@GROOVISIONS.COM
FAX: +81 (0)3-5723-6356

デザイン会社名：グルーヴィジョンズ
メンバー名(生年)：伊藤弘(63年)/原徹(66年)/住岡謙次(72年)/矢部綾子(71年)/近藤朋幸(69年)/ミルクマン斉藤(63年)
会社設立日：1993年
住所：東京都目黒区
ウェブサイト：http://www.groovisions.com/
Eメールアドレス：grv@groovisions.com
ファックス番号：+81 (0)3-5723-6356

BIOGRAPHY / 10 QUESTIONS/ANSWERS

HOW DOES JAPAN SMELL TODAY?
Like tobacco.

HOW DOES YOUR DAY START AND HOW DOES YOUR DAY END?
Start: I buy some bread and go to work in the afternoon. End: I work until dawn and then go home (occasionally I drink beer).

IS THERE SOMETHING THAT YOU REALLY LOVE AND THAT YOU REALLY HATE ABOUT JAPAN?
Love: How busy we are. Hate: How busy we are.

WHAT DO YOU THINK ARE THE DIFFERENCES BETWEEN AMERICAN, EUROPEAN AND JAPANESE PEOPLE?
The Japanese language.

WHAT DO YOU THINK IS THE DIFFERENCE BETWEEN JAPANESE, AMERICAN AND EUROPEAN DESIGN?
The Japanese language.

WHAT WOULD YOU DO, IF GRAPHIC DESIGN DID NOT EXIST?
Stationer's shop. (Hara).

CAN YOU TELL US YOUR 3 MOST IMPORTANT THINGS/OBJECTS/ACTIVITIES?
To have a go anyway. To keep on thinking. To take a break when you get tired.

WHAT IS BEAUTIFUL AND WHAT IS UGLY?
Beautiful: Fuller's geodesic dome house. Ugly: unfortunately, the dome that we built on the roof of the office is quite dirty.

TO WHICH QUESTION YOU WOULD NEVER GIVE AN ANSWER?
None in particular.

IS THERE ANYTHING YOU WOULD LIKE TO TELL THE READERS OF THIS BOOK?
This year, we've got more opportunity to do the exhibition overseas. Please come to the show if you have a chance.

(interview with groovisions)

Q1: 今日の日本はどんな匂いがしますか？
A1: たばこ。

Q2: あなたの1日はどの様に始まり、どの様に終わりますか？
A2: 始まり―お昼すぎに、パンを買って仕事に出かける。終わり―明け方まで仕事して家に帰る（たまにビールを飲む）。

Q3: 日本の好きな部分、嫌いな部分を挙げて下さい。
A3: 好き―忙しいところ。嫌い―忙しいところ。

Q4: アメリカ人、ヨーロッパ人、日本人の違いは何だと思いますか？
A4: 日本語。

Q5: 日本のデザイン、アメリカのデザイン、ヨーロッパのデザインの違いは何だと思いますか？
A5: 日本語。

Q6: グラフィックデザインが存在していなかったら、あなたは何をしていますか？
A6: 文房具用品店。(原)

Q7: あなた大事なことを3つ教えて下さい。
A7: とりあえず、やってみること。あきらめず、考えること。つかれたら、少し休むこと。

Q8: 何が美しくて、何が醜いと思いますか？
A8: 美しい―フラー型ドーム。醜い―事務所の屋上に建てたドームは、残念ながらかなり汚い。

Q9: あなたが絶対に答えない質問は何でしょう？
A9: 特にない。

Q10: 読者に何か伝えたいことがあれば書いて下さい。
A10: 今年は海外での展示が増えました。機会があれば、ぜひご覧下さい。

（インタビュー：グルーヴィジョンズ）

PROFILE / BUSINESS CARD / SELFPORTRAIT

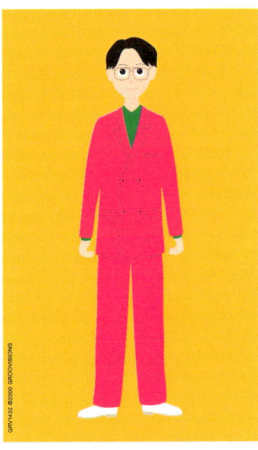
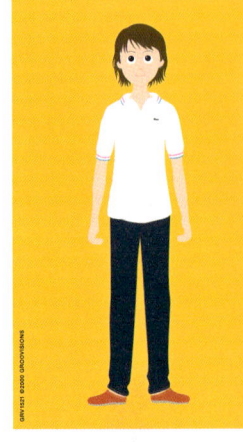

TITLE OF WORK: MONOGRAME GIFT
DESIGNER: MIYAJIMA TAKAFUMI
DESIGN COMPANY: LIVING
YEAR: 2001
CLIENT: SAL MAGAZINE VOL.02

TITLE OF WORK: TOKYO STATION LOGOS
DESIGNER: KENTARO «ANI» FUJIMOTO
DESIGN COMPANY: NENDO
YEAR: 1999

B4   02 GIF   COPYRIGHT(C)1998-2001 LIVING td.
                ALL RIGHTS RESERVED.

SALmagazine Vol.02 "Monograme(GIFT)"

GROOVISIONS グルーヴィジョンズ

groovisions

WORKSPACES ↓   LOGOTYPE ↑

→ TITLE OF WORK: MICHAEL YOUNG EXHIBITION
IN KYOTO
DESIGN COMPANY: GROOVISIONS
YEAR: 1996
CLIENT: E&Y

→ TITLE OF WORK: GRV1546
(OTHER VERSION)
DESIGN COMPANY: GROOVISIONS
YEAR: 2001
CLIENT: JAM EXHIBITION
AT BARBICAN ART GALLERY

→ TITLE OF WORK: GRV1503
S.M.P.KO2 STRIKES BACK!
DESIGN COMPANY: GROOVISIONS
YEAR: 2001
CLIENT: HIROPON FACTORY
PUBLISHED BY KAIYODO CO., LTD.
(C) TAKASHI MURAKAMI, KAIKAIKIKI 2000-2001
PRODUCED BY KAIYODO

HIDEKI INABA DESIGN

Born in Shizuoka in 1971. Started as a graphic designer and, since 1997, has worked on many visual creations, fonts, and art directions . +81magazine (97-2001), gasbook (97-00), img src 100 by shift.jp.org (98), FONTROM (98-99), SALmagazine (01). Released original fonts such as NOTE, SHEET, DIRECTION (97-01) etc. A wide range of activities including the exhibition MOVEMENT at Sendai Mediatheque (01) etc.

1971年静岡県に生まれる。97年からグラフィックデザイナーとしてスタート。以後、ビジュアル制作、FONT、アートディレクションを多く担当。+81magazine(97-2001年)、gasbook(97-00年)、shift.jp.orgによるimg src 100(98年)、FONTROM(98-99年)、SALmagazine(01年)、NOTE、SHEET、DIRECTION(97-01年)等、オリジナル書体の発表。仙台メディアテークで開催されたMOVEMENT(01年)作品出展等、活動は多岐に渡る。

NAME OF DESIGN COMPANY: HIDEKI INABA DESIGN
NAME/YEAR OF BIRTH: HIDEKI INABA (71)
COMPANY SINCE: 1997
ADDRESS: 2-32-13 PK108/B1F, MATSUBARA, SETAGAYA-KU, TOKYO 156-0043, JAPAN
EMAIL ADDRESS: INABA@T3.RIM.OR.JP
FAX: +81 (0)3-3321-1766

デザイン会社名：稲葉英樹
メンバー名(生年)：稲葉英樹(71年)
会社設立日：1997年
住所：〒156-0043 東京都世田谷区松原2-32-13 PK108/B1F
ウェブサイト：-
Eメールアドレス：inaba@t3.rim.or.jp
ファックス番号：+81 (0)3-3321-1766

BIOGRAPHY ↑
10 QUESTIONS/ANSWERS ↓

HOW DOES JAPAN SMELL TODAY?
—

HOW DOES YOUR DAY START AND HOW DOES YOUR DAY END?
I start with working on what I had in my mind the night before. I end with thinking about what I have to do next.

IS THERE SOMETHING THAT YOU REALLY LOVE AND THAT YOU REALLY HATE ABOUT JAPAN?
Love: Wabi, Sabi (which is a Japanese expression meaning subtle taste, elegant simplicity). Chaos.
Hate: Wabi, Sabi (which is a Japanese expression meaning subtle taste, elegant simplicity). Chaos.

WHAT DO YOU THINK ARE THE DIFFERENCES BETWEEN AMERICAN, EUROPEAN AND JAPANESE PEOPLE?
Cultural differences. Educational differences. Physical differences.

WHAT DO YOU THINK IS THE DIFFERENCE BETWEEN JAPANESE, AMERICAN AND EUROPEAN DESIGN?
Cultural differences. Educational differences. Physical differences. Each of them has its own appropriate form of design. Each of them is mixed slowly and has its own purity.

WHAT WOULD YOU DO, IF GRAPHIC DESIGN DID NOT EXIST?
—

CAN YOU TELL US YOUR 3 MOST IMPORTANT THINGS/OBJECTS/ACTIVITIES?
Purity. Time. Oneself.

WHAT IS BEAUTIFUL AND WHAT IS UGLY?
Individuality is beautiful, but something impure is created when the number of people increases. Something that is pure is considered to be beautiful, something that is impure is considered to be ugly.

TO WHICH QUESTION YOU WOULD NEVER GIVE AN ANSWER?
—

IS THERE ANYTHING YOU WOULD LIKE TO TELL THE READERS OF THIS BOOK?
—

(interview with Hideki Inaba)

Q1: 今日の日本はどんな匂いがしますか？
A1: —

Q2: あなたの1日はどの様に始まり、どの様に終わりますか？
A2: 睡眠前に考えていた事を実行 → 次の事を考えて寝る。

Q3: 日本の好きな部分、嫌いな部分を挙げて下さい。
A3: 好き―わびさび。カオスなところ。
嫌い―わびさび。カオスなところ。

Q4: アメリカ人、ヨーロッパ人、日本人の違いは何だと思いますか？
A4: 文化の違い。教育の違い。身体の違い。

Q5: 日本のデザイン、アメリカのデザイン、ヨーロッパのデザインの違いは何だと思いますか？
A5: 文化の違い。教育の違い。身体の違い。それぞれが母国に似合ったデザイン形態をもっている。それぞれが少しずつ混ざりあい、それぞれ純度が違う。

Q6: グラフィックデザインが存在していなかったら、あなたは何をしていますか？
A6: —

Q7: あなた大事なことを3つ教えて下さい。
A7: 純粋。時間。自分。

Q8: 何が美しくて、何が醜いと思いますか？
A8: 個人は美しく、人数が増えると純粋でない部分が存在してしまう。純粋なものは美しく、純粋でないものは醜い。

Q9: あなたが絶対に答えない質問は何でしょう？
A9: —

Q10: 読者に何か伝えたいことがあれば書いて下さい。
A10: —

(インタビュー：稲葉英樹)

PROFILE ↑
BUSINESS CARD →
SELFPORTRAIT ↓

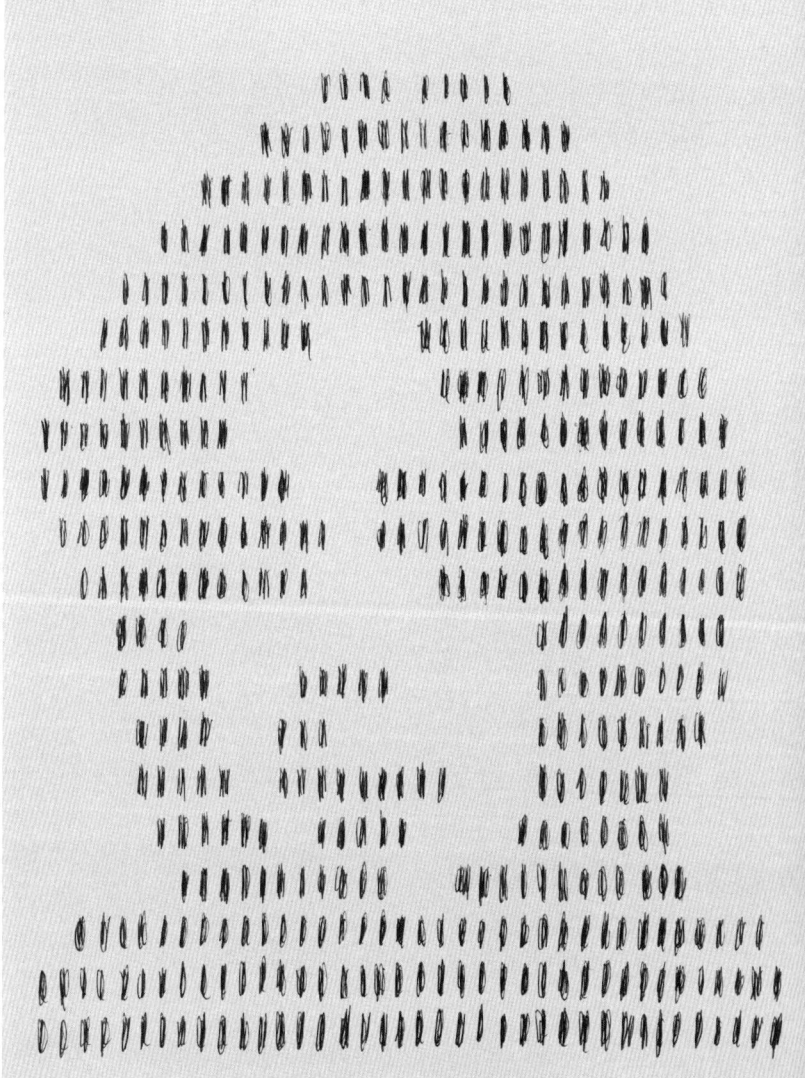

HIDEKI INABA DESIGN　　　稲葉英樹

HIDEKI INABA Design

WORKSPACES ↓　　　　LOGOTYPE ↑

NOTEFONT (HIRAGANA)

DIRECTION

This font has meaning that guides a new kind of direction. (created in 20th.)

SHEET

This font is imaged from "mark sheet" "check sheet". Gathering dots of 7X7 assigned to blank key, everyone can erase the dots or arrange.
Created in 1999.

SHEET2000

This is a new family of "SHEET" and used in "+81" magazine etc.

TITLE OF WORK: NOTEFONT
DESIGNER: HIDEKI IANABA
YEAR: 1997

TITLE OF WORK: DIRECTION
DESIGNER: HIDEKI IANABA
YEAR: 2001

TITLE OF WORK: SHEET
DESIGNER: HIDEKI IANABA
YEAR: 1999

TITLE OF WORK: PACKAGE
DESIGNER: HIDEKI INABA
YEAR: 2000
<CLIENT: ABAHOUSE INTERNATIONAL

TITLE OF WORK: SHEET 2000
DESIGNER: HIDEKI IANABA
YEAR: 2000

TITLE OF WORK: EDITORIAL WORK
DESIGNER: HIDEKI INABA
YEAR: 2001
<CLIENT: +81, D.D.WAVE CO., LTD.

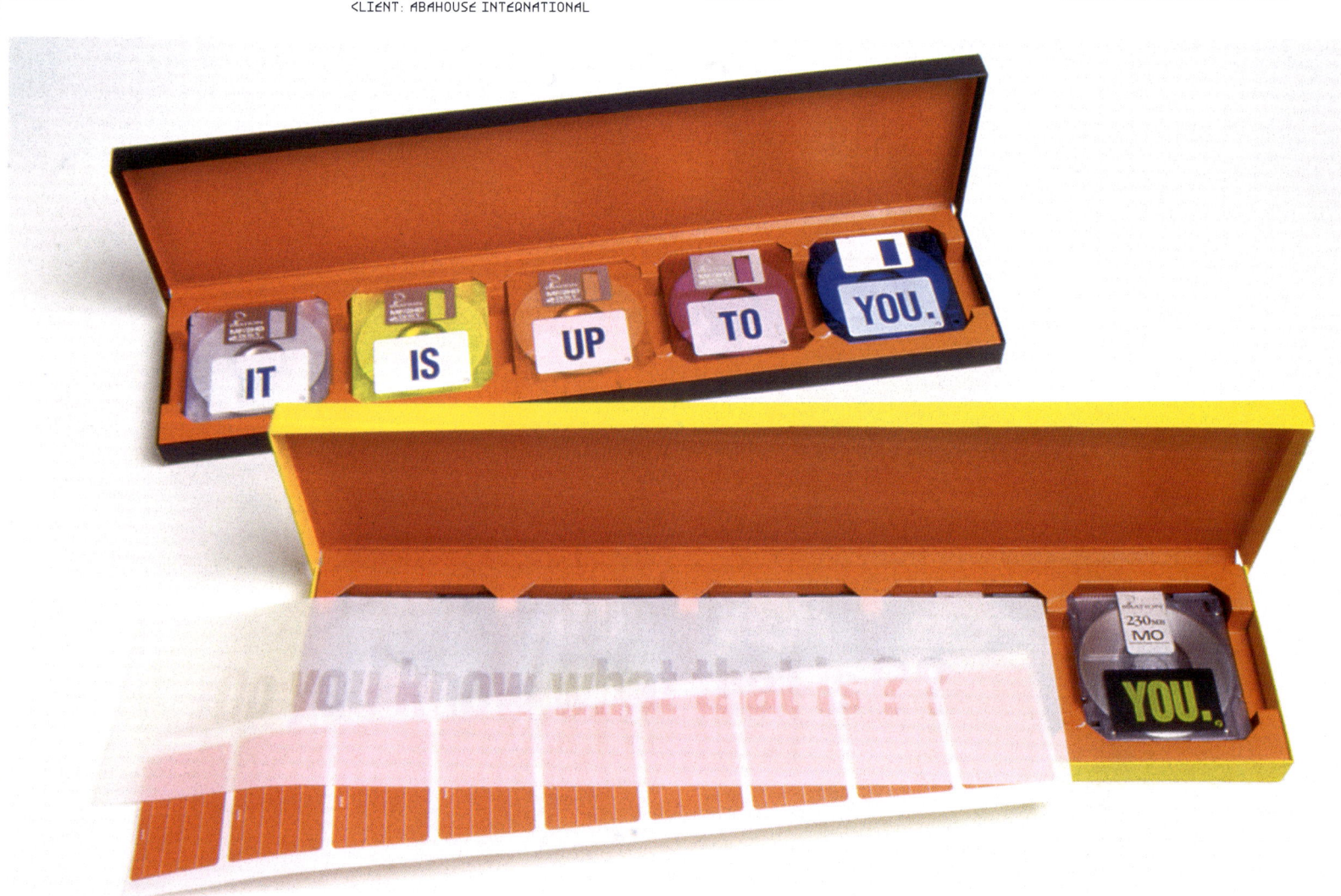

BOLD INC.

Bold Inc. is made up two parts. The one part lays emphasis on individual skills, and the other on teamwork. This is the company's most unique. Sometimes they work individually like a freelancers, sometimes they work with outside business partners. For example, Masataka Kurashina's custom paint work is one of the projects that strongly displays his personal side, and Toru Tachizawa's INHABITANT and LOOP- WHEELER are projects that were built on relationship and mutual trust with outside partnesr. Actually their personal sides feature strongly in all lines of activity. Bonzaipaint has become the main activity of Bold Inc. – a team effort involving all the members.

ボールドでは個人個人の能力を重要視した活動と、チームワークを活かした活動に大きく分かれている。これが当社の最もユニークな点でもある。まるでフリーランスのように個人的に、または外部のビジネスパートナーと活動することもある。例えば倉科昌高のカスタムペイントワークは彼のパーソナルな面が強く表れる仕事の一つでもあるし、立沢トオルのINHABITANTやLOOPWHEELERの仕事は外部パートナーとの信頼関係のうえに築かれた仕事で、どちらにしても個人の顔が強く全面に出るような内容になっている。一方、Bonzaipaintはボールドの中心的な活動として全員のチームワークのうえに成り立っている。

BIOGRAPHY
10 QUESTIONS/ANSWERS

HOW DOES JAPAN SMELL TODAY?
The smell of soy sauce. That's what I smell when I arrive at Narita Airport from abroad. (Tachizawa).
Exhaust fumes. (Kurashina).

HOW DOES YOUR DAY START AND HOW DOES YOUR DAY END?
Everyday is different. (Tachizawa).
I remember waking up, but I don't remember falling asleep. (Kurashina).

IS THERE SOMETHING THAT YOU REALLY LOVE AND THAT YOU REALLY HATE ABOUT JAPAN?
Nature is beautiful, and the same goes for other countries. There may be a tendency to spread the epidemic in Japan. (Tachizawa).
I love the delicious food. But I find there are not many people capable of exchanging their opinions. (Kurashina).

WHAT DO YOU THINK ARE THE DIFFERENCES BETWEEN AMERICAN, EUROPEAN AND JAPANESE PEOPLE?
I don't really think about this matter because there are many things that don't make any sense in themselves, I think. (Tachizawa).
I am not conscious of the differences. (Kurashina).

WHAT DO YOU THINK IS THE DIFFERENCE BETWEEN JAPANESE, AMERICAN AND EUROPEAN DESIGN?
I think it is no longer possible to distinguish between their design. (Tachizawa).
I think differences in design can be created by different characters or languages. (Kurashina).

WHAT WOULD YOU DO, IF GRAPHIC DESIGN DID NOT EXIST?
What I would like to be is a surgeon, chef or athlete. (Tachizawa).
I would be doing some kind of expressive work. (Kurashina).

CAN YOU TELL US YOUR 3 MOST IMPORTANT THINGS/OBJECTS/ACTIVITIES?
Snowboarding. Audio. Design. Tokyo life with friends too. (Tachizawa).
To eat. To paint. To chat. (Kurashina).

WHAT IS BEAUTIFUL AND WHAT IS UGLY?
As they say, beauty is in the eye of the beholder, that's exactly what I think. Beauty and ugliness are what grow in the mind. (Tachizawa).
What I think is beautiful is children. What I think is ugly is discrimination. (Kurashina).

TO WHICH QUESTION YOU WOULD NEVER GIVE AN ANSWER?
I wouldn't answer questions about my private life. (Tachizawa).
That's a secret. (Kurashina).

IS THERE ANYTHING YOU WOULD LIKE TO TELL THE READERS OF THIS BOOK?
Just like the posters from Switzerland or Poland inspired me to become a graphic designer when I was a child, I will find pleasure again if Japanese graphic design can make an impact in the eyes or the minds of the young readers of this book in anyway. (Tachizawa).
I think that an information trade fair is in Tokyo. I am very glad to be able to receive the information on Tokyo itself in the situation where the information around the world is flying about. (Kurashina).

(interview with Tachizawa/Kurashina)

Q1: 今日の日本はどんな匂いがしますか？
A1: お醤油の匂い。海外から成田に戻るとすごく感じる。(立沢)
排気ガス。(倉科)

Q2: あなたの1日はどの様に始まり、どの様に終わりますか？
A2: 日々によって違う。(立沢)
起きたのは憶えているが、寝たのは憶えていない。(倉科)

Q3: 日本の好きな部分、嫌いな部分を挙げて下さい。
A3: 他所でも同じことが言えるが、やはり自然は素晴らしい。日本では流行という伝染病が蔓延するきらいが少しあるのかもしれない。(立沢)
食べ物が美味しいという部分が好き。自分の意見を言える人が少ないと感じる。(倉科)

Q4: アメリカ人、ヨーロッパ人、日本人の違いは何だと思いますか？
A4: その事自体ナンセンスな部分の方が多いと思うのであまり考えない。(立沢)
違いについては意識していない。(倉科)

Q5: 日本のデザイン、アメリカのデザイン、ヨーロッパのデザインの違いは何だと思いますか？
A5: 3つの地域に分けてデザインの違いを表すことはもはや出来ないと思う。(立沢)
文字や言語の違いによるデザインの違いはあると思う。(倉科)

Q6: グラフィックデザインが存在していなかったら、あなたは何をしていますか？
A6: なりたい職業としては外科医、料理人、スポーツ選手。(立沢)
表現をする仕事をしていると思う。(倉科)

Q7: あなた大事なことを3つ教えて下さい。
A7: スノーボーディング。オーディオ。デザイン。友人たちとのトーキョーライフも。(立沢)
喰う。塗る。喋る。(倉科)

Q8: 何が美しくて、何が醜いと思いますか？
A8: 「美は見る人の目のなかにあり」と言われるが、僕も美と醜は心の中に芽生えるものと考える。(立沢)
美しいのは子供、醜いのは差別。(倉科)

Q9: あなたが絶対に答えない質問は何でしょう？
A9: 答えたくないのはプライベートに関する質問。(立沢)
それは秘密です。(倉科)

Q10: 読者に何か伝えたいことがあれば書いて下さい。
A10: スイスやポーランドのポスター等を見て、小学生だった僕がグラフィックデザインという仕事に憧れたように、この本の若い読者の目と心の中に、日本のグラフィックデザインが多少なりとも同じような影響を与えることができたら、僕がこの仕事を選ぶきっかけを与えてくれた先人たちに、改めて感謝できる喜びが生まれることでしょう。(立沢)
僕は情報の見本市は東京だと考えています。世界中の情報が飛び交っている中で、東京自体の情報が受信されることが嬉しく思います。(倉科)

(インタビュー: 立沢/倉科)

NAME OF DESIGN COMPANY: BOLD INC.
NAMES/YEAR OF BIRTH: MASATAKA KURASHINA (62)/ TORU TACHIZAWA (62)
COMPANY SINCE: 1999
ADDRESS: 2-15-3-201 MEGURO, MEGURO-KU, TOKYO 153-0063, JAPAN
WEBSITE: -
EMAIL ADDRESS: TORU-T@TKA.ATT.NE.JP
FAX: +81 (0)3-5768-0832

デザイン会社名：有限会社ボールド
メンバー名(生年)：倉科昌高(62年)/立沢トオル(62年)
会社設立日：1999年
住所：〒153-0063 東京都目黒区目黒2-15-3-201
ウェブサイト：—
Eメールアドレス：toru-t@tka.att.ne.jp
ファックス番号：+81 (0)3-5768-0832

PROFILE ↑
BUSINESS CARD →
SELFPORTRAIT ↓

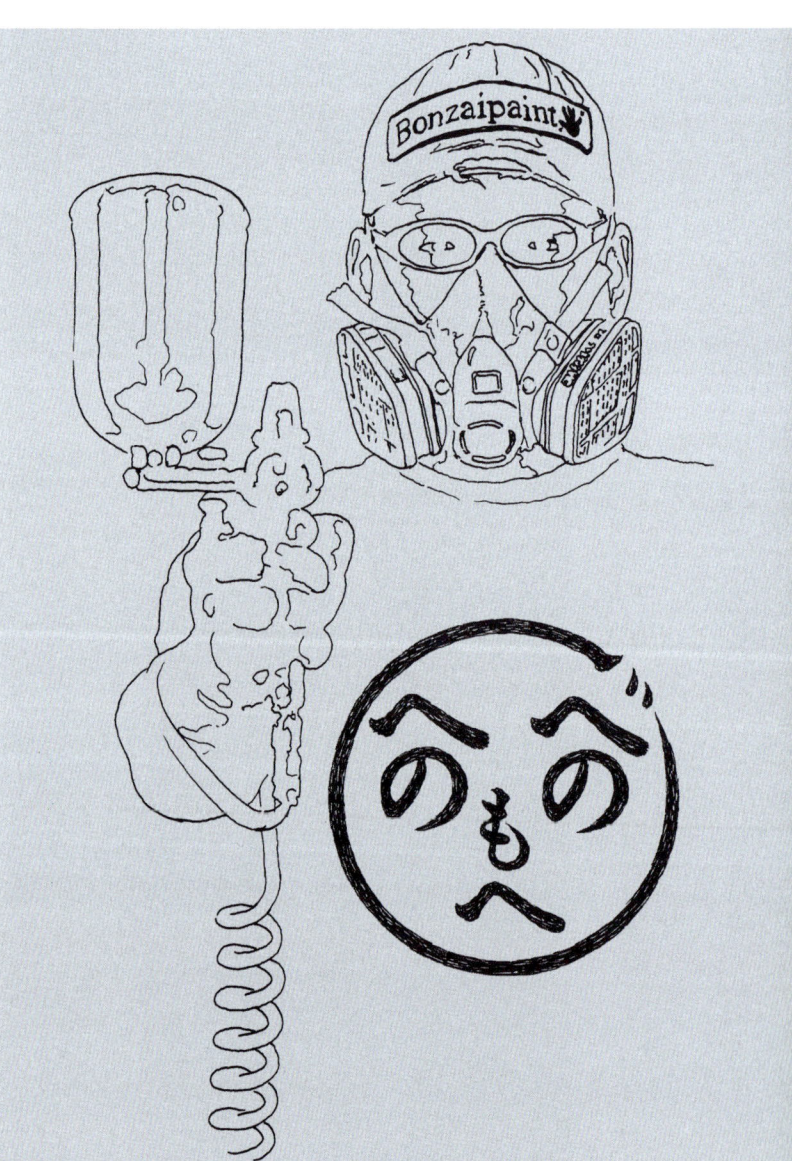

有限会社ボールド

Bold Inc.

↓
TITLE OF WORK: INHABITANT LOGO,
MARK AND TAG
DESIGNER: TORU TACHIZAWA
DESIGN COMPANY: BOLD INC.
YEAR: 1999
CLIENT: PHENIX CO., LTD.

→
TITLE OF WORK: MESSENGER
DESIGNER: TORU TACHIZAWA
DESIGN COMPANY: BOLD INC.
YEAR: 1997
CLIENT: BONZAIPAINT

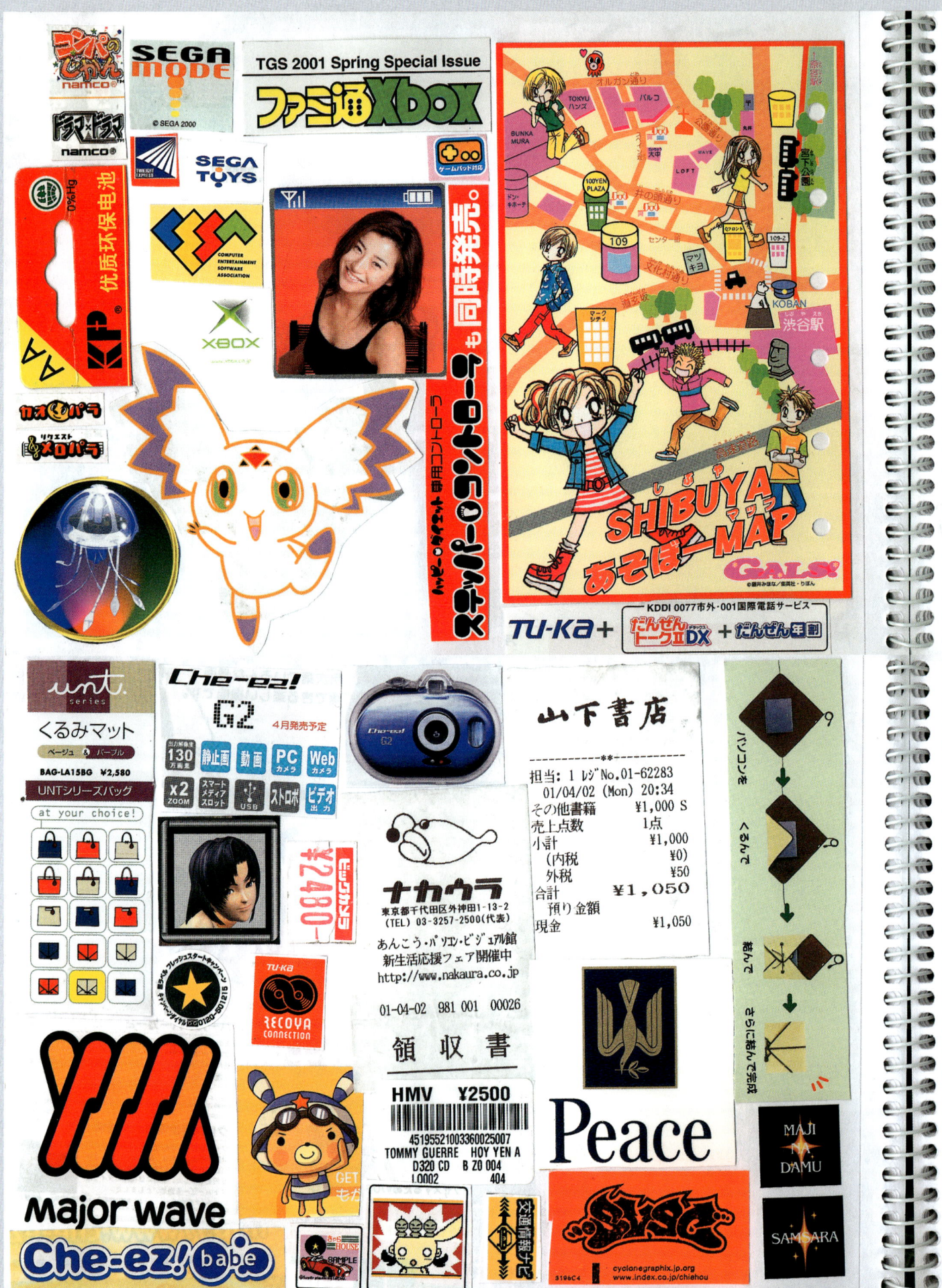

TGB DESIGN

Founded in 1995. A unique design unit consisting of 3 guys who rarely collaborate with each other (although we have collaborated recently). The motto is to do your own thing in your own field. The work of TGB design includes CD jackets, editorial design, advertising, motion graphics, web design etc., and DJing once in a while.

95年結成。基本的に共同作業は行わないという異色の3人組デザインユニット。(最近は共同も多い) それぞれが好きな分野で好きなことをするのがモットー。CDジャケット、エディトリアル、広告、映像、ホームページ等を制作する。最近は少ないが、たまーにDJ活動もする。

TGB design

NAME OF DESIGN COMPANY: TGB DESIGN
NAMES/YEAR OF BIRTH: MASARU ISHIURA (75)/
HIDEAKI KOMIYAMA (75)/MASASHI ICHIFURU (76)
COMPANY SINCE: 1995
ADDRESS: 3-45-11-#103 HONMACHI, SHIBUYA,
TOKYO 151-0001, JAPAN
WEBSITE: HTTP://WWW.TGBDESIGN.COM/
EMAIL ADDRESS: INFO@TGBDESIGN.COM
FAX: +81 (0)3-5333-6027

デザイン会社名：TGB design
メンバー名(生年)：石浦克(75年)/小宮山秀明(75年)/市古斉史(76年)
会社設立日：1995年
住所：〒151-0071 東京都渋谷区本町3-45-11 セントヒルズ清水橋103
ウェブサイト：http://www.tgbdesign.com/
Eメールアドレス：info@tgbdesign.com
ファックス番号：+81 (0)3-5333-6027

BIOGRAPHY
10 QUESTIONS/ANSWERS

HOW DOES JAPAN SMELL TODAY?
Since I have chronic allergic rhinitis...

HOW DOES YOUR DAY START AND HOW DOES YOUR DAY END?
I start with a yawn and I end with a yawn. (~o~)>

IS THERE SOMETHING THAT YOU REALLY LOVE AND THAT YOU REALLY HATE ABOUT JAPAN?
Fujiyama, Geisha, Akihabara!

WHAT DO YOU THINK ARE THE DIFFERENCES BETWEEN AMERICAN, EUROPEAN AND JAPANESE PEOPLE?
Where they live!

WHAT DO YOU THINK IS THE DIFFERENCE BETWEEN JAPANESE, AMERICAN AND EUROPEAN DESIGN?
I don't know.

WHAT WOULD YOU DO, IF GRAPHIC DESIGN DID NOT EXIST?
Research at Xerox Palo Alto Research Center.

CAN YOU TELL US YOUR 3 MOST IMPORTANT THINGS/OBJECTS/ACTIVITIES?
«T» and «G» and «B»!

WHAT IS BEAUTIFUL AND WHAT IS UGLY?
That's too difficult to answer.

TO WHICH QUESTION YOU WOULD NEVER GIVE AN ANSWER?
I have no idea.

IS THERE ANYTHING YOU WOULD LIKE TO TELL THE READERS OF THIS BOOK?
Thanks for supporting TGB design!

(interview with TGB design)

Q1: 今日の日本はどんな匂いがしますか？
A1: 慢性アレルギー性鼻炎なので…。

Q2: あなたの1日はどの様に始まり、どの様に終わりますか？
A2: あくびで始まってあくびで終わります。(￣O￣)>

Q3: 日本の好きな部分、嫌いな部分を挙げて下さい。
A3: フジヤマ、ゲイシャ、アキハバラ！

Q4: アメリカ人、ヨーロッパ人、日本人の違いは何だと思いますか？
A4: 住んでいる場所っ！

Q5: 日本のデザイン、アメリカのデザイン、ヨーロッパのデザインの違いは何だと思いますか？
A5: 分かりません。

Q6: グラフィックデザインが存在していなかったら、あなたは何をしていますか？
A6: パロアルトで研究。

Q7: あなた大事なことを3つ教えて下さい。
A7: 「T」と「G」と「B」！

Q8: 何が美しくて、何が醜いと思いますか？
A8: 難しすぎて答えられません。

Q9: あなたが絶対に答えない質問は何でしょう？
A9: 特に思いつきません。

Q10: 読者に何か伝えたいことがあれば書いて下さい。
A10: TGB designをよろしくネ！

(インタビュー：TGB design)

PROFILE
BUSINESS CARD →
SELFPORTRAIT ↓

TGB design

WORKSPACES ↓   LOGOTYPE ↑

 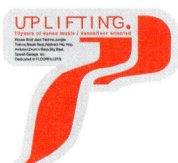   

↑↑↓
TITLE OF WORK: TGB LOGOTYPE WORKS
DESIGNER: MASARU ISHIURA, HIDEAKI KOMIYAMA, MASASHI ICHIFURU
DESIGN COMPANY: TGB DESIGN
YEAR: 1996-2001
CLIENT: DIVERSE

→
TITLE OF WORK: THE DESERT MOM
DESIGNER: HIDEAKI KOMIYAMA
DESIGN COMPANY: TGB DESIGN
YEAR: 1998

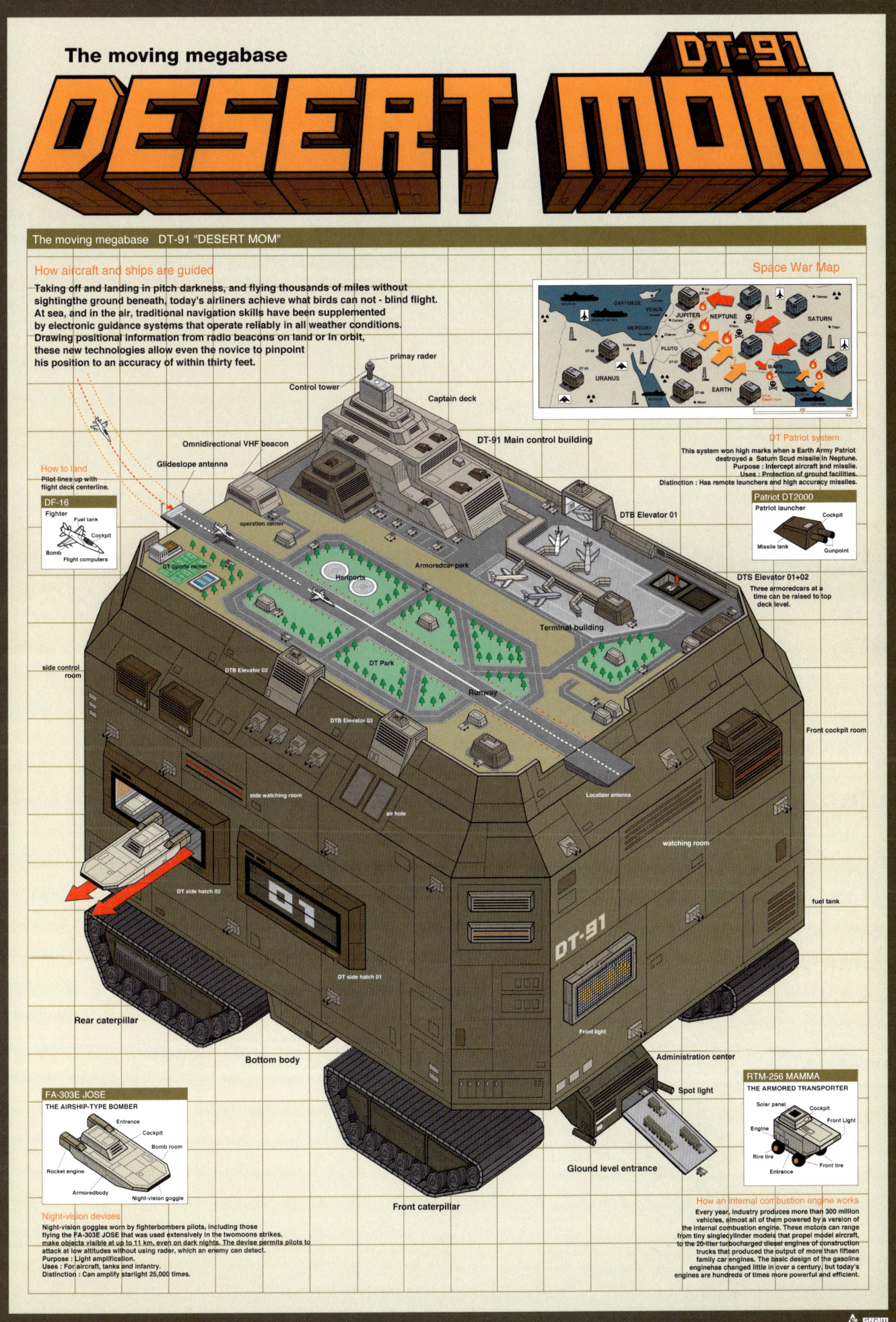

ASTRO GRAPHICA

ASTRO graphica is a graphic design team established in 1997 by Koji Takeuchi and Tetsuro Sano, who had been working in printed media such as posters and flyers. The main designer Kouji Takeuchi, typography-savvy Tetsuro Sano, and Tatsuya Hama, who has worked with computers since childhood, have teamed up and temporary members come in to help occasionally. Their unique sense of anime and pop culture and the delicate artwork created in a pixel unit has been critically acclaimed. Have worked on all different types of media such as posters, CD jackets, flyers, editorials, character design, illustration, C.I. logos, fonts, web design, motion graphics, sound design etc.

ポスターやフライヤーなど印刷媒体で活躍して来た竹内光司と佐野哲郎により1997年に結成されたグラフィックデザインチーム。現在はメインデザイナーの竹内光司、タイポグラフィに精通した佐野哲郎、幼少よりコンピュータと親密な関係を築いてきた浜達也から編成され、さらに臨時的なメンバーが加わることもある。アニメやポップカルチャーが生み出したその特異なセンスとピクセル単位の緻密な仕事ぶりが評価されている。ポスター、CDジャケット、フライヤー、エディトリアル、キャラクターデザイン、イラストレーション、CI製作、フォント製作、WEBデザイン、映像製作、サウンドデザインなど、部門を問わず活躍中。

BIOGRAPHY ↑
10 QUESTIONS/ANSWERS ↓

HOW DOES JAPAN SMELL TODAY?
As usual there is a smell of exhaust fumes here in Shinjuku. (Takeuchi)

HOW DOES YOUR DAY START AND HOW DOES YOUR DAY END?
Recently day and night have been almost reversed. I sometimes don't get any sleep, so I often can not see the line between yesterday and today. (Takeuchi).
I wake up in the morning, I go to sleep when it gets dark. Having a regular life is the secret to good health. (Sano).

IS THERE SOMETHING THAT YOU REALLY LOVE AND THAT YOU REALLY HATE ABOUT JAPAN?
I love how easily we can get cutting-edge computers and games and how closely our life is always linked to technology. I hate the national character which unconsciously tries to eliminate individual character. (Hama).. I love the peaceful vibe of Japan. I hate the overbearing, young kids. We should all respect our elders. (Sano).

WHAT DO YOU THINK ARE THE DIFFERENCES BETWEEN AMERICAN, EUROPEAN AND JAPANESE PEOPLE?
Compared to people from other countries, many Japanese are clumsy in how they enjoy life and treat ladies, I think. American people are the most modern. They are lucky to be able to show their individuality freely. European people can give you the history and the vibe of other nations. (Takeuchi). Nothing is different except the historical background. The only difference is that most Japanese people cannot speak English at all. (Hama).

WHAT DO YOU THINK IS THE DIFFERENCE BETWEEN JAPANESE, AMERICAN AND EUROPEAN DESIGN?
Japanese: the design looks like it's from skillful hands. American: generally rational design but in many cases also prosaic. European: design which is elegant and well established. (Takeuchi).
Japanese: introverted/national isolation. American: consumptive/fast food. European: historical/conservative. (Sano).

WHAT WOULD YOU DO, IF GRAPHIC DESIGN DID NOT EXIST?
Teacher, musician, journalist, explorer or cartoon artist. (Takeuchi). I'd go to work at 9 o'clock everyday, have a cup of coffee, and smoke. I'd go home at 5 o'clock. Or live a life without a computer. (Hama).

CAN YOU TELL US YOUR 3 MOST IMPORTANT THINGS/OBJECTS/ACTIVITIES?
To strive. To be gentle. To be honest. (Takeuchi).
Friends. Hours of sleep. Curiosity. (Hama).
Passion. Equality. Money. (Sano).

WHAT IS BEAUTIFUL AND WHAT IS UGLY?
The past and future are beautiful. The present is ugly. (Hama).
I consider equilibrium as a beauty, and sweating and looking desperate as ugly. You should be flexible in everything you do. (Sano).

TO WHICH QUESTION YOU WOULD NEVER GIVE AN ANSWER?
About my first kiss. (Hama).
About my habits. (Sano).

IS THERE ANYTHING YOU WOULD LIKE TO TELL THE READERS OF THIS BOOK?
I usually have a high reputation abroad, especially for my character design work. It seems almost to be hard to get accepted in Japan. So, I would love to work with people from other countries via phone and e-mail. Or if you send me an air ticket, I will fly over. (Takeuchi).

(interview with Takeuchi/Hama/Sano).

Q1: 今日の日本はどんな匂いがしますか?
A1: ここ新宿はいつものように排気ガス臭い。(竹内)

Q2: あなたの1日はどの様に始まり、どの様に終わりますか?
A2: 最近はほとんど昼夜逆転気味。寝ないこともあるので昨日今日の区別がつかないことも多い。(竹内)
朝起きて、暗くなったら眠る。規則正しい生活が健康の秘訣。(佐野)

Q3: 日本の好きな部分、嫌いな部分を挙げて下さい。
A3: 最先端のコンピュータやゲームが苦労することなく手に入り、常に生活がテクノロジーに密接しているところが大好き。突出した個性を無自覚に潰そうとする国民性が大嫌い。(浜)
日本の平和な空気感が好き。傍若無人な若者が嫌い。年長者は敬うべき。(佐野)

Q4: アメリカ人、ヨーロッパ人、日本人の違いは何だと思いますか?
A4: 多くの日本人は他国の人に比べて人生を楽しむことが下手、女性の扱いも下手だと思う。アメリカ人は一番現代的。個性を存分に発揮できて羨ましい。ヨーロッパ人は各国々が持つ歴史や空気感を個人から感じることができる。(竹内)
歴史的背景以外に違いはないと思う。ただ一つの違いは、ほとんどの日本人が英語を話せないこと。(浜)

Q5: 日本のデザイン、アメリカのデザイン、ヨーロッパのデザインの違いは何だと思いますか?
A5: 日本─手先が器用そうなデザイン。アメリカ─大味でもある場合も多いが概して合理的なデザイン。ヨーロッパ─エレガントでしっかりとしたデザイン(竹内)
日本─内向的/鎖国。アメリカ─消費的/ファーストフード。ヨーロッパ─歴史的/保守的。(佐野)

Q6: グラフィックデザインが存在していなかったら、あなたは何をしていますか?
A6: 教師かミュージシャンかジャーナリストか探検家か漫画家。(竹内)
毎日9時に会社に出勤し、コーヒーを飲んで煙草を吸い、5時に帰宅。あるいはコンピュータの無い生活。(浜)

Q7: あなた大事なことを3つ教えて下さい。
A7: 努力すること。優しくあること。正直であること。(竹内)
友人。睡眠時間。好奇心。(浜)
情熱。落ち着き。お金。(佐野)

Q8: 何が美しくて、何が醜いと思いますか?
A8: 過去と未来が美しくて、現在は醜い。(浜)
冷静さを美徳と考えている。汗かき焦る様は醜い。何ごとも余裕が必要。(佐野)

Q9: あなたが絶対に答えない質問は何でしょう?
A9: ファーストキスのこと。(浜)
癖について。(佐野)

Q10: 読者に何か伝えたいことがあれば書いて下さい。
A10: 私の作品、特にキャラクターデザインに対しては外国人のほうがはるかに高い評価をします。日本だといまいち受け入れられにくいようです。ということで海外の方、私と仕事をしましょう。仕事は電話とメールのやりとりで。もしくは航空券を送ってくれるのならそちらに伺います。(竹内)

(インタビュー: 竹内/浜/佐野)

NAME OF DESIGN COMPANY: ASTRO GRAPHICA
NAMES/YEAR OF BIRTH: KOUJI TAKEUCHI (76)/ TATSUYA HAMA (73)/ TETSURO SANO (75)
COMPANY SINCE: 1997
ADDRESS: 5-1-18-903 NISHISHINJUKU, SHINJUKU-KU, TOKYO 160-0023, JAPAN
WEBSITE: HTTP://WWW.ASTRO-G.COM/
EMAIL ADDRESS: INFO@ASTRO-G.COM
FAX: +81 (0)3-5334-0586

デザイン会社名:アストロ・グラフィカ
メンバー名(生年):竹内光司(76年)/浜達也(73年)/佐野哲郎(75年)
会社設立日:1997年
住所:〒160-0023 東京都新宿区西新宿5-1-18 Urban White House 903
ウェブサイト:http://www.astro-g.com/
Eメールアドレス:info@astro-g.com
ファックス番号:+81 (0)3-5334-0586

PROFILE ↑
BUSINESS CARD →
SELFPORTRAIT ↓

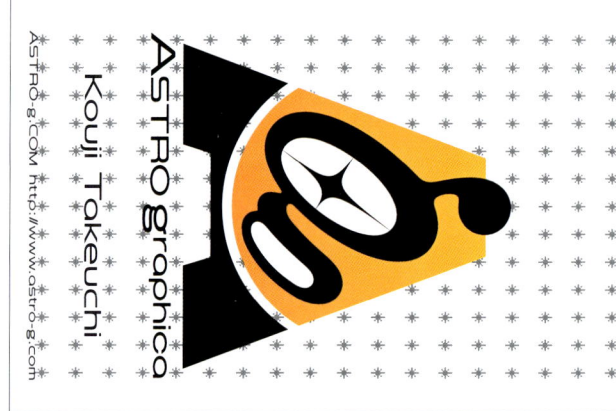

ASTRO GRAPHICA   アストロ・グラフィカ

WORKSPACES ↓　　　　　　　　　　　　　　　　　　　　　　　　LOGOTYPE ↑

↓
TITLE OF WORK: PCI-FI MACHINES
NIGHTEXPLORER/SONICSPORTS/GUNMOBILE
DESIGNER: KOJI TAKEUCHI
DESIGN COMPANY: ASTRO GRAPHICA
YEAR: 1998

→
TITLE OF WORK: SUMMER BOY
DESIGNER: KOJI TAKEUCHI
DESIGN COMPANY: ASTRO GRAPHICA
YEAR: 1998
CLIENT: ASCII

→→
TITLE OF WORK: FOR ASTRO-G.COM
DESIGNER: KOJI TAKEUCHI
DESIGN COMPANY: ASTRO GRAPHICA
YEAR: 2000

→→→
TITLE OF WORK: THE MAN OF PELA
DESIGNER: KOJI TAKEUCHI
DESIGN COMPANY: ASTRO GRAPHICA
YEAR: 1999
CLIENT: CASIO & STUDIO VOICE

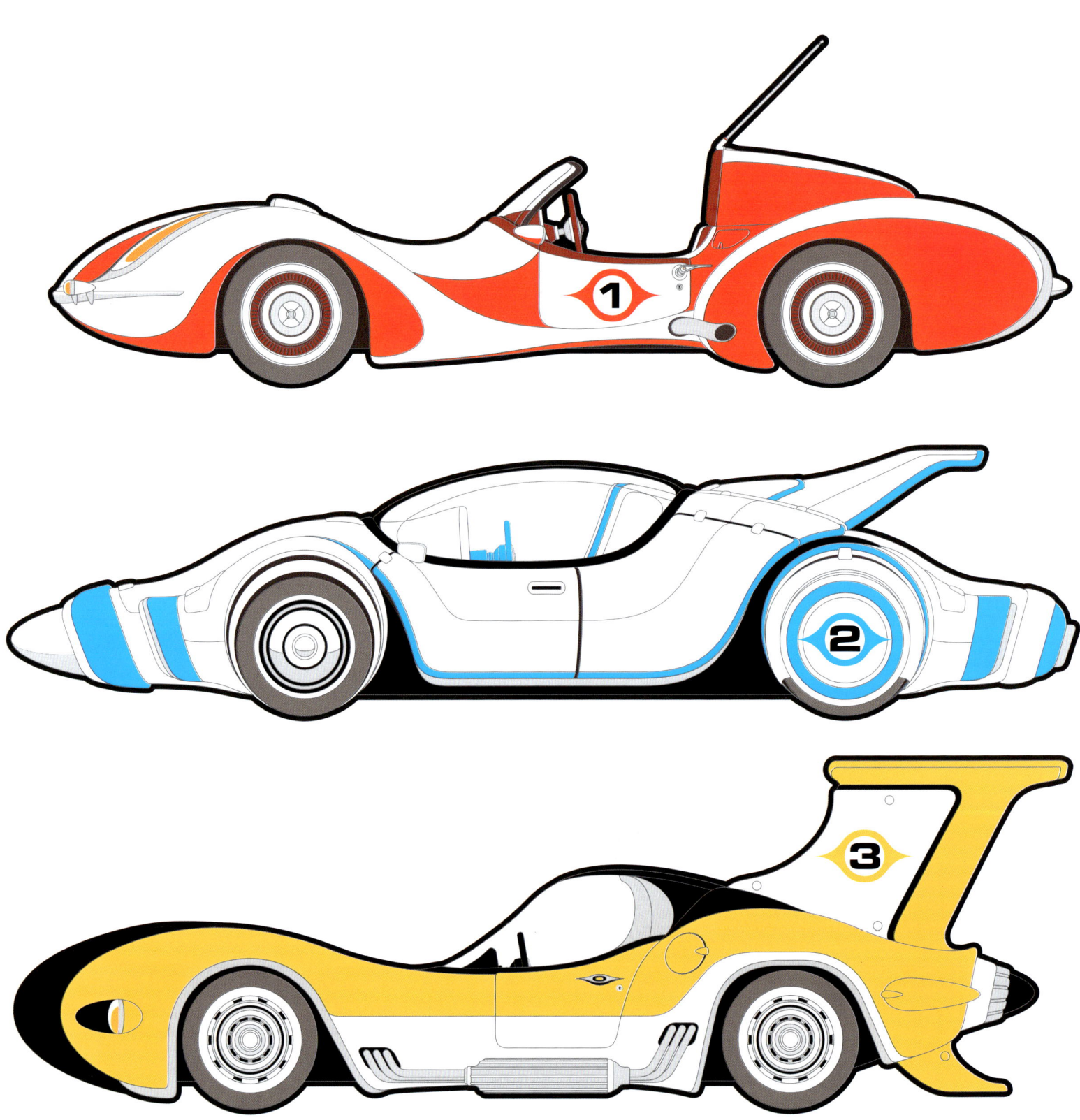

KAITEKI

Launched in January, 2000 and established the office in October, 2001. Started off working for the same ad/web production company at first. Although Club VJing formed the greatest part of the work in the early days, they now also work in various other fields such as motion graphics (CM/TV titles, events), web animation, advertising media etc. They have each specialized in completely different things, so they often collaborate with external designers rather than each other, depending on the format of the project. Work is based in Shibuya, Tokyo.

2000年01月発足、2001年10月事務所設立。もともと同じ広告・ウェブ制作会社に属していたのがきっかけ。発足当初の活動内容はクラブVJが大半を占めていたが、現在ではそれに留まる事なく映像（CM、番組タイトル、イベント）、ウェブアニメーション、広告媒体など多岐にわたり活動。個々で得意としているものが全く異なり、手がけるモノの形態によってメンバー以外のデザイナーとのコラボレーションもよく行う。東京渋谷を拠点に活動中。

BIOGRAPHY
10 QUESTIONS/ANSWERS

HOW DOES JAPAN SMELL TODAY?
Of rain. (Hagiuda).

HOW DOES YOUR DAY START AND HOW DOES YOUR DAY END?
I wake up with the sunset, and I go to sleep after sunrise.

IS THERE SOMETHING THAT YOU REALLY LOVE AND THAT YOU REALLY HATE ABOUT JAPAN?
Love: peace. Hate: narrow. (Yamaya).

WHAT DO YOU THINK ARE THE DIFFERENCES BETWEEN AMERICAN, EUROPEAN AND JAPANESE PEOPLE?
Basically, there are no differences. (Matsunaga).

WHAT DO YOU THINK IS THE DIFFERENCE BETWEEN JAPANESE, AMERICAN AND EUROPEAN DESIGN?
Culture. (Yamaya).

WHAT WOULD YOU DO, IF GRAPHIC DESIGN DID NOT EXIST?
I would probably get involved in music. (Awano).

CAN YOU TELL US YOUR 3 MOST IMPORTANT THINGS/OBJECTS/ACTIVITIES?
Oneself. Friends. Thinking. (Hagiuda).

WHAT IS BEAUTIFUL AND WHAT IS UGLY?
I think everything has both of these sides to it. (Matsunaga).

TO WHICH QUESTION YOU WOULD NEVER GIVE AN ANSWER?
What would you do if you found out that you were going to die tomorrow? (Awano).

IS THERE ANYTHING YOU WOULD LIKE TO TELL THE READERS OF THIS BOOK?
Let's have some fun.

(interview with Awano, Hagiuda, Yamaya, Matsunaga)

Q1: 今日の日本はどんな匂いがしますか？
A1: 雨の匂い。（萩生田）

Q2: あなたの1日はどの様に始まり、どの様に終わりますか？
A2: 夕日で目覚めて、朝日で眠る。

Q3: 日本の好きな部分、嫌いな部分を挙げて下さい。
A3: 好き―平和。嫌い―狭い。（山屋）

Q4: アメリカ人、ヨーロッパ人、日本人の違いは何だと思いますか？
A4: 基本的には変わらないと思う。（松永）

Q5: 日本のデザイン、アメリカのデザイン、ヨーロッパのデザインの違いは何だと思いますか？
A5: カルチャー。（山屋）

Q6: グラフィックデザインが存在していなかったら、あなたは何をしていますか？
A6: 音楽をやっているかも。（粟野）

Q7: あなた大事なことを3つ教えて下さい。
A7: 自分。友人。考えること。（萩生田）

Q8: 何が美しくて、何が醜いと思いますか？
A8: どんなものでも、その両方の面を持っていると思う。（松永）

Q9: あなたが絶対に答えない質問は何でしょう？
A9: 明日死ぬと知ったらどうしますか？（粟野）

Q10: 読者に何か伝えたいことがあれば書いて下さい。
A10: 楽しみましょう。

（インタビュー：粟野/萩生田/山屋/松永）

NAME OF DESIGN COMPANY: KAITEKI
NAMES/YEAR OF BIRTH: JUN AWANO (73)/ SHINJI HAGIUDA (74)/KOJI YAMAYA (74)/ HIROKI MATSUNAGA (76)
COMPANY SINCE: 2000
ADDRESS: 2-9-19-101 HIGASHI, SHIBUYA, TOKYO 150-0011, JAPAN
WEBSITE: HTTP://KITK.ORG/
EMAIL ADDRESS: INFO@KITK.DESIGN.CO.JP
FAX: +81 (0)3-5766-3180

デザイン会社名：快的
メンバー名(生年)：粟野順(73年)/萩生田晋司(74年)/山屋光司(74年)/松永大樹(76年)
会社設立日：2000年
住所：〒150-0011 東京都渋谷区東2-9-19 カントリーハイツ10
ウェブサイト：http://kitk.org/
Eメールアドレス：info@kitk.design.co.jp
ファックス番号：+81 (0)3-5766-3180

PROFILE
BUSINESS CARD
SELFPORTRAIT

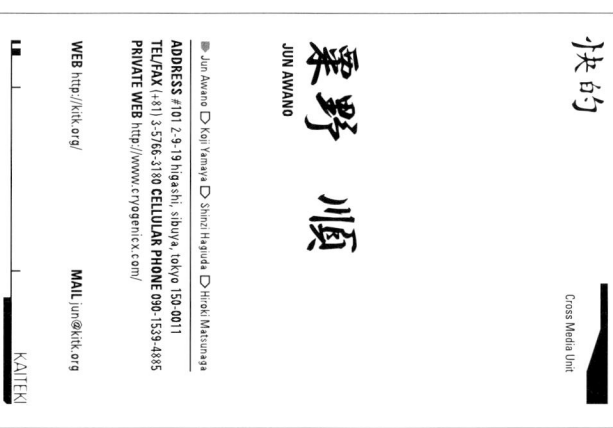

KAITEKI 快的

WORKSPACES ↓ LOGOTYPE ↑

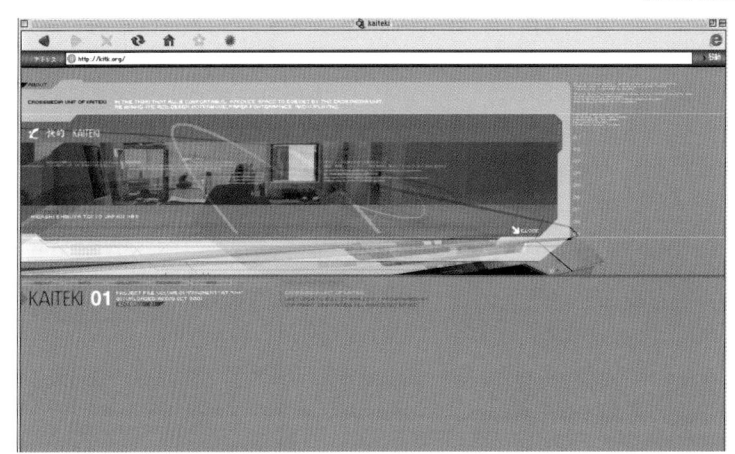

TITLE OF WORK: 1999 VIBE STATION ID CONTEST
WINNING A PRIZE
DESIGNER: KOJI YAMAYA, SHINZI HAGIUDA
DESIGN COMPANY: KAITEKI
YEAR: 1999
CLIENT: VIBE

TITLE OF WORK: KAITEKI WEB
DESIGNER: JUN AWANO
DESIGN COMPANY: KAITEKI
YEAR: 2001

LIVING TD.

In 1995 Developed new font stlye for Katakana & Alphabet at Flokke exhibition.
In 1998 Released the work collection «LIIVNG typedrive1.0J».
In 1999 Released the work collection «LIIVNG typedrive2.0J».
In 2000 Released the work collection «LIIVNG typedrive3.0J».
In 2001 Participated in Font 1000.

1995年 フロッケ展にてカタカナ＋アルファベットの新しいフォントスタイルを提案
1998年 「LIIVNG typedrive1.0J」の作品集を発売
1999年 「LIIVNG typedrive2.0J」の作品集を発売
2000年 「LIIVNG typedrive3.0J」の作品集を発売
2001年 「FONT1000」に参加

BIOGRAPHY ↑
10 QUESTIONS/ANSWERS ↓

HOW DOES JAPAN SMELL TODAY?
Like concrete.

HOW DOES YOUR DAY START AND HOW DOES YOUR DAY END?
12:00pm wake-up – 6:00am bedtime.

IS THERE SOMETHING THAT YOU REALLY LOVE AND THAT YOU REALLY HATE ABOUT JAPAN?
Love: Japanese language. Hate: Japanese language.

WHAT DO YOU THINK ARE THE DIFFERENCES BETWEEN AMERICAN, EUROPEAN AND JAPANESE PEOPLE?
Food.

WHAT DO YOU THINK IS THE DIFFERENCE BETWEEN JAPANESE, AMERICAN AND EUROPEAN DESIGN?
Language.

WHAT WOULD YOU DO, IF GRAPHIC DESIGN DID NOT EXIST?
Craftsman.

CAN YOU TELL US YOUR 3 MOST IMPORTANT THINGS/OBJECTS/ACTIVITIES?
Food, clothing and shelter.

WHAT IS BEAUTIFUL AND WHAT IS UGLY?
Beautiful: Bezier curve. Ugly: spline curve.

TO WHICH QUESTION YOU WOULD NEVER GIVE AN ANSWER?
–

IS THERE ANYTHING YOU WOULD LIKE TO TELL THE READERS OF THIS BOOK?
We should all cherish the Japanese language.

(interview with Takafumi Miyadima)

Q1: 今日の日本はどんな匂いがしますか？
A1: コンクリート。

Q2: あなたの1日はどの様に始まり、どの様に終わりますか？
A2: 12:00pm起床→6:00am就寝。

Q3: 日本の好きな部分、嫌いな部分を挙げて下さい。
A3: 好き―日本語。嫌い―日本語。

Q4: アメリカ人、ヨーロッパ人、日本人の違いは何だと思いますか？
A4: 食べ物。

Q5: 日本のデザイン、アメリカのデザイン、ヨーロッパのデザインの違いは何だと思いますか？
A5: 言葉。

Q6: グラフィックデザインが存在していなかったら、あなたは何をしていますか？
A6: 職人。

Q7: あなた大事なことを3つ教えて下さい。
A7: 衣食住。

Q8: 何が美しくて、何が醜いと思いますか？
A8: 美しい―ベジェ曲線。醜い―スプライン曲線。

Q9: あなたが絶対に答えない質問は何でしょう？
A9: ―

Q10: 読者に何か伝えたいことがあれば書いて下さい。
A10: 日本語を大切にしよう。

（インタビュー：ミヤヂマタカフミ）

NAME OF DESIGN COMPANY: LIVING TD.
NAME/YEAR OF BIRTH: TAKAFUMI MIYADIMA (71)
COMPANY SINCE: 1998
ADDRESS: 4-9-10-101 SAKURAGAOKA, SETAGAYA-KU, TOKYO 156-0054, JAPAN
WEBSITE: –
EMAIL ADDRESS: LIVING@QB3.SO-NET.NE.JP
FAX: +81 (0)3-3425-3903

デザイン会社名：リビングティーディー
メンバー名（生年）：ミヤヂマタカフミ（71年）
会社設立日：1998年
住所：〒156-0054 東京都世田谷区桜丘4-9-10 桜丘レヂデンス101
ウェブサイト：―
Eメールアドレス：living@qb3.so-net.ne.jp
ファックス番号：+81 (0)3-3425-3903

PROFILE ↑
BUSINESS CARD →
SELFPORTRAIT ↓

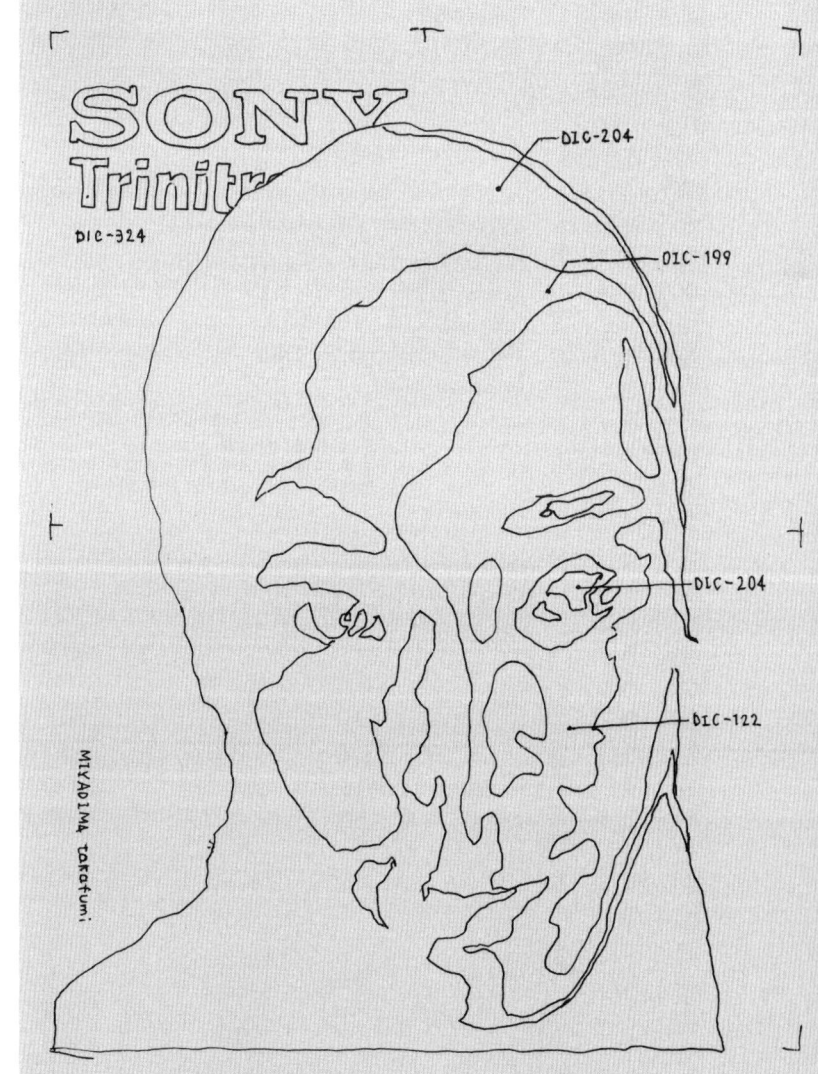

LIVING TD.

WORKSPACES ↓   LOGOTYPE ↑

TITLE OF WORK: 2021 ACRYLIC KAT/ALP
DESIGNER: MIYADIMA, TAKAFUMI
DESIGN COMPANY: LIVING TD.
YEAR: 2000

TITLE OF WORK: 2110 TITANIUM KAT/ALP
DESIGNER: MIYADIMA, TAKAFUMI
DESIGN COMPANY: LIVING TD.
YEAR: 2000

TITLE OF WORK: 2170 GLUCOSE KAT/ALP
DESIGNER: MIYADIMA, TAKAFUMI
DESIGN COMPANY: LIVING TD.
YEAR: 2000

TITLE OF WORK: 2010 SILICONE KAT/ALP
DESIGNER: MIYADIMA, TAKAFUMI
DESIGN COMPANY: LIVING TD.
YEAR: 1999

TITLE OF WORK: 2040 CONCRETE KAT/ALP
DESIGNER: MIYADIMA, TAKAFUMI
DESIGN COMPANY: LIVING TD.
YEAR: 1999

TITLE OF WORK: 2130 URANIUM KAT/ALP
DESIGNER: MIYADIMA, TAKAFUMI
DESIGN COMPANY: LIVING TD.
YEAR: 1999

TITLE OF WORK: 1120 REG-JPN
DESIGNER: MIYADIMA, TAKAFUMI
DESIGN COMPANY: LIVING TD.
YEAR: 2000

TITLE OF WORK: 1130 CPU-JPN
DESIGNER: MIYADIMA, TAKAFUMI
DESIGN COMPANY: LIVING TD.
YEAR: 2001

TITLE OF WORK: 1140 DIS-JPN
DESIGNER: MIYADIMA, TAKAFUMI
DESIGN COMPANY: LIVING TD.
YEAR: 2001

TITLE OF WORK: LIVING PLAN
DESIGNER: MIYADIMA, TAKAFUMI
DESIGN COMPANY: LIVING TD.
YEAR: 1998

TITLE OF WORK: LOGOTYPES
DESIGNER: MIYADIMA, TAKAFUMI
DESIGN COMPANY: LIVING TD.
YEAR: 1998-2001
CLIENT: VARIOUS

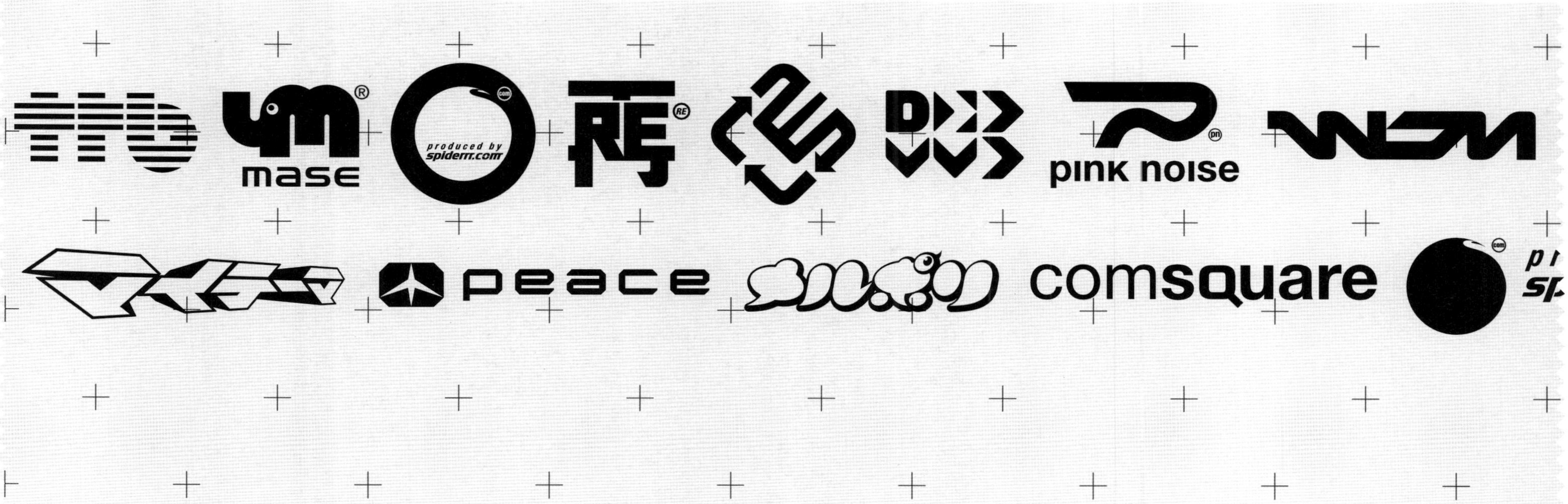

NARITA INSPECTED

mase · **RE** · **peace** · **pink noise** · **comsquare**

LIVING PLAN 1:250

- BED ROOM / ベッドルーム
- TERRACE / テラス
- HALLWAY / ホールウェイ
- LIVING ROOM / リビングルーム
- HALL / ホール
- ENTRANCE / エントランス
- DINING KITCHIN / ダイニングキッチン
- TOILET / トイレット
- BATH ROOM / バスルーム
- PLAY ROOM / パーティールーム
- PARK / パーキ

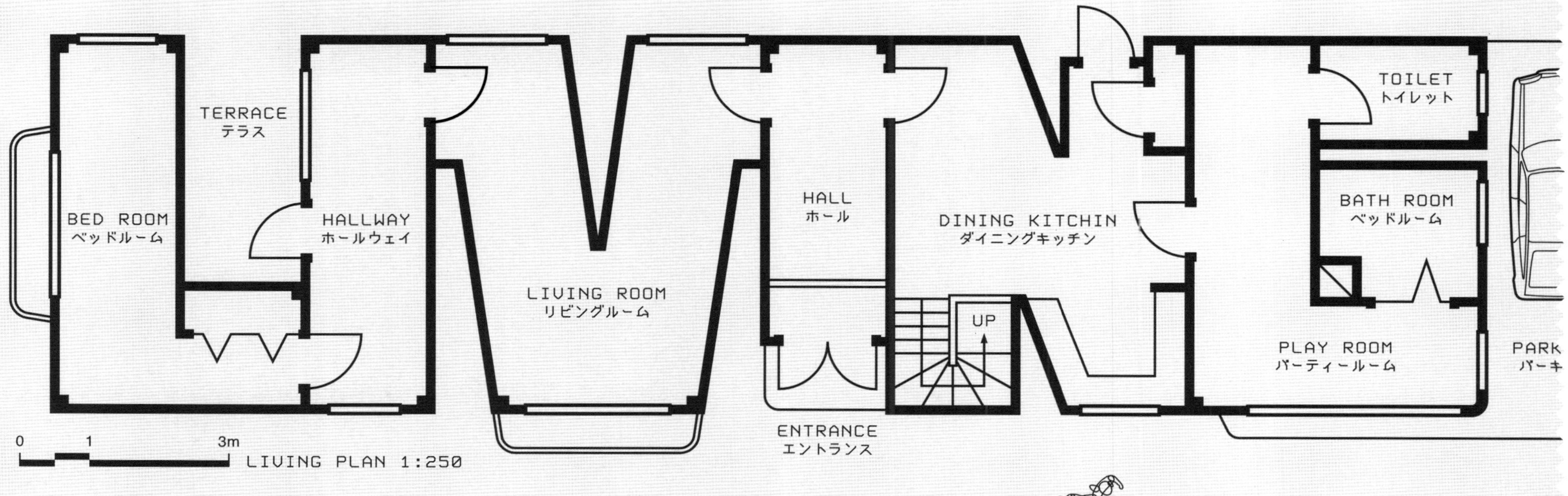

0 — 1 — 3m

COPYRIGHT(C)1998-2001 LIVING td.
ALL RIGHTS RESERVED.

EXTRA DESIGN

Established by Nobutaka Sato in 1997. Shin Sasaki has been a member since 1998. Have been working in the field of logo design, editorial, web design, fonts, t-shirt designs etc. The main project includes an opening title for the MTV2 programme, CD jacket of Simplest Preasures Free, an opening movie for Macromedia wwwhat award, and a cover design of Design Plex magazine. Have participated in projects such as a free paper called Selfish, and RMX Extended Play (www.rmxxx.com) etc. also.

1997年佐藤暢孝により設立。1998年より佐々木信が加入。ロゴデザイン、エディトリアル、ウェブデザイン、フォント制作、Tシャツデザインなどの分野で活動中。主な仕事にMTV2の番組オープニングタイトル、Simplest Preasures FreeのCDジャケットデザイン、Macromedia wwwhat awardのオープニングムービー、デザインプレックスのカバーデザインなどがある。その他、フリーペーパーセルフィッシュ、RMX Extended Play(www.rmxxx.com)などのプロジェクトにも参加。

BIOGRAPHY / 10 QUESTIONS/ANSWERS

HOW DOES JAPAN SMELL TODAY?
The scent of the perfume that Prime Minister Koizumi wears.

HOW DOES YOUR DAY START AND HOW DOES YOUR DAY END?
Turn on my Macintosh – Turn off my Macintosh.

IS THERE SOMETHING THAT YOU REALLY LOVE AND THAT YOU REALLY HATE ABOUT JAPAN?
Love: city, countryside, people. Hate: overwork.

WHAT DO YOU THINK ARE THE DIFFERENCES BETWEEN AMERICAN, EUROPEAN AND JAPANESE PEOPLE?
The number of days off.

WHAT DO YOU THINK IS THE DIFFERENCE BETWEEN JAPANESE, AMERICAN AND EUROPEAN DESIGN?
I don't think it has anything to do with national differences.

WHAT WOULD YOU DO, IF GRAPHIC DESIGN DID NOT EXIST?
Wear a tie, and go to work at 9am.

CAN YOU TELL US YOUR 3 MOST IMPORTANT THINGS/OBJECTS/ACTIVITIES?
The vibe of the community. Macintosh. Design.

WHAT IS BEAUTIFUL AND WHAT IS UGLY?
Friendship. Ego trip.

TO WHICH QUESTION YOU WOULD NEVER GIVE AN ANSWER?
Question 11.

IS THERE ANYTHING YOU WOULD LIKE TO TELL THE READERS OF THIS BOOK?
Do what you want and what you like, and have a nice life!

(interview with Extra Design)

Q1: 今日の日本はどんな匂いがしますか?
A1: 小泉さんの香水の香り。

Q2: あなたの1日はどの様に始まり、どの様に終わりますか?
A2: マッキントッシュを起動→マッキントッシュを終了。

Q3: 日本の好きな部分、嫌いな部分を挙げて下さい。
A3: 好き—都市、田舎、人。嫌い—過労。

Q4: アメリカ人、ヨーロッパ人、日本人の違いは何だと思いますか?
A4: 休暇の日数。

Q5: 日本のデザイン、アメリカのデザイン、ヨーロッパのデザインの違いは何だと思いますか?
A5: 国はあまり関係ないと思う。

Q6: グラフィックデザインが存在していなかったら、あなたは何をしていますか?
A6: ネクタイして9時出社。

Q7: あなた大事なことを3つ教えて下さい。
A7: その土地の空気。MAC。デザイン。

Q8: 何が美しくて、何が醜いと思いますか?
A8: 友情。エゴ。

Q9: あなたが絶対に答えない質問は何でしょう?
A9: 11問目。

Q10: 読者に何か伝えたいことがあれば書いて下さい。
A10: やりたいこと→自分の好きなことをやって良い人生を!

(インタビュー: エクストラ・デザイン)

NAME OF DESIGN COMPANY: EXTRA DESIGN
NAMES/YEAR OF BIRTH: NOBUTAKA SATO (73)/ SHIN SASAKI (74)
COMPANY SINCE: 1997
ADDRESS: C/O SHIMOOKA OFFICE, S2E2 DAITO-BLDG. 9F, CHUO-KU, SAPPORO 060-0052, JAPAN
WEBSITE: HTTP://WWW.EXTRA.JP.ORG/
EMAIL ADDRESS: INFO@EXTRA.JP.ORG
FAX: +81 (0)11-210-4330

デザイン会社名:エクストラ・デザイン
メンバー名(生年):佐藤暢孝(73年)/佐々木信(74年)
会社設立日:1997年
住所:〒060-0052 札幌市中央区南2条東2丁目大都ビル9F 下岡事務所内
ウェブサイト:http://www.extra.jp.org/
Eメールアドレス:info@extra.jp.org
ファックス番号:+81 (0)11-210-4330

PROFILE / BUSINESS CARD / SELFPORTRAIT

c/o Shimooka Office
9F Daito bldg / S2E2
Chuo-ku / Sapporo
Japan 060-0052

Tel +81.(0)11.210.4320
Fax +81.(0)11.210.4330

Shin Sasaki

shin@extra.jp.org
www.extra.jp.org

EXTRA DESIGN　　　　エクストラ・デザイン

WORKSPACES ↓　　　　　　　　　　　　　　　　　　　　　　　　　　　　　LOGOTYPE ↑

TITLE OF WORK: KITTY HOUSE
DESIGN COMPANY: EXTRA DESIGN
YEAR: 2000
<LIENT: IDN MAGAZINE

TITLE OF WORK: EAT
DESIGN COMPANY: EXTRA DESIGN
YEAR: 2000
<LIENT: SELFISH MAGAZINE

あきっぽいコーヒーちがう

IMAITOONZ

Born in 1971. Graduated from Tama Art University. Has worked on the TV opening movie for MTV's «TOP OF JAPAN», CF character design/poster design for SUNTORY «C.C.Lemon», character design for the SEGA arcade game «FIGHTING VIPERS2», cassette character/package illustration for SONY's «GIG», E-CD animation for NIKE's «PRESTO» etc. He has acquired a reputation for his confident, original and detailed imagary using various forms such as character design, comic, art and anime. Recently he has been invited to show his original animation at film festivals and international exhibitions and has expanded his activities both at home and abroad.

1971年生。多摩美術大学研究科修了。MTV「TOP OF JAPAN」番組オープニングアニメ、サントリー「C.C.Lemon」CFキャラクターデザイン/ポスター制作、SEGAアーケードゲーム「FIGHTING VIPERS2」キャラクターデザイン、SONY「GIG」カセットキャラクター/パッケージイラスト、NIKE「PRESTO」E-CDアニメーションなど、キャラクターデザイン、コミック、アート、アニメと様々な形態を用い、枠にとらわれない斬新で緻密な表現には定評がある。最近では映画祭、国際展などにオリジナルアニメーション、作品を招待出品されるなど国内外ともにその活躍の場を拡げている。

今井トゥーンズ

NAME OF DESIGN COMPANY: –
NAME/YEAR OF BIRTH: IMAITOONZ (71)
COMPANY SINCE: 1995
ADDRESS: MEGURO-KU, TOKYO JAPAN
WEBSITE: HTTP://WWW.IMAITOONZ.COM
EMAIL ADDRESS: TOONS@DIN.OR.JP
FAX: +81 (0)3-3714-8799

デザイン会社名：—
メンバー名(生年)：今井トゥーンズ(71年)
会社設立日：1995年
住所：東京都目黒区
ウェブサイト：http://www.imaitoonz.com
Eメールアドレス：toons@din.or.jp
ファックス番号：+81 (0)3-3714-8799

BIOGRAPHY ↑
10 QUESTIONS/ANSWERS ↓

PROFILE ↑
BUSINESS CARD →
SELFPORTRAIT ↓

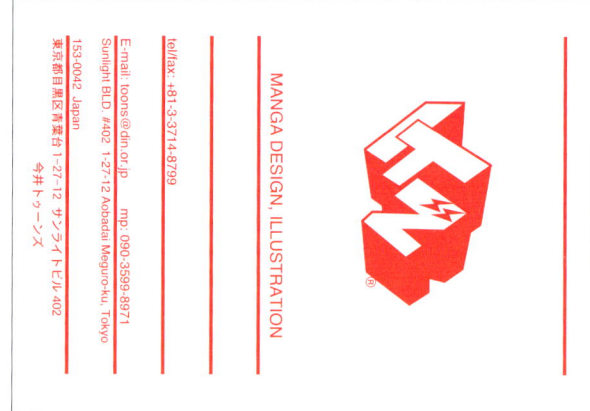

HOW DOES JAPAN SMELL TODAY?
The mixed smell of earth, rain, sun and soy sauce.

HOW DOES YOUR DAY START AND HOW DOES YOUR DAY END?
If you count playing as work; wake up at 10:00am – take a shower – work – have breakfast – work – have lunch – work – have dinner – take a shower – go to sleep at 6:00am.

IS THERE SOMETHING THAT YOU REALLY LOVE AND THAT YOU REALLY HATE ABOUT JAPAN?
Love: four seasons. Japanese culture. Climate. Hate: how easy it is. How people go with the trend. Policy of following the crowd. Nothing-is-wrong policy. The living environment which allows you to live like a dead man. How narrow it is in all senses.

WHAT DO YOU THINK ARE THE DIFFERENCES BETWEEN AMERICAN, EUROPEAN AND JAPANESE PEOPLE?
Japanese: people look like they are obsessed with something, but they actually aren't. Somehow exclusive, but momentary in a good mood. Others: confidence which is built in a determined way. Vast history, and cultural accumulation. Things that Japanese people have forgotten...

WHAT DO YOU THINK IS THE DIFFERENCE BETWEEN JAPANESE, AMERICAN AND EUROPEAN DESIGN?
Japanese people hesitate to choose a design from their own personal viewpoint, they simply have no choice. Therefore unreasonable design spills over into the way of life. For example, the streamlined rice cooker which looks like a motorcycle helmet (pointless insistence). Pearl-white cellular phone (the design is only for the demand of certain people). Another thing is environmental difference. In Japan, people purposelessly ask you «what is this» each time. Is this because everyone is speaking flattering words?

WHAT WOULD YOU DO, IF GRAPHIC DESIGN DID NOT EXIST?
I would have enough sleep.

CAN YOU TELL US YOUR 3 MOST IMPORTANT THINGS/OBJECTS/ACTIVITIES?
Ambition for creation. Sane vision straight into tomorrow. Mind.

WHAT IS BEAUTIFUL AND WHAT IS UGLY?
People's good hearts. People who are jealous of it.

TO WHICH QUESTION YOU WOULD NEVER GIVE AN ANSWER?
«What do you think will happen when you die?»

IS THERE ANYTHING YOU WOULD LIKE TO TELL THE READERS OF THIS BOOK?
Take care of yourself.

(interview with Imaitoonz)

Q1: 今日の日本はどんな匂いがしますか？
A1: 土の匂、雨の匂、太陽の匂、醤油の匂、の混ざった匂。

Q2: あなたの1日はどの様に始まり、どの様に終わりますか？
A2: 遊びも仕事のうちと言うなら、10:00am起床→風呂→仕事→飯→仕事→散歩→飯→仕事→飯→風呂→仕事→就寝6:00am。

Q3: 日本の好きな部分、嫌いな部分を挙げて下さい。
A3: 好き—四季。日本の文化。風土。嫌い—イージーなところ。風潮に流される。右にならえ主義。そしてことなかれ主義。死んだように生きていても許される生活環境。いろんな意味で狭い！

Q4: アメリカ人、ヨーロッパ人、日本人の違いは何だと思いますか？
A4: 日本人—こだわっているようでこだわっていない。なんだか排他的。良くいえば刹那的。
他国の人—確固たるものの上にある自信。膨大な歴史、文化の蓄積。日本人は忘れちゃったみたい…。

Q5: 日本のデザイン、アメリカのデザイン、ヨーロッパのデザインの違いは何だと思いますか？
A5: 日本人はパーソナルな考えでデザインをチョイスできないし、選択肢もない。ライフスタイルの中に訳の分からないデザインが横行してしまう。例えばバイクのヘルメットに似た流線型の炊飯器（←意味のない主張）。パールホワイトの携帯電話（←需要のある層オンリーのデザイン）。環境の違い。いちいち日本では「これは何？」と、しかもイージーに聞かれる。社交辞令？

Q6: グラフィックデザインが存在していなかったら、あなたは何をしていますか？
A6: 睡眠を今よりもよく取っている。

Q7: あなた大事なことを3つ教えて下さい。
A7: 創造する想い。突き抜けるような明日への揺らがないビジョン。マインド。

Q8: 何が美しくて、何が醜いと思いますか？
A8: 人の良き心。それを妬む人。

Q9: あなたが絶対に答えない質問は何でしょう？
A9: 「人間、死んだらどうなる？」

Q10: 読者に何か伝えたいことがあれば書いて下さい。
A10: 体には気をつけてね。

（インタビュー：今井トゥーンズ）

:IMAITOONZ   今井トゥーンズ

WORKSPACES ↓   LOGOTYPE ↑

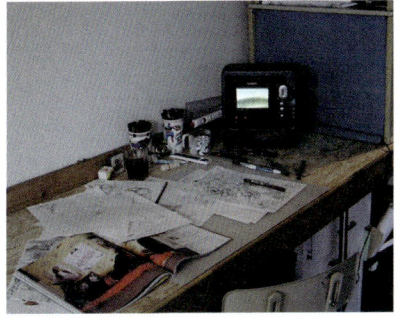

TITLE OF WORK: TOONZ CAMP 1-4
DESIGNER: YOSUKE IMAI
DESIGN COMPANY: IMAITOONZ
YEAR: 2001
CLIENT: GALLERY SPEAK FOR/
ABA HOUSE INTERNATIONAL CO., LTD.

TITLE OF WORK: SPIDEAD POSTER
(FROM TO TOKYO, TO TOKYO EXHIBITION)
DESIGNER: YOSUKE IMAI
DESIGN COMPANY: IMAITOONZ
YEAR: 1998
CLIENT: BEAMS CO., LTD.

YUTANPO SHIRANE

Born in 1968 in Saitama. After graduating from the Graduate Course in Graphics, Kuwasawa Design School, became a freelance illustrator. Has been working mainly on illustration for magazines, book covers, and advertisement in all areas from adult material to kids stuff, and men's magazines to women's fashion magazines. Exhibition «YUTANPOINT» at HB gallery (1993), «Shirane vs Kurone» at Degitalogue Gallery (1998). Released the book «Nama-Nuru Panorama Edition» (Parco Publishing). Recent work includes the Tokyo Metropolitan Election campaign poster for the Democratic Party.

1968年埼玉生まれ。桑沢デザイン研究所グラフィック研究科卒業後フリーのイラストレーターとなる。現在、大人向けから子供向け、男性誌から女性ファッション誌までジャンルを問わずイラストを雑誌、書籍表紙、広告等に提供。個展「YUTANPOINT」HBギャラリー(1993年)、「白根VS黒根」デジタローグギャラリー(1998年)。著書に「ナマヌル パノラマエディション」(パルコ出版)がある。最近の仕事に民主党都議選用ポスター等。

BIOGRAPHY ↑
10 QUESTIONS/ANSWERS ↓

HOW DOES JAPAN SMELL TODAY?
It smells like summer approaching, hey! midsummer is coming.

HOW DOES YOUR DAY START AND HOW DOES YOUR DAY END?
I wake up at 10 in the morning, have a cup of coffee and breakfast (usually it's rice, natto, egg, and miso soup) while checking my e-mails. In the afternoon, I start working on my drawing while meeting with a visitor. When I have enough time, I have dinner and beer at night. I work until midnight and go to sleep. Since I live in a home-office, my work begins right after I get out of my bed.

IS THERE SOMETHING THAT YOU REALLY LOVE AND THAT YOU REALLY HATE ABOUT JAPAN?
Love: I don't know exactly because I basically love Japan. I'm happy that I live in Japan when I bathe in a hot spring (especially an open-air bath). Hate: it's not something that I hate or anything, but I feel disappointed as one of Japanese men who are not popular compared with Japanese women who are very popular worldwide.

WHAT DO YOU THINK ARE THE DIFFERENCES BETWEEN AMERICAN, EUROPEAN AND JAPANESE PEOPLE?
Some American people want to be European, some Japanese people want to be American, and some European people think they are the best.

WHAT DO YOU THINK IS THE DIFFERENCE BETWEEN JAPANESE, AMERICAN AND EUROPEAN DESIGN?
Europe: immovable foundation. America: infinite foundation. Japan: reasonable foundation.

WHAT WOULD YOU DO, IF GRAPHIC DESIGN DID NOT EXIST?
I think an illustration itself persists by some kind of format even if there was no graphic design existing. So I guess I would be working on an illustration. If there was no illustration existing too, I guess I would try to create a figure in three dimensions by clay or whatever.

CAN YOU TELL US YOUR 3 MOST IMPORTANT THINGS/OBJECTS/ACTIVITIES?
Normal reflexes. Vitality. Bright mind.

WHAT IS BEAUTIFUL AND WHAT IS UGLY?
Beautiful: sense of speed (fast and slow). Ugly: Nothing in particular. The feeling of thinking something is ugly, if I have to say one.

TO WHICH QUESTION YOU WOULD NEVER GIVE AN ANSWER?
Well, if you can get me drunk I would answer most questions about me.

IS THERE ANYTHING YOU WOULD LIKE TO TELL THE READERS OF THIS BOOK?
I think there are a lot of Japanese artists who can take an active part not just in Japan but also worldwide. I hope you will be interested and support them if you ever have a chance to see them.

(interview with Yutanpo Shirane)

白根ゆたんぽ

NAME OF DESIGN COMPANY: —
NAME/YEAR OF BIRTH: YUTANPO SHIRANE (68)
COMPANY SINCE: 1991
ADDRESS: 1-30-1-214 HATAGAYA, SHIBUYA-KU, TOKYO 151-0072, JAPAN
WEBSITE: HTTP://WWW07.U-PAGE.SO-NET.NE.JP/JA2/YUTAN-PO/
EMAIL ADDRESS: YUTAN-PO@JA2.SO-NET.NE.JP
FAX: +81 (0)3-3465-8795

デザイン会社名：—
メンバー名(生年)：白根ゆたんぽ(68年)
会社設立日：1991年
住所：〒151-0072 東京都渋谷区幡ヶ谷1-30-1-214
ウェブサイト：http://www07.u-page.so-net.ne.jp/ja2/yutan-
Eメールアドレス：yutan-po@ja2.so-net.ne.jp
ファックス番号：+81 (0)3-3465-8795

Q1: 今日の日本はどんな匂いがしますか？
A1: 夏が近い、そろそろ真夏になるぞ〜という匂い。

Q2: あなたの1日はどの様に始まり、どの様に終わりますか？
A2: 午前10時頃に起きてメールチェックなどしつつ、コーヒーと食事(大体ご飯と納豆、卵、味噌汁など)。午後から来客と打ち合わせなどしつつ、合間に絵を描く。夜になり余裕があるときは晩飯を食べつつ、ビールも飲んだりして深夜まで仕事を続けて寝ます。住居と仕事場が一緒なので、起きたらそこで仕事開始です。

Q3: 日本の好きな部分、嫌いな部分を挙げて下さい。
A3: 好き—基本的に日本が好きなのでどこが好きなのかもよくわかりませんが、温泉(特に露天風呂)に入っていると、日本に生きているという充実感を感じます。
嫌い—大嫌いというほどでは無いのですが、日本人女性は世界的にモテるのに日本人男性は全くその逆、ということに日本人男性として少し残念な気持ちになります。

Q4: アメリカ人、ヨーロッパ人、日本人の違いは何だと思いますか？
A4: アメリカ人の一部はヨーロッパ人になりたがっていて、日本人の一部はアメリカ人になりたがっていて、ヨーロッパ人の一部は自分たちが一番だと思っている。

Q5: 日本のデザイン、アメリカのデザイン、ヨーロッパのデザインの違いは何だと思いますか？
A5: ヨーロッパ—土台がしっかりしている。アメリカ—土台がとても大きい。日本—土台が適当。

Q6: グラフィックデザインが存在していなかったら、あなたは何をしていますか？
A6: グラフィックデザインが存在していなくても絵は何かしらの形で残っていると思うので、適当なところで絵は描いてると思います。でも仮に絵がなかったとしたら粘土で立体を作るとか。

Q7: あなた大事なことを3つ教えて下さい。
A7: 反射神経。体力。明るい心。

Q8: 何が美しくて、何が醜いと思いますか？
A8: 美しい—スピード感(速い遅い含めて)。
醜い—特にありません。強いて言うなら醜いと思う気持ち。

Q9: あなたが絶対に答えない質問は何でしょう？
A9: う〜ん。お酒を飲ませれば自分に関する大抵の事は答えます。

Q10: 読者に何か伝えたいことがあれば書いて下さい。
A10: これからは日本国内に限らず世界でも活躍できる日本の作家がどんどんと出てくると思います。そういう人を見たら面白がって、出来れば応援してください。

(インタビュー：白根ゆたんぽ)

PROFILE ↑
BUSINESS CARD →
SELFPORTRAIT ↓

YUTANPO SHIRANE 白根ゆたんぽ

 WORKSPACES 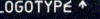 LOGOTYPE

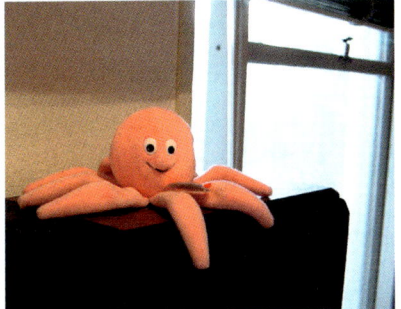

↑
TITLE OF WORK: THE ALIEN FRIED #6
(THE ALIEN FRIED APPEARS AT TOKYO BIGSIGHT)
DESIGNER: YUTANPO SHIRANE
YEAR: 1997
CLIENT: «COMICKERS» MAGAZINE
(BIJUTSU SHUPPAN CO., LTD.)

←
TITLE OF WORK: SEXUAL FANTASIES
DESIGNER: YUTANPO SHIRANE
YEAR: 2001
CLIENT: «WEEKLY SPA!» MAGAZINE
(FUSOSHA PUBLISHING INC.)

↑
TITLE OF WORK: THE ALIEN FRIED #5
(THE ALIEN FRIED MEETS CURRY RICE)
DESIGNER: YUTANPO SHIRANE
YEAR: 1997
CLIENT: «COMICKERS» MAGAZINE
(BIJUTSU SHUPPAN CO., LTD.)

→
TITLE OF WORK: «KOMEZUKURI SHAKAI TO BUSINESS SHAKAI»
BOOK COVER
DESIGNER: YUTANPO SHIRANE
YEAR: 2001
CLIENT: NIKKEI BUSINESS PUBLICATIONS, INC

«NARITA RESPECTED»

```
EA  ET  OE  ET  FK   ET  AE
ON  OO  OF  OO  OE   OO  FT
NR  OR  NO  OR  OU   OR  NO
D   M   OR  M   RN   M   OD
    TR  P   TI  TY   TH  R
HE  H.  AH  AC  TI   EA  J
IS  EI  TÉ  HK  HA   JI  HH
SN  IS  GH  E<  Q<   AT  UE
NA  RT  EE  <O  HK   PA  EE
TL  T   W   AS  EO   AN  NR
RY  XD  S   AN  II   HE  KO
US  RA  I   DI  RK   SE  OE
TO  LA  PD  TU  <<   2A  VN
    EY  /O  RO  Q«   AT  TE
IR  R   2T  RI  AN   WY  EG
NO  SA  /S  GI  AA«  AP  OR
BM  UP  1   AN  WO   TE  LZ
EY  PD  3   EA  N<   S   AI
RT  PO  4/  LT  IT    AL
    OR  13  EX  Y»   TR  SK
PR  T.  5/  TT  <    AA  LH
KO      15  ÉO  NI   NN  I
LJ  WU  0/  SU  AO   SS  JS
AE  TH  19  I.  MT   LL  UA
NC  RI  8/  HA  TI   AL  PP
TT  CH  19  <H  O»    AO
ÉN  .   9.  HI  JN    NR
.       .   IG  OI     ET
            A   YT     .S
                MA     E-
                NA     TR
                 .     AN
                       SL
                       AT
                       IO
                       NS
```

THIS BOOK IS DEDICATED TO A GIRL CALLED NARITA

DOMO ARIGATO GOZAIMASU

MATANE